chasing portraits

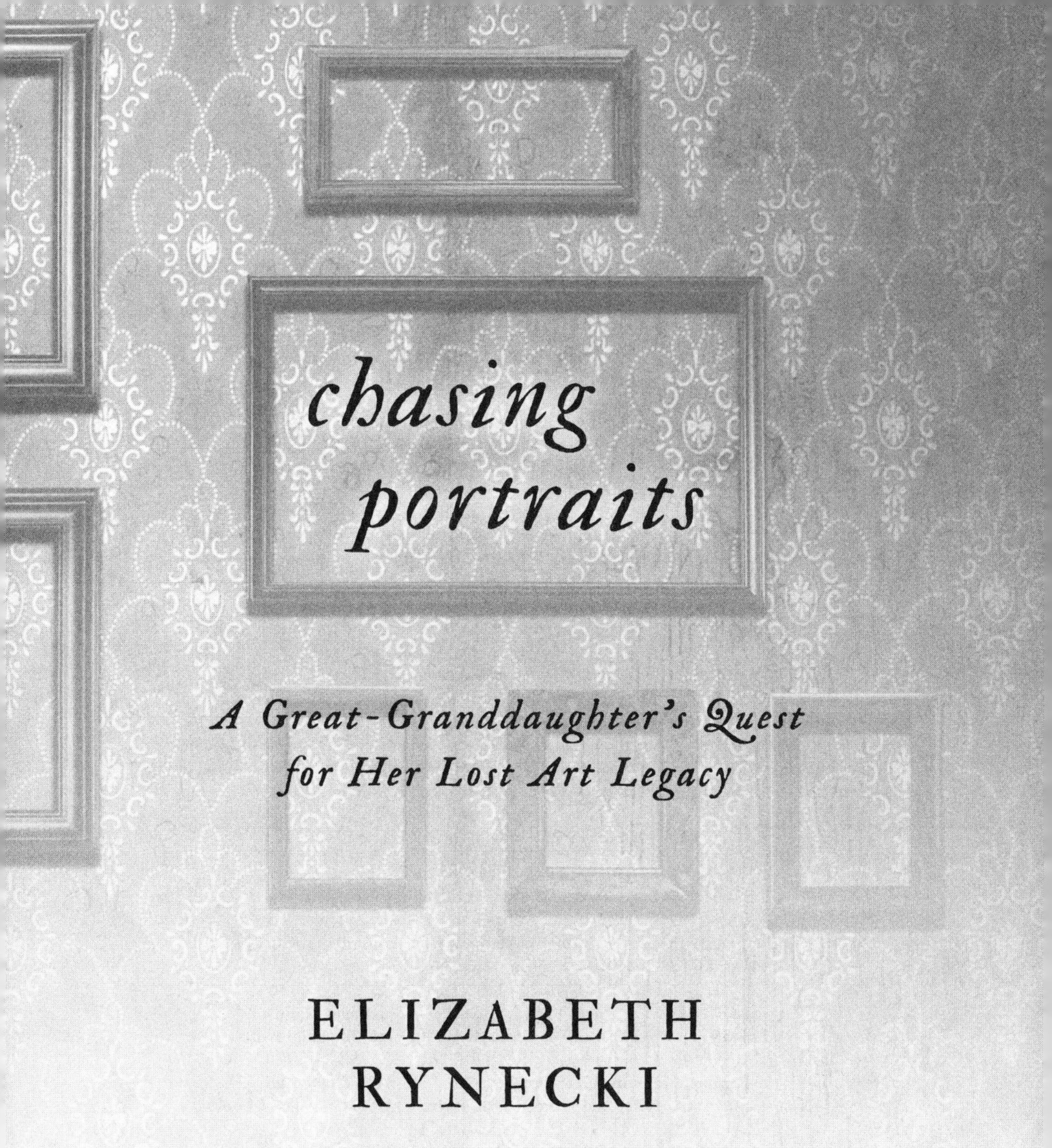

chasing portraits

A Great-Granddaughter's Quest for Her Lost Art Legacy

ELIZABETH RYNECKI

NEW AMERICAN LIBRARY

New York

NEW AMERICAN LIBRARY
Published by Berkley
An imprint of Penguin Random House LLC
375 Hudson Street, New York, New York 10014

Text photos courtesy of the Rynecki family except as follows: p. 95 courtesy of Mitchell Schwarzbach; pp. 226–228, 237–38, and 267 courtesy of the Thomas Fisher Rare Book Library, University of Toronto; p. 247 courtesy of Elizabeth Rynecki Fisher.

Library of Congress Cataloging-in-Publication Data

Names: Rynecki, Elizabeth, author.
Title: Chasing portraits: a great-granddaughter's quest for her lost art legacy/Elizabeth Rynecki.
Description: First edition. | New York: NAL, New American Library, [2016] | "2016"
Identifiers: LCCN 2016012588 (print) | LCCN 2016013257 (ebook) | ISBN 9781101987667 (hardback) | ISBN 9781101987681 (ebook)
Subjects: LCSH: Rynecki, Moshe, 1881–1943. | Rynecki, Moshe, 1881–1943—Appreciation. | Jewish artists—Poland—Biography. | Art, Polish—20th century. | Jews in art. | BISAC: BIOGRAPHY & AUTOBIOGRAPHY/Personal Memoirs. | HISTORY/Jewish. | HISTORY/Holocaust.
Classification: LCC N7255.P63 R9637 2016 (print) | LCC N7255.P63 (ebook) | DDC 700.92—dc23
LC record available at http://lccn.loc.gov/2016012588

First Edition: September 2016

Printed in the United States of America
1 3 5 7 9 10 8 6 4 2

Jacket artwork by Moshe Rynecki; courtesy of the author
Jacket design by Emily Osborne
Title page art © Valentin Agapov/Shutterstock Images
Book design by Laura K. Corless

For my great-grandfather
who persisted in his passion for painting.
Culture belongs to all of us.

CONTENTS

chasing portraits

PREFACE

I was born in San Francisco on a summer day in 1969, just over twenty-five years after my great-grandfather perished in the Holocaust. My life began in a modern hospital with the prospect of a war-free childhood. Until I was forty-five I had never visited Poland. I tell you this to emphasize the fact that I am not a Holocaust survivor; I cannot bear witness to a past I did not personally experience and which seemed distant and tangential to me. I am, however, distinctly connected to the history of the Holocaust through the legacy of my great-grandfather's art.

I grew up with many of my great-grandfather's paintings on the walls of my childhood home. Moshe Rynecki (1881–1943) painted scenes detailing the everyday lives of Polish Jews in the 1920s and 1930s. His depictions of woodworkers, water carriers, women sewing, men studying the Talmud, even street performers, were the background of my childhood.

Moshe was a prolific artist whose work was exhibited in Warsaw and featured in a number of newspapers (both Polish and Yiddish) in his lifetime. Although he was known in Warsaw before the Second World War, he was not particularly famous.

Moshe was never supposed to be an artist. He had been born into a religious Jewish family in Poland, and painting was not on the short list of acceptable career options. My great-grandfather didn't care. He loved to draw and paint, even if it got him in trouble, which it sometimes did.

Moshe eventually grew up and left home. He lived in Warsaw, in a non-Jewish part of town, and led a surprisingly assimilated life. He and his wife, Perla Rynecki (née Mittelsbach), ran an art supply store. To be fair, Perla managed the store and family life, while Moshe went out into the world to paint. He painted constantly. By the time the Nazis invaded Poland on the first of September in 1939, he had painted more than eight hundred artworks and sculpted a number of pieces as well.

Moshe continued to paint after the Nazi invasion, but as conditions for Jews worsened, he became worried about protecting his body of work. At that point my great-grandfather made the fateful decision to divide his paintings and sculptures into bundles and to ask friends and acquaintances to hide them. To those who agreed, he promised he would return after the war ended (whenever that might happen) to retrieve the bundles. Soon after, Moshe willingly went to live in the Warsaw Ghetto. His son, my Grandpa George, who lived with false papers in a Polish neighborhood in Warsaw, begged his father not to go. And when conditions in the ghetto worsened, George offered to find a way to get Moshe out. But Moshe didn't want to leave—he wanted to "be with his people"—and whatever happened to them would happen to him. "If it's death, so be it," he said the last time he ever spoke with his son.

Though Moshe was ultimately deported and murdered by the Nazis, his wife, Perla, managed to survive the Holocaust. After the war she did her best amid the near total devastation in and around Warsaw to recover her husband's art. Ultimately, she found only 120 paintings, stashed in a cellar in the Praga district of the city. Grandpa George wrote in his reminiscences of the war years that his mother finding them was a "miracle." For more than fifty years, my family assumed all that remained of my great-grandfather's collection was the work Perla had recovered.

In 1999 I built a website dedicated to sharing my great-grandfather's art. At first not much happened, but over time, with the help of information I found posted on the Internet, friendships I made on social media, and the kindness of strangers, I began to find clues that more of my great-grandfather's paintings had survived the Second World War. Sometimes I discovered accession numbers of works held by museums, but no other information; other times I found photos of the works but no clues as to the location or holders of the originals; and sometimes I lucked out and private collectors with my great-grandfather's paintings contacted me. Of course, not everyone who had my great-grandfather's artwork wanted to speak to me. Some were afraid of the great-granddaughter asking for pictures and information about how the paintings were obtained. Others were more generous, sending photographs of Rynecki paintings in their possession and even allowing me into their homes to see the works and interview them. As my project gained momentum, and I spoke to more people about my search, I heard from others what I'd always felt personally: not only was the story amazing, but the art was beautiful.

There would be no story to tell if the Holocaust had not happened, but this story is less about the Shoah and more about my great-grandfather's art and what happened to his body of work in the aftermath of the Second World War. If the paintings could speak, it would be their story to tell. But they cannot, and so I wrote this book to share my story of discovery.

I am uniquely situated to tell the *Chasing Portraits* story. I grew up surrounded by my great-grandfather's paintings. I studied his art and learned to discern his ethnographic and impressionistic documentation of Polish-Jewish life from a young age. For more than fifteen years I have researched and written about Moshe's work to make the archival information, history, and narrative connections come alive.

Over the past several years, there has been a lot of publicity about lost and looted art from the Nazi era. While much of the recent interest centers around the astronomical value of famous artworks both lost and found, there are much greater numbers of lesser known pieces that vanished during the war, and each has its own tale to tell. *Chasing Portraits* seeks to tell one of those stories in order to share the rich history in the scenes my great-grandfather painted as well as what the paintings themselves represent as survivors.

ONE

A Jewish Girl Should Know

"Echh, what is friendship? There are never good friends. They all want something," Grandpa George said to me from where he sat on the couch in my grandparents' living room.

"But, Grandpa, I have friends at school."

"You just think they're friends. There are no such things as friends. Never trust anyone," he said, wagging his finger at me.

Grandma, who sat next to me, put her arm around my shoulders and came to my defense. "Why do you say this to her? She's just a girl," she told Grandpa.

"A girl?" Grandpa half stated and half asked. He pursed his lips, shrugged his shoulders, and lifted his hands to question. "Alex," he said, and pointed at Dad, "was younger than she is now when the Nazis marched into Poland. Alex watched me dig ditches to slow down the advancing German forces, and he wasn't even three yet! She should know these things. A Jewish girl. She should know," he said to Grandma.

"Never trust anyone? But, Grandpa, that's mean. You shouldn't say bad things about my friends." I tried to say it with conviction, but I felt uncertain. The girls at school were not always so nice. Sometimes they made fun of me. They called me "Elizabeth ding-dong" because my middle name is Bel. And that was Grandpa's fault. He had asked my parents to give me a middle name after his sister. My great-aunt's actual name was Bronisława, so Bel was a nickname. She had died a long time ago, in Warsaw, a place I had never been and wasn't certain I could locate on a map. After all, I was only in third grade and we had spent much of the school year studying California Native Americans like the Miwok tribe, not world geography. I thought being named after her was supposed to be an honor. I wasn't sure. I wondered if people had called her "ding-dong."

Grandpa looked at me, looked at Grandma, and then switched from English into Polish. I recognized the sounds and rhythm even though I didn't understand a word. I knew *tak* meant "yes," and *na zdrowie* (*Nahzdrovya*), which is said in a toast or after someone sneezes, meant something like "to your health." But those were not the words they used. I might not have understood the details, but I got the gist. Grandpa said something. Grandma fidgeted with her rings and gave a short response. Grandpa raised his voice and spoke emphatically. Grandma stood up from the ten-foot-long blue couch where we had been sitting side by side, looked across the room at Grandpa, and made some sort of plea. Grandpa raised his voice and slammed his glass of cognac on the redwood coffee table, which made the amber liquid slosh about. His words came out powerfully, forcefully. Grandma started to cry.

"Please, no war stories," she said. She ran from the room. Dad said something in Polish to Grandpa, and I looked to Mom for an explanation, as much for comfort as for understanding. Frightened, I pulled a pillow close to my body, hoping to find reassurance in its soft contours. The cookie and glass of juice I had been enjoying were forgotten.

I stood to go after Grandma. I wanted to console her, tell her that everything was okay. Mom grabbed my hand.

Me with Grandpa George and Grandma Stella.

"Let her be alone for a bit. She needs some private time," Mom told me. She looked unsure what to do, but before I could ask any questions, Grandpa began.

"I'm going to tell you a story," he said, pulling his glasses off his mostly bald head and onto his nose so he could see me clearly.

Though I was still confused, I perked up somewhat. I liked stories.

Fifteen years later, looking back, I couldn't remember the details. I remembered it had something to do with the Second World War, an arrest, and how the Nazis almost sent Dad and Grandma to a concentration camp. As a child, I hadn't thought the details were important, but now, too late, I realized how important, and yet how ephemeral, they were. Dad had called me at work to tell me Grandpa had died, and I was keenly aware I would never hear the story again. I was stuck in a recurring loop of regret and sadness, punctuated by mostly futile attempts to piece together more of my grandfather's story. I was bubbling over with questions I could no longer ask.

I was still stuck in that line of thinking that evening as I flew from Washington, D.C., to San Francisco. I had left work early to catch the flight. I was headed to Humboldt County, the farthest coastal reaches of Northern California, an outpost of redwood forests and former logging towns where Grandpa George had died and would be buried. Humboldt is only 250 miles from San Francisco, but it's a hard place to get to by car or airplane. It hugs Highway 101, which for much of its length north of the San Francisco Bay is a narrow two-lane road. As it approaches Humboldt County, it twists and turns its way through the Eel River canyon, and ultimately breaks through the "Redwood Curtain," as locals call it. The forests of enormous trees are both a physical barrier to travel and a symbol representing the cultural distance from the rest of California.

I had mixed feelings about the trip. On one hand, Dad had said I didn't need to be there.

"It's more important to be around for someone when they're living," he told me.

While I agreed with his sentiment, I thought he had missed the point, at least for me. I wasn't going for Grandpa; I was going to support Dad. Our family was small and getting smaller. I'm an only child, and Dad is an only child too. I also felt a need to support Grandma. I knew Grandma had her own mixed feelings about attending the funeral, in large part because my grandparents had divorced about a decade earlier.

I arrived early in the morning and ate a breakfast of toast and hot tea at the Eureka Inn. After breakfast, Mom and Dad chatted with me while I checked in, asking about the flight and giving me a rundown of the day's events. They then headed off to meet with the rabbi about the funeral, confirm the plot selection at the cemetery, invite a few more people to the graveside funeral service, and sort out the details for the reception we would host. My role was much simpler; I would spend the morning with Grandma.

Grandma met me in the lobby at ten, wearing a suit and heels. I felt sloppy in my jeans and T-shirt. She wanted to walk to the florist a few blocks away. "Elżbieta," she said and gave me a large hug. She took my hand, and we were off.

I loved Grandma, but I didn't know her very well. Or, rather, I did know her, but not the same way I imagined other kids knew their grandparents. Grandma spoke English with a strong Polish accent. She spoke very quietly because she feared making mistakes. She was so different than Grandpa, who figured if he kept talking everything would all come together and work itself out. Grandma was soft-spoken, seemingly doubting her skills, herself, and her place in the world. I wondered if she was more assertive when she spoke Polish.

"You help me pick out some flowers," Grandma said.

"Of course," and then we headed off to look at the local offerings.

The floral shop was small and didn't have a great deal of inventory. Grandma scoffed at the bouquets. Some were too big and said the wrong thing about Grandma's relationship to Grandpa.

"Red roses are too much?" Grandma both told and asked me at the same time. She meant they expressed love when what she really wanted to say was "We had a life together. We survived hell together." I picked up irises, but Grandma dismissed the bouquet. She pointed to yellow and white roses.

"Together," she announced to the florist. "The white is somber, the yellow is friendship," she said. With flowers in hand, we began our walk back to the hotel. "You flew a long way for the funeral," she said.

"You came a long way too, Grandma."

"It was a mistake." She shook her head and her eyes welled up.

"What was a mistake?" I asked. But I knew. I didn't really need to ask. The divorce. After the trauma of the war, they had built a new life together in America, and then they divorced. It was too much.

"Nothing, oh . . . Just nothing." She shook her head, embarrassed her inner thoughts had escaped her lips. "Oh, Elżbieta . . ." She bit her lower lip and grabbed on to my arm.

I looked at Grandma, waiting for her to finish the sentence, but she didn't and we walked back to the hotel in silence.

Around three o'clock the telephone in my hotel room rang.

"Are you ready?" Dad asked. "Meet in the lobby in fifteen minutes."

I stood and straightened my suit. It wasn't great, but it was what I owned. Blue pencil skirt and matching jacket with shoulder pads. Post-college interview outfit. I put on my flats and walked down to the lobby.

Dad didn't want to drive to the service, so we piled into a limousine. We rode south along Highway 101 through Eureka. The freeway went through the center of town. It was a vaguely depressing series of strip malls, offices, and light industrial workspaces supporting a slowly fading timber-based economy.

We arrived at Sunset Memorial Park just off Broadway, the main street. The cemetery was up on the hill. The limo went all the way to the top to reach the Jewish part of it, where the driver let us out.

"There's a nice view from up here," Dad said to no one in particular, and gestured toward the bay, which was visible on the horizon. "Dad will have a view from his final resting place." I nodded my head, not sure what to say. He won't ever see the view, I thought, but I was careful to keep the words to myself.

The rabbi was there. So were many longtime friends and acquaintances. I didn't know many of them because I had never lived here. Eureka was where Grandpa lived, worked, and put down roots in the Jewish community when he settled here in the mid-1950s. People had come to remember him, to pay their respects. The rabbi approached. In a hushed tone, he welcomed us to the cemetery and asked Dad if he was ready for the service to begin.

"Yes," Dad said softly.

"May I perform *keriah*?" the rabbi asked. Dad nodded.

The *keriah*, or the tearing of the mourner's clothes, is an ancient

Jewish ritual that is meant to give a physical way of expressing grief. We didn't actually tear our clothes. Instead, the rabbi pinned a black, torn ribbon to each of us. The ribbon was a symbol, a powerful one, indicating separation and finality. Prior to this moment, my family had taken the responsibility for the funeral details. With the *keriah* the responsibility shifted to the community. They must take care of us. The *keriah* was a way for us to express our anger and grief. It was a way to express loss and to begin the healing process.

"*Baruch atah Adonai, Dayan Ha-Emet*—Blessed are You, Adonai, Truthful Judge," the rabbi recited. We were to wear the torn ribbon for the first seven days of mourning—the period of shiva. I touched the ribbon, hoping it would impart wisdom, hoping for some sort of sign about how to mourn Grandpa, help my father, and aid my grandmother.

The rabbi began the service with a prayer, and then offered kind words of remembrance of Grandpa George as an individual and as a member of the community. Grandpa's casket was lowered to the bottom of the grave. The rabbi invited us to recite the mourner's kaddish.

"Yitgadal v'yitkadash sh'mei raba. B'alma di v'ra chirutei, v'yamlich malchutei, b'chayeichon uv'yomeichon, uv'chayei d'chol beit Yisrael, baagala uviz'man kariv. V'im'ru: Amen." [Exalted and hallowed be God's great name in the world which God created, according to plan. May God's majesty be revealed in the days of our lifetime and the life of all Israel—speedily, imminently, to which we say: Amen.]

As the prayer continued—there were several more stanzas—I stared toward the edge of the grave. I saw where the coffin had gone down. It was so final. After a time, I couldn't watch it anymore, and focused on the distance, toward the view Dad had pointed out when we arrived. I didn't want to be here. I didn't want to think about death.

The mourner's kaddish came to a close. The rabbi paused and then spoke to the mourners in English.

"It is tradition," he said, "for mourners to place earth in the grave. Using the back side of this shovel," he said, holding it up, "we scoop the earth onto the casket to show that this is not an easy task to perform. The Rynecki family invites you to be part of this important tradition."

Grandma went first. She shoveled a small piece of dirt onto the casket. Mom and Dad walked to the edge of the grave and each took a turn. I came next. The sound of the clods of dirt hitting the casket unnerved me. It was somehow both strangely comforting and deeply disturbing. I passed the shovel to someone else and walked away from the pile of dirt that would eventually completely cover the casket.

I lost track of how many people helped us bury Grandpa. When the last one had taken a turn at the shovel, the rabbi faced us and recited another Hebrew prayer. Then he issued an announcement from my family.

"You are all," he told the gathered crowd, "invited to join the Rynecki family at the Eureka Inn for a reception." The graveside service over, Dad, Mom, Grandma, and I climbed into the limousine for the return trip to the hotel. No one spoke. I stared out the window, uncomfortable at the silence. Everything I would normally think to talk about—my new job, my housemates, life in D.C.—seemed inappropriate given the circumstances.

The Eureka Inn had a room off the main lobby where we gathered. I played hostess and offered people glasses of wine, bottles of water, cheese and crackers. People I had met once, long ago, asked me questions about where I lived, what I did, how I got to Eureka in time for the funeral. I heard a lot of "your grandpa was quite a man" comments. They told me stories about his scrap metal business, about building construction, and cattle ranching. I smiled and listened politely, although it got harder and harder to do so. The toll of the late night flight and the emotional exhaustion of the funeral started to wear me down.

Dad made his way over to me. "How you doing, Ace?" he asked. I looked at Dad in his crisp dark suit and his tie done just so. Not exactly a dapper dresser, but at five-ten, with a trim build, Dad always looked dashing and classy.

Me with my parents and grandparents in the early 1970s.

"I think I've talked to almost everyone," I said.

"Thanks for helping out."

"That's what families do," I told him.

"Well, but you made a big effort to come out and be here today. I didn't think it would matter if you missed the funeral, but now I know it was good that you came. Thanks for making the effort."

"Of course," I said, breaking into a yawn.

"Go get some rest," he offered. "We have a big day of packing tomorrow." Although the funeral was over, it was just the first step, and in some ways the easiest.

Calling Grandpa George's property "the Ranch" was sort of a stretch, or maybe it was wishful thinking. It made it sound grander than it was. The land itself was a long, skinny strip totaling twenty or so acres next to Highway 101. Access to the property was up a narrow, curving driveway lined with Monterey pine trees. The driveway was unmarked. You had to know it was there in order to find it.

The house on the ranch was a dreadful L-shaped structure that needed a lot of work. It had begun as a pump house: a small square building with a door on one side and windows on two of the other sides. It had a small sink and running water. When Grandpa added on to the pump house, he had joined a new rectangular structure to the existing square. The new part was like the long side of a capital L, with the old pump house as the short stubby end. Adding a master bedroom, bathroom, kitchen, and living room had made the house livable. But I hated it, finding it depressing and uninspired even under the best of circumstances. Now knowing Grandpa had died there just a few days ago made being there emotionally exhausting.

The ranch wasn't far from Eureka, maybe a half hour away, but we left early to get a good start on the day. Although we had buried Grandpa yesterday, we had to take on the task of clearing out his personal property from the home. Eureka was too far from the Bay Area to put this task off for another trip. Dad also worried about leaving the house full but unoccupied. The plan was to pack up valuable personal items and donate everything else, so our focus was on sorting. There were a couple of moving vans and crews to help with the heavy lifting and packing.

Grandpa had a lot of art in his home. He was an avid art collector. I segmented the collection in my head into three distinct parts: his father's art painted in Poland in the 1920s and 1930s, paintings purchased since he arrived in the United States, and sculpture. Dad didn't have a clue where he was going to put it all, but for now we placed it into boxes to have it trucked down to the Bay Area. The moving crew pulled out "mirror" boxes and asked Dad where they should start. He pointed them to the pump house room, where the majority of the Moshe Rynecki art had been stored.

Dad wandered aimlessly from room to room and asked Mom where he should start. She was naturally very organized. She still teased Dad that her dowry was her filing cabinet. She loved sorting, filing, and labeling. It gave her a great sense of accomplishment when each and every item had a predictable home and place. She pulled a pen out of her purse and put a yellow legal pad of paper on the kitchen counter.

"We'll number the boxes and create a chart here"—she tapped the pad of paper—"of what goes into each box."

"We could start in the kitchen," I said. "I can pack the dishes, glasses, and pots and pans."

"I'm happy to work in the bedroom," Mom offered. "I'm assuming you're donating most of those items."

Dad nodded in agreement. He had already scheduled a pickup from the house later in the afternoon.

The three of us headed off to our assigned tasks. The movers gave me flattened boxes and tape. I found a pile of newspapers to stack between dishes and began emptying the cabinets into the boxes. I worked quickly. I didn't have any attachment to the items in the kitchen, but as the boxes grew full and the cabinets more empty, I became increasingly melancholy. After an hour or so, Mom came into the kitchen.

"Do you need help in here?" she asked. "I need a break from the bedroom."

"Sure," I said, and I pointed to the pots and pans in the lower cabinets that needed packing.

"It's tough going through his clothes," Mom said. "It's so personal. Some clothes I don't remember well, but others remind me very much of your grandpa."

Dad came in through the front door. He had been supervising the movers. Frankly, I hadn't seen him pack anything himself yet.

"Want to walk down to the barn with me?" he asked.

"Sure," I said. The three of us headed toward the gate that led into the field and down to the barn.

The barn wasn't visible from the house. It was down the hill and hidden away by trees and the slope of the land. The ground was bumpy and the footing uneven as we headed down the hill. The wild grasses were tall and tickled me when they brushed my hands, but I liked the feel of them against my skin. Although the barn no longer had a practical purpose, it was my favorite place on the property. Aged by the constant exposure to damp air, its loose boards creaked and groaned as the fog blew in from Northern California's Lost Coast.

"The roof on the barn should be replaced," Dad said. "I'm afraid it's been neglected for too long and might fall down."

I nodded. It was neglected, and had a ramshackle look, but that's what I liked about it. It was authentic. It felt well connected to the land, as if it had been here forever.

"We aren't going to be able to pack up everything today," Mom said, sidestepping Dad's focus on the barn. She was a city girl at heart, far more comfortable in Ferragamo heels and a tailored suit, and ranching questions weren't her forte. But Mom was also practical. She had a Midwestern sensibility acquired growing up in Minnesota, and Dad liked that about her.

Dad nodded, but seemed not to hear her as he looked up at the roof of the barn and pointed to the beams.

"It's amazing it has held up so well for so long," he said. "Maybe a steel roof on the barn would be good. A red one would be classic, don't you think?"

I looked at Mom. She shrugged her shoulders. She knew Dad didn't want to talk about packing. She didn't push the topic.

We stood in silence for a few moments and, without words, headed back. We returned to the house by a different path, a way I liked somewhat better. The longer route went through a grove of trees and passed by an abandoned fort and tree swing. I liked looking at both even though I was too old for them.

I went back into the kitchen and tackled the drawers. There was a pretty beat-up set of cutlery and old steak knives. I wrapped the knives in a dishtowel and put them into a box.

Dad walked by the kitchen with a bronze sculpture of a horse he had wrapped in towels.

"I think I'll put this in the trunk of the car," he said. "It's too awkward for the crew to pack."

I turned back to finish up with the pots and pans. I taped up my last box and turned to walk to the bedroom to see if Mom needed help.

She sorted through the sock drawer. She tried to find mates to the singletons. She had a pile of dark socks, white socks, and unpaired socks. She was very thorough. I would have probably just thrown all the socks into the donation bag and called it a day.

"I think you better take a look at this," Dad said to both of us as he walked into the bedroom right behind me with a pile of papers in his hands.

"What is it?" I asked.

"I'm not sure. I found it in the trunk of Grandpa's car when I went to put the sculpture away," he said. "It looks like he wrote some things. I just flipped through it a bit. It looks like a memoir."

"Can I see?" I asked.

Dad handed me the collection of paper. The stack was a printout from a dot matrix printer. Some of the edges with the holed margins that guided the paper through the printer were still attached. The font was small and looked similar to the text from an old-fashioned typewriter. Some of the words were crossed out. I recognized Grandpa's handwriting.

Flipping through the pages, not actually stopping to read any of it, I saw words that caught my attention: Jews, Warsaw, anti-Semitism, hiding, Germans, Majdanek, and Hitler. I looked up at Dad.

"Oh my God," I said. "It *is* a memoir. He wrote about the war years." I felt an intense desire to read every single page at once, which made it almost impossible to focus. I sat down, thinking it would help me concentrate, but I kept flipping pages. I couldn't stop to actually read an entire page.

A number of years before, when I was sixteen, Grandpa had shown me some of his writing. He had wanted my opinion about whether or not it was any good. His use of English was confusing and sloppy. He had commingled stories, so that a tale about Poland in 1480 was intersected with a memory of the Second World War. I hadn't understood the thread of his story. I couldn't make out his goal in storytelling. I don't exactly think I was mean in my critique, but I didn't offer praise or insist he keep writing.

"I know I'm not talented like James Michener, and who am I to even compare myself to a writer of such magnitude?" Grandpa had said. "I never spent a single day in an English-speaking school, but I have stories to tell. And I must, because I am a survivor, and if I do not write them, who will?"

I recalled this exchange as I looked at his journal and realized he had continued writing despite my lack of enthusiasm. Grandpa had felt the importance of his story and of passing on this written history to his granddaughter. He had been wise in ways I didn't comprehend. He had written so that when he was gone, I would know.

How did I know this? Because as I turned the pages, unable to read any one in its entirety, I spotted a paragraph, one that had my name in it. Grandpa wrote:

> *Some say it will never happen again. Well, it's too easy. It did happen. They killed openly without fear. Where and how did they have that much hatred toward us? It could happen again. We cannot and will not forget. We will carry it, like the Bible, forever. There are hundreds of books on the subject. Nevertheless, I am a Jew and I write. I'll do it till the end of my days. If only for my granddaughter, Elizabeth, to know the truth, and not to be afraid of it.*

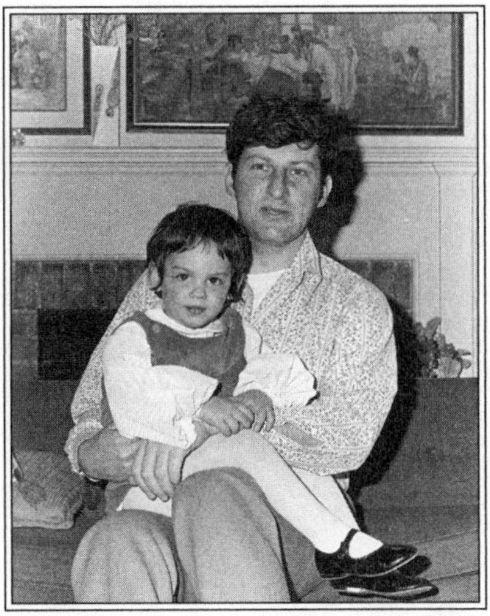

Me and Dad.

Time stopped for a moment. The nostalgia and sadness I felt weighed upon me. If history and legacy make a sound as they fall upon your shoulders, the clamor of Grandpa's words landing on mine was deafening.

For a long while I was torn, unsure of how to even begin to bear the responsibility I felt, and only fitfully engaged with my family history. Over time, I realized how deeply I yearned to learn more, and I began to pursue the lost fragments of my family's history—a journey that eventually came to be called *Chasing Portraits*. This book is that story. But the story doesn't start with me; it begins around 1890 with my great-grandfather Moshe, in the Polish town of Siedlce.

TWO

The Trouble with Moshe

Moshe didn't mean to pain his father. The boy gave him trouble, or as he sometimes said in Yiddish, *tsures*, the *t* slurring into the *s* and the hissing *s* at the end somehow hanging guilt over the young child's head. He'd been at it again, drawing a figure from memory—a scene he knew well—the rabbi leading the congregation in prayer—and now his father stood over him, scowling. Moshe held his breath. Would Father scold him, again, for drawing, for disregarding the second commandment, "thou shalt not make graven images"?

His father peered closely at the paper. The work was good. A sketch of the rabbi at temple.

"It shouldn't be quite so stiff in the shoulders. It's fabric. You need to drape it more, let it fall more effortlessly," his father said and pointed to the tallith (the Jewish prayer shawl).

Moshe heaved a sigh of relief. At least he wasn't in trouble this time. And his father was right, it was too stiff. As a prominent tailor of uniforms, Moshe's father, Avraham, worked with fabric every day. He knew how to pick out well-made bolts of cloth that would hold up through pattern cutting and all the wear and tear the clothing would endure over the course of its life. His clothing factory did everything by hand, and he knew how hard soldiers and schoolchildren were on their uniforms. Avraham made sure what he made was of the finest quality. Good workmanship meant pleased customers and more orders.

"It's so hard," he told his father. Moshe picked up his pencil and found a part of the paper where he had not yet sketched. "The tallith starts out straight, and has parallel blue lines, but once it's draped over the rabbi's shoulders, it changes," he said. He shook his head and tried again. He'd been working on this particular scene for several days, but just couldn't get it right. And now his father had confirmed what he had already suspected. The tallith in his drawing looked wrong. Thinking about it gave him a headache. He put down the pencil and looked up at his father. He thought again about asking if he might apprentice with someone who could teach him, but he knew better than to plead. The last time he'd begged for lessons his father had scoffed.

"You're lucky I don't forbid you from drawing altogether! This is a hobby, not a trade."

Moshe knew what his father meant. He was supposed to be like the craftsmen in town—the cobbler, the elderly toymaker who painted his creations unusual colors because he had limited access to paint, the wheelwright, the blacksmith, or even the bookbinder. Tradespeople fascinated Moshe. He loved watching them work, observing how they hunched over their workbenches and held their tools, but he didn't want to *be like* the tradespeople, he wanted to *paint* them. Unfortunately, he knew his father would say no.

Siedlce wasn't the only town Moshe knew. He spent his early childhood in Międzyrzecze, a place whose name meant "Between Rivers." It was a shtetl, a small Jewish settlement a little less than one hundred kilometers (about sixty miles) east of Warsaw, off the main roads, surrounded

Lathe *(1934). Held by the Rynecki family.*

by Polish farmers and their fertile farmlands. The community had few inhabitants: some landlords lived in the countryside, a few Russian soldiers and police, a doctor, a rabbi, a few midwives, a small Catholic church with a priest, and a tiny slaughterhouse for the *shochet*, the butcher who followed strict Jewish rules and rituals for the slaughter of poultry and cattle.

The Rynecki family moved to the larger but still primarily agricultural town of Siedlce when Moshe was about ten years old. The town's Polish residents said the name of the town "Shed-lits-a," and its Jewish residents preferred the pronunciation "Shedlitz." The town sat between the Vistula and Bug rivers on flat land with extensive marshes in the north and southeast. Four railways ran through the town, making it an economic hub.

Siedlce's Jewish population was both significant and long-standing, including the presence of innkeepers, merchants, and artisans from the mid-sixteenth century. In the eighteenth century, both a Jewish hospital and *Beit Midrash* (a Jewish place of study) were founded, and there was a large Jewish cemetery. Until 1819, the Siedlce rabbis oversaw the Jewish community in Warsaw.

Leaving Międzyrzecze for Siedlce meant a better life and more

Untitled (1929). Whereabouts of this painting are unknown.
It was last part of the Rynecki collection in Italy in the late 1940s.

opportunities for the family. The wide tree-lined boulevards and public gathering spots were a source of pride to its residents. In the Jewish neighborhood, homes and businesses along the streets stood close to sewer ditches, with a near constant stench of waste. For Avraham, the move gave him a chance to expand his business holdings to real estate and to parlay his own talent for drawing into making architectural drawings for the construction of a few houses and apartment buildings. For Moshe the move translated into the chance at an education beyond the *cheder* (the Jewish religious school).

When the family relocated to Siedlce, they moved into a three-story brick house. It was a remarkable home, even without running water or plumbing. While the outhouse was a nice feature, the home's best asset was its cellar. It was a cool, damp space with compacted dirt floors, divided by two long dark corridors that created different rooms. The temperature in the basement was constant all year long, making it possible to store potatoes, cabbage, and barrels and barrels of pickles.

"We really don't need to bother him," Moshe said, knowing his father wouldn't heed his words. They'd been at it for days, this arguing about his drawing. Somehow, his father had gotten it into his head to visit Marian Trzebiński at his home studio in Warsaw. Trzebiński had the double distinction of having attended high school in Siedlce and working as an artist in Warsaw.

"If anyone knows whether or not a boy artist from Siedlce can make a living doing this work, it's him. We're going," said Moshe's father. "Now, get your things." Moshe reached for his sketch pad. He didn't want to go, yet perhaps he might make the most of it by sketching on the train ride into Warsaw.

The walking distance from the train station to Trzebiński's address wasn't far. Before long, Moshe's father announced their arrival. "This is it." He pointed to Marian Trzebiński's name written on the building's directory and knocked.

Moshe stood with his father in the street waiting for someone to answer the door, but secretly hoping the artist wasn't home. He felt awkward standing in this neighborhood in his traditional black cassock and a Jewish black cap. Warsaw had Jewish neighborhoods, he was certain, but he felt out of place in front of this particular door. He disliked how his clothing defined him: that it indicated, and to some summarized, the whole of who he was. He wanted people to understand him as a person, for his passion for painting, not because of his religion.

"I am certain we are in the right place. Perhaps I should knock louder," his father said. Moshe sneaked glances at his father while mostly staring at the door of Trzebiński's studio. As things stood, he still had a chance at being an artist. What if Trzebiński said he was no good, told him to pack it up and forget his dreams of being a painter? Maybe it would be a blessing if Trzebiński did not answer the door. His father banged more loudly on the door, three times in a row.

"Maybe we should come back later," Moshe said.

"Wait. I hear something," Avraham said, and in a moment, the door opened.

Moshe immediately felt embarrassment. Trzebiński appeared to still be wearing his nightclothes. Perhaps they'd awakened him from a nap? Moshe wanted to leave, but his father clearly wasn't going anywhere except inside. Trzebiński peered into the street at Moshe and his father.

"Good day, Marian. I'm sorry to have disturbed you. We wish to come inside, to speak to you about my son's art."

"Of course, of course, please, come in." Trzebiński motioned for both of them to enter his studio. He closed the door and then pointed to two chairs for them to take. There was not a third chair. The artist crawled into his bed. "What can I do for you?" he asked Moshe's father.

"I hope you remember me. I certainly remember you! Your mother used to bring you to my shop. I sewed you several shirts and uniforms when you were younger. I remember your mother well. She used to go on and on about how your older brother was doing so well in school and how he would someday become someone, but you . . ." Avraham Rynecki's voice trailed off. "Well, she used to complain about how you had no interest in school, that you would spend all day drawing. I remember I used to laugh at her. Back then I didn't know God would send me the same punishment. Now I know."

Trzebiński stared blankly at Moshe's father as he told this story, but then suddenly his expression changed. "I remember," he exclaimed. "I haven't seen you in at least twenty years! You were always running around with half-stitched clothes in your hands. You used to repair clothes for the students at the Siedlce Gymnasium [High School]."

Moshe's father sat in his chair a little bit taller, prouder.

"Yes!" he told Trzebiński. "I'm so pleased you've remembered me."

"What brings you here? What can I do for you?" Trzebiński asked Avraham.

"It's him," Moshe's father said, pointing at him. "It's nothing but trouble with him and nothing helps to bring a stop to the art! He studied for a bit with Ignacy Gajewski in Siedlce, but"—and he shrugged his shoulders and shook his head—"he didn't really learn anything there."

Moshe tried to block out the unpleasant tone to his father's voice. How could he say Moshe hadn't learned anything from Gajewski, when he had gained so much from the experience? He learned about perspective and color, and that was just the start. Moshe could teach himself only so much. Other artists understood why it was so important for him to paint. He tried to set aside his passion for putting the images in his head onto paper. He knew it would make his father happier if he would stop drawing. He couldn't stop. Not ever. The passion to paint eclipsed everything else in his life.

Trzebiński seemed to be listening to Moshe's father, but he stole a glance at the young man. His father noticed.

"He can show you," Avraham Rynecki said, gesturing at his son. "You just ask him. Tell him what to draw!"

Trzebiński seemed a bit surprised at the command, but recovered quickly.

"All right," he said. "Can you draw arguing Jews?"

"Of course," Moshe told Trzebiński, but as he moved into the other room to avoid his father's line of questioning about how much money an artist makes, Moshe wondered why he must draw them arguing. This was not a scene that spoke to him. He preferred to show them praying. He sat down and sketched, maybe fifteen to twenty minutes went by, and he got lost in his drawing. When he realized his father had stopped talking, he stood up and returned to Trzebiński. He handed him the sketch pad with his drawing.

Trzebiński placed it on the bed in front of him. He pursed his lips and nodded his head, left to right, up and down.

"Well," Moshe's father asked, "what do you think?"

"It's good," Trzebiński said. He looked right at Moshe. "It's raw, but he's got talent."

"Ehh," his father said dismissively. "Perhaps, but this drawing. It's a hobby, not a career. I hoped you'd dissuade him from this line of work."

"Good luck with your art. You have much to learn, but your talent can take you far," Trzebiński said to Moshe.

Moshe mumbled a "Thank you," and then looked down, uncertain what he could or should say next.

"Thank you for your time, Marian," his father said. "We'll be on our way. We've taken enough of your morning. Sorry to have troubled you."

Moshe's father grabbed his arm and pushed him toward the front door. When they were outside, he turned to his son.

"Did you hear what he told me when I asked how much money he makes from his art? I'll tell you what he said . . . just about one hundred rubles a month. Nothing else! You see, this is not a business. No business at all! I sent you to schools in Kraków, Munich, and Paris, and what can you earn? Just twenty-five rubles a week! This is no business."

"I don't care," Moshe said, but his father did not listen.

"This is no life for you," his father insisted. "Look at these stone stairs! They need repairing. And did you see how Trzebiński lives? I'll tell you how he lives. In an attic, with no servants. He had to open the door by himself. And did you see the bed? He sleeps under a thin cover. He doesn't even have a comforter."

"I don't care," Moshe said again, but his father didn't pay any attention. He was ten steps ahead of his son, who could still hear him.

"Twenty-five rubles a week! That's what I pay my employees. This isn't a job, a career. This is a waste. This will never do."

"Why not?" Moshe asked. "I like to paint. It makes me happy."

"You know what, Mojsiele . . ." His voice trailed off.

Moshe sighed. His father's use of his nickname always made him feel like a child. His irritation was quickly chased away by fear of answering the question and, even more, fear of a future about which he would apparently have little say.

"I'll tell you what. I'll buy you a paper store just like Celnik in Siedlce has. An art store. This will make you happy and make you money. Celnik owns eleven houses already. He is doing well and you are going to do well also. Quit painting. Painting is for a stupid goy, not for a smart Jew."

"Please, no," Moshe pleaded. A store? What would he ever do with a store? Moshe imagined he would be chained to it all day, waiting for customers, stocking inventory, staring out its windows. A store would never do. "Please, Father," Moshe asked, "sign me up for drawing school."

Avraham Rynecki shook his head from side to side.

"I'm not promising anything, but I thought you might say that. I'll make an appointment with Professor Kotarbiński at the Municipal Drawing School."

A few days later, setting off for Teatralny Square, the hub of Warsaw's art and culture scene, Moshe could hardly believe it.

Professor Kotarbiński gave Avraham Rynecki and his son a tour of the school, showed them the models students drew from and the plasters they used in class assignments. Moshe wanted to enroll right away, but before the tour was even over his father started in again.

"Listen to what I have to tell you, Mojsiele. This art world, you already did models in Siedlce and even plaster at Gajewski's. Even if they teach you a practical skill like how to paint a candlestick, this is not a business. I remember what that painting you did of Napoleon sold for in Siedlce. Do you remember?"

"Of course," Moshe said, "I remember."

"Twelve rubles, to Dr. Frumkinow. You can't make money selling a painting for twelve rubles."

They left the Municipal Drawing School and Moshe had a bad feeling about how it would all end. Over the next several months, his father relentlessly told him both that he could not make a living as an artist and that he had a plan to fix it. He seemed so pleased with himself Moshe didn't ask for details. His future was slowly hammered into place by his father, a future he felt shifting from his dream of art to his father's dream of commerce. And it was a future that arrived all too soon.

Maybe it was pride that made Moshe's father insist they return to Trzebiński's studio to share the news. Moshe really did not want to go, but his father insisted. "He'll be your first customer," he proclaimed.

Back at the doorstep to Trzebiński's apartment Moshe waited while his father knocked on the door. Once again, they roused the artist from his bed. When they were settled inside Avraham made the announcement.

"My problem is solved! Mojsiele wouldn't listen to me, so I took care of it. He is now married." He smiled triumphantly. Moshe stared at his hands.

Trzebiński tried to hide his surprise, but from the way he looked at Moshe, he felt pity. Moshe felt like crying. Trzebiński was quiet. Avraham was jubilant with his solution to the "problem" of what to do with his son.

"If he takes care of his wife, he won't need to live from his painting. I've purchased a paper store for Mojsiele and his wife, Perla. She is from a merchant family. They will be a happy couple. Come visit them sometime. The store is at 24 Krucza Street."

THREE

Paintings

The apartment building at 24 Krucza offered tenants a fashionable art nouveau structure with a modern architectural flair. Built in a vibrant and thriving new neighborhood, it was a place where Gentiles lived. It was just a five-minute walk to Jerozolimskie Avenue, one of the newer prosperous neighborhoods in Warsaw, and only a bit farther to Krasiński Park, a verdant, shady expanse where Moshe enjoyed painting in the afternoons. The location seemed ideal for the newlyweds.

Moving from Siedlce to Warsaw both excited and intimidated Moshe. Establishing residency in the city gave him the chance to discover new places and people to paint. As a city of more than a million residents, of which about 30 percent were Jewish, Warsaw offered Moshe the opportunity to recast himself in a more secular, metropolitan guise. Although still a man of faith, he no longer wore the traditional black cassock and Jewish black cap. Instead, he accented his slim build and modest stature with a small beard and neat mustache, preferring to wear a button-down shirt and dress pants.

Moshe and Perla settled smoothly into domestic life in a two-bedroom street-level apartment behind their retail shop while they went about the business of setting up and running their art supply store. Moshe had strong opinions on the numbers, types, and brands of brushes, pencils, paints, and paper the store should stock. Perla considered his views, then placed orders for items she determined would sell best and make the business profitable. While Moshe painted, Perla invested time and energy in the shop. Perhaps it was unfair Perla took care of business and financial concerns so Moshe could paint without a care, but honestly the arrangement worked out well for both. As the daughter of merchants, Perla understood the life of a store owner and took on these responsibilities with practiced authority. Running the store gave Perla her own domain, and she liked the independence it afforded her. Similarly, while Moshe was deeply invested in the world of art, he didn't have the kind of focus needed to run a successful business. So while both Moshe and Perla had been apprehensive about marriage, the union worked because their disparate interests allowed each a surprising level of freedom and autonomy for the culture in which they lived.

With the business flourishing under Perla's guidance, Moshe focused on his art. In 1906, he enrolled at the School of Fine Arts in Warsaw. The school, founded by Professor Kazimierz Stabrowski (1869–1929) among others, did more than train students in classical art techniques; it engaged and developed the broader Warsaw art community and culture. Some of this stemmed from Stabrowski's cosmopolitan perspective, gained from his time at the Academy of Fine Arts in St. Petersburg and his master's workshop completed in Paris.

Moshe wasn't so sure about some of Stabrowski's views on art and technique, but he loved to paint, and at art school he was able to focus on painting every day. Whereas his earlier art teachers, such as Ignacy Gajewski, offered encouragement, it was instruction with the professors at the Warsaw academy that helped him develop his talent and hone his style. Moshe spent much of his schooling under the tutelage of Marian Trzebiński and Professor Adolf Eduard Herstein. Trzebiński, the artist for whom his father had little respect, offered encouragement and optimism that he might transition from a hobby painter from Siedlce into a Warsaw-based artist. Professor Herstein exposed Moshe to different styles of painting as a means to bring expressiveness to his works. In Professor Herstein's personal case, this was the use of heavy impasto, an impressionism technique, to control light and to give a real sense of depth and dimension to the subject. Although exposure to different styles, approaches, and techniques appealed to Moshe as he developed his own, in the end he mostly rejected Herstein's approach. One thing that intrigued Moshe about Herstein, and that really stuck with him as he moved forward as an artist, was that in addition to being a painter, Herstein was an engraver. Moshe liked the idea that artists could move across media, particularly when he discovered he enjoyed experiments in wood, clay, and much later (in the 1930s), in plastics, which were just becoming commercially available.

While learning about and experimenting with different styles and techniques was important to Moshe, he didn't use new techniques just to be fashionable. For example, Cubism, an enormously influential movement that revolutionized many artists' approach to painting and sculpture before the First World War, held little appeal for Moshe. Moshe didn't want to be in the studio studying and practicing technique, cross-pollinating with other artists. Instead, he wanted to be out observing and painting what he called "Jewish folktales."

He was at home in the alleys of small Jewish neighborhoods in the large city of Warsaw.

These neighborhoods were a window into a silent but powerful cultural struggle between the metropolitan culture of Warsaw and traditional Jewish life. As a big city, Warsaw exerted a strong pull toward mixing and assimilation, by providing jobs and other opportunities for those who learned Polish language and customs. The resulting tension fascinated Moshe. He observed the strange mixture of culture and change for Jews who were shifting in various ways between traditional and contemporary secular society. He saw the world changing around him, changes that were reflected in his own life. He knew his own movement away from the traditional Jewish life his parents preferred was increasingly common.

While Moshe saw change all around him, his painting focused much more on traditional Jewish life, and that focus was reflected in his choice of style. Moshe didn't want those who saw his paintings to ask questions about the artist; he wanted them to focus on the people in his paintings—the beggars, laborers, draymen, toy makers, and water carriers—and ultimately the culture and religious life that surrounded them. As an ethnographically inspired painter, he thought that abstract or avant-garde styles would detract from the world he wanted to portray.

Two years after Moshe began his studies at the School of Fine Arts in Warsaw, Perla became pregnant, and in August of 1908 a daughter, Bronisława, arrived. Bronisława, whom Perla and Moshe often called Bronisia or Isia, was the apple of Moshe's eye. A year and nine months later, in April 1910, a son, Jerzy, was born. The family squeezed into the two-bedroom apartment on the ground floor behind the store for quite some time, but as the children got bigger and Moshe's art continued to eat up space, the apartment was just too small. They were eventually able, given the store's success, to move into a larger apartment, a suite of six rooms on the third floor. The larger apartment managed to fit Moshe's art, as well as an upright ebony piano and red mahogany furniture, with only modest overcrowding. Perhaps the greatest feature of the apartment was its large kitchen, which served both as the family's dining room and as the center of the household. It was where everyone gathered when they were home, and at least in the winter, that was because it was the warmest room in the house. Although the apartment had a heating system, it was a rudimentary one, consisting of a tall oven between each pair of rooms. One side featured white porcelain tile; the other was dominated by an opening for coal. Because the ovens had no fans or other means to circulate air, each oven only heated the air nearest it, so Jerzy and his sister crowded close to the heater to keep warm.

Coal was a precious commodity kept deep in a subbasement. Somebody had to bring it up four flights of stairs, and that job fell to Jerzy and Isia. Not surprisingly, neither sibling particularly enjoyed the task. It was scary, cold, damp, unlit, and deep underground, which made the journey to get coal quite creepy. They generally went down as a pair, since they found it frightening, but as they got older, they began to see the basement as a weird sort of playground, since no one else went down there.

Although Isia and Jerzy bonded over their shared dislike of the basement and their coal delivery responsibilities, the two were not particularly close, in part because Jerzy was jealous of what he saw as favoritism toward his sister. Isia, a petite and lovely girl who treasured books and excelled in school, could, in Moshe's eyes, do no wrong. Jerzy, however, was often in trouble with his parents, both because of his almost daily clashes with Isia and because of his disputes with neighborhood kids. Perla and Moshe tried to warn both Isia and Jerzy that as the only Jewish children in the apartment house, they ought to steer clear of the Gentile neighbors and their anti-Semitic jabs. It was a pronouncement both meant to protect and shelter their family. Isia took the message to heart and did her best to avoid the neighbors. Although Jerzy and Isia were both chased by the Gentile children, Isia otherwise stayed away from them, while Jerzy often got into fights. Fortunately for Jerzy, no one at his school knew, or at least no one told the school headmaster, about his Jewish ancestry. Jerzy attended a prestigious private school, Kretchmar, where the headmaster, Mr. Wilczek, sometimes called for lice inspections. Whenever this happened, all the students had to strip down to their underwear to be inspected. During inspections, Mr. Wilczek would invariably call forward the few known Jewish children in the school and send them home. Jerzy looked Gentile, his name was Gentile, and so when Wilczek examined him for lice he said, "Even if I see one or two lice on your head, I won't send you home. Only the dirty Jews!" Jerzy was scared and embarrassed. He kept quiet in order to stay in school. It was the first time he really understood his parents' warnings about Gentiles: that anti-Semitism was rampant and its consequences were significant.

While Jerzy and Isia were growing up, Perla always had a live-in maid, typically a girl from Moshe's place of birth, Międzyrzecze, in the apartment to help tidy up and cook. The maids were hired because Perla needed the additional set of hands to help around the apartment while she was busy in the store, but also as a *mitzvah*, a good deed. The job offered the girls, who were often from very poor families, and who could be as young as sixteen or seventeen, work, a place to live, and a steppingstone toward a better life. It also made it easier for their families to make ends meet, since there were few job opportunities for young women in smaller towns and villages. Often the girls who came to live with them arrived at the family home with not much more than the clothes on their backs. One such girl, Rachel, was amazed by all the new and surprising things she found in the city. She seemed particularly fascinated by water coming out of pipes in the walls, as well as the drainpipes which whisked wastewater away. Perla provided what she could to the young girls, but Rachel presented a particularly challenging problem since upon her arrival she had outgrown her shoes. Perla had trouble finding replacement shoes. Until they could find a pair to fit her, Rachel borrowed shoes from Moshe. Since they were several sizes too large, she found moving around awkward, and struggled to stand close to the stove as she prepared the family's dinner. Young Jerzy, much to Rachel's embarrassment, found the scene hilariously funny.

Having help in the home was not only good for Perla, who received vital assistance keeping the household functioning; it also made it possible for the family to entertain, which they did frequently. Although Jerzy and Isia were not allowed to attend, they would listen in, and were fascinated by the adults' conversation around current events and art. The maid would feed the children and, if the dinner party went late, would help them get ready for bed. Being economically fortunate enough to have a maid was the key element that allowed the household to function smoothly, particularly with Perla focused on the business, and Moshe working on his art.

Jerzy and Moshe attended the wedding of Bela Cucker, Jerzy's cousin. Bela's fiancé was a baker's son. The baker, a wealthy man with a big belly and a long mustache, was a good man who indulged the children with sweets, candy, and cookies; however, many of the kids were scared of him anyway. Maybe it was because he was so large.

The wedding began with the rabbi blessing the couple under the chuppah, and then quickly turned into a festive party. First, the bride and groom danced, whirling really, with a kerchief held between them. Then there was a *błazen* ("clown") and musicians. People danced the waltz, polka, and Argentine tango. The more religious men even danced the *Kazatsky*, the Russian squatting dance. The tables were laden with food, wine, and sweet liquor. Later the bride opened presents with her mother.

People ate, spent time with loved ones whom they rarely got to see, laughed, and reveled in the hiatus from the monotony of their everyday lives. As Moshe sketched Jerzy on a notepad, a man across the room told a joke, and the musical notes of laughter filled the room with delight. This made Jerzy even more eager to have fun and get away from his father.

"Sit still, Jerzy. You're making this awfully difficult," Moshe said.

"Why can't you paint Isia instead?" Jerzy asked. "Or why not paint Mother? I want to go play with the other children."

"I painted Isia last week and your mother yesterday. Just give me a few more minutes so I can sketch an outline."

Jerzy rolled his eyes and tried holding still. Father constantly painted. Anytime he thought he could get away with sketching someone, out came paper and pencil. Drawings of faces, hands, all kinds of animals. Even people he barely knew but saw at temple ended up in his sketch pad.

"Why do you paint if it's forbidden?" Jerzy asked.

Moshe looked up from his sketch and sighed. "Have you been talking to Grandpa Avraham again about my painting?"

"No. I am just curious, that's all," said Jerzy.

Moshe put the sketch pad on the table and rested the pencil beside it. "I'm a religious man," he began. "Some would say it's against God's will to make these images. But I also know God gave me a talent and I can't deny my passion for it." He could see he hadn't answered his son's question. "I simply have to do it."

"Do you think you'll get in trouble with God if you keep painting?" Jerzy asked.

"No, because if God didn't want me to paint, I wouldn't feel an irresistible urge to put on paper or canvas all that I see. I am a writer, of sorts. Instead of words, I leave my message in pictures," Moshe explained.

"But why? What is it that makes you want to paint all the time?" Jerzy asked.

"You know, I'm not sure. Some people give back to the world by making shoes, by carrying water. Others make their way in life through stories, inventions, or music. Me? I paint. My gift is finding a single spark, something tiny and precious in the details of everyday life, and portraying it."

"But why paint it if it's ordinary—when you can just see it again tomorrow?"

"You ask an important question, Jerzy." Moshe paused, momentarily stumped. "I don't know. I don't have a perfect answer. I feel a sense of responsibility for my people, even though I don't agree with them. Maybe I feel guilty about living a secular life. I have responsibility for the customs and history of our people. Painting gives me a way to give them a voice—to

Self-Portrait *(November 6, 1936). Held by the Rynecki family.*

preserve them. To say that people's work, lives, and religion are important, worth thinking about, and worth remembering."

Jerzy peered at the sketch pad on the table. "Are you done?"

"I suppose," Moshe said. "If I let you go, you need to go and congratulate Bela. This is an exciting day for her."

"I want to see what my cousins are doing," Jerzy said.

"Of course you do," Moshe said. "Go."

And so off Jerzy ran, while Moshe contentedly sat at the table, pen in hand, sketching and observing.

Moshe painted his family numerous times over the years. He marked birthdays and special family gatherings with paintings, along with spontaneous sketches, studies, and the like, even added the occasional self-portrait. Most days, he would also go out into the city and paint whatever struck his fancy—chess players, children playing, scenes inside the synagogue, workers at an endless variety of tasks. He painted annual Passover gatherings, including a series of pictures based on the Passover Haggadah, a text that sets forth the rituals of the annual Passover feast, or seder.

Seder *(circa 1938).*
Whereabouts of this painting and whether it survived World War II are unknown.

Moshe found inspiration nearly everywhere, from the streets to the temple, even in other representations of the arts. In 1920 the Vilna troupe premiered *The Dybbuk* in Warsaw. The play so moved Moshe that after he got home from the theater, he stayed up all night to paint a scene from memory.

While Moshe continued to paint, and Perla ran the business, Jerzy and Isia grew up, and in that time Isia's academic accomplishments and ambitions grew by leaps and bounds. She wanted to attend Warsaw University. Even though she was bright and had an exceptional academic background, there were substantial barriers to entry. This was partially because women were not commonly educated, but an even larger problem was the existence and enforcement of tight quotas for Jews. In most cases, Jews were rejected without consideration of their academic records. The combination seemed potentially insurmountable, and Isia was rejected more than once.

Moshe, as a Jewish painter from a traditional family, had a deep understanding of the need to pursue one's dreams despite difficult obstacles. He was also very proud of his daughter and wanted to help her reach her goal. Eventually, he went to see a friend named Singer, whose son was a professor at the university. Moshe was able to persuade this man and his son to use their influence to get Isia admitted.

Isia thrived at the university. She graduated in 1933 at the age of twenty-five with two doctorates, one in dentistry and one in surgical medicine. She eventually married another dentist named Jasha, and they started a practice on Tamka Street, not far from Moshe and Perla. They had no children. Isia was known to provide services for those who couldn't afford other dentists, and as a result, she worked very long days providing dentistry to laborers.

While Isia was still at the university, Jerzy left home in 1929, at the age of eighteen. He wasn't academically inclined and wanted a measure of independence. He moved to the northern part of Poland, to Gdynia, a port on the Baltic Sea, to establish himself. He worked a variety of jobs while trying to build up capital to start a business. From time to time, he would visit Warsaw to see his parents and sister. Age and maturity melted away the siblings' rivalry, and the two eventually became close.

During one of Jerzy's visits to Warsaw, he met Stanisława (Stasia) Bortman at a friend's party, and fell in love. Their courtship was soon interrupted, but fortunately not derailed, by Jerzy's compulsory military service. After attending officer training school, he was posted in the 63rd Regiment, about 250 kilometers west of Warsaw in Toruń, along the Vistula River. It certainly helped that the Polish Army, and most of his comrades-in-arms, were unaware he was Jewish. Although Jerzy found the service extremely hard, he was strong, young, and in love, and made it through relatively unscathed. When he'd completed his service, he and Stasia planned a wedding. The two of them were married

Aleksander and Jerzy in Gdynia, 1939.

on December 24, 1934. There was no real honeymoon, just a move for the newlyweds to Gdynia. On January 16, 1935, they settled into a home on ulica Świętojańska, and in October of 1936 Stasia gave birth to a son, Aleksander.

In the meantime, shortly after getting out of the army, Jerzy worked for Paul Stockhammer-Rosenfeld, a Jewish man from Germany and Holland, who bought and sold fresh fish. While working at the fish business, he met Herman Mathiesen. A tall, good-looking Norwegian salesman with gray wavy hair, Mathiesen had numerous business connections in England and Scandinavia. Gregarious, and with a great facility for languages—speaking flawless Norwegian, Swedish, and Danish and good German, English, French, and Spanish, and some Polish—he was also well connected with North Sea fishing captains. Mathiesen and Jerzy hit it off immediately. Both saw Gdynia's geography, travel routes, and the desire for those in landlocked places in middle Europe—Romania, Hungary, Austria, Czechoslovakia—to eat fish from the Baltic Sea. With Mathiesen's connections and Jerzy's business knowledge of Eastern Europe and culture, Mathiesen convinced Jerzy they should form a company together. With ten thousand zloty, of which Jerzy put up 45 percent, the company registered for business on August 14, 1936, with the number RHB 399. The company was called Herman Mathiesen & Co.

Jerzy, to his great chagrin, was the "& Co." He was almost thirty years younger than Mathiesen, and reluctantly took a smaller holding in the company for the opportunity to work with a more experienced businessman. Together their joint enterprise aimed to import and export frozen, salted, and fresh herring and cod. Theirs was a small company, and the competition against the larger companies was tough, but they believed in their initiative and potential to grow.

Cuisine, geography, and years of shifting politics and borders strongly influenced the Polish palate. While influences from across Europe could be found in Polish gastronomy, traditional Polish meals consisted of vegetables, fruits, and meats, all of which could easily be preserved by drying, pickling, or fermenting for later consumption in the long, cold, dark winter months. Over the course of its history, Poland repeatedly lost access to the Baltic Sea. This meant that Poles who wanted to eat fish were often only able to obtain local freshwater fish. But when trade routes allowed access, Poles adored a variety of saltwater fish including herring (a particular favorite) as well as codfish and sprat. These were the fish Mathiesen & Co. aimed to sell.

Jerzy ran the office in Gdynia. Herman kept up his connections in Sweden, Norway, and England. The business structure was basic—they received shipments of fresh fish from Lowestoft-Yarmouth (a town in England on the North Sea), sprat (a fish related to sardine and herring) from Sweden, and frozen herring from Norway, and Jerzy sold it as fast as it arrived on the docks in Gdynia, if not before. Their partnership worked and they made good money. Their success led to more commercial accounts, which enabled them to expand their credit in England, Holland, and Belgium.

For three years the company did well, and they began to add staff, a clerical worker and a dockworker, onto the payroll. But as quickly as things took off, Jerzy's relationship with Mathiesen began to sour. First Jerzy discovered Mathiesen had been hiding cash commissions he'd received as part of the fish deals, which amounted to more than two thousand English pounds. Furthermore, Jerzy learned that Mathiesen had not only seduced the company secretary, but gotten her pregnant. A married man, Mathiesen ran off, leaving Jerzy with a difficult and expensive mess to resolve. Jerzy opted to fire the pregnant employee "not because of prudishness, just as an example to others." The last thing Jerzy needed in a small town like Gdynia, where everyone knew everyone else's business, was a scandal, and he thought firing the young woman was the best solution. She did not agree, and she sued. She won, and the small fish import business was ordered by the court to pay her severance, support for medical care during her pregnancy, hospital expenses, and other charges to help the single mother raise the child.

Jerzy wanted to find a way for the business to succeed without Mathiesen, as well as pay ongoing support to the former secretary and her child. Unfortunately, he didn't have the resources he needed to run the business solo, and as the summer of 1939 passed, rumors of war swirled. Soon, trade ground to a halt, and as a result there were few fish to buy or sell. The business of Mathiesen & Co. came to an end. The Polish Navy abandoned the port and the few ships that remained didn't stay in the wharf for long. By mid-August, with rumors of war everywhere, Gdynia was a ghost town.

There was one exception—at dock was the MS *Batory*, a large, luxurious ocean liner, named after Stefan Batory, the famous sixteenth-century king of Poland. The ship, preparing for imminent departure for New York, was an impressive sight with a last stream of supplies being loaded into its holds. Paul Stockhammer-Rosenfeld, Jerzy's good friend, who was to depart on the *Batory*, asked Jerzy to drive him to the dock. Jerzy took him in his small car, a Ford Eifel.

Aleksander in Gdynia before the war.

"You should come with me," Paul said.

"I can't. My passport is outdated, and I don't have visas," Jerzy said.

"This is the last ship. The hour is very late. Come with me, and stay in my cabin. No one cares in a time like this about papers at all, you'll see."

"No, I'm just back from business in Göteborg and I haven't seen Stasia or Aleksander in quite a while. I can't abandon them," Jerzy said.

"At least walk me aboard," Paul said. "Maybe being on board will change your mind."

Jerzy and Paul walked up the *Batory*'s gangplank. She was an impressive passenger liner built in Trieste, Italy, for Polish Ocean Lines, and paid for, in part, by shipments of coal. Capable of carrying just over seven hundred passengers, she ran a regular service between Gdynia and New York. Although Paul worried about the impending invasion, and tried to get Jerzy to stay, eventually the ship's bell rang, reminding nonpassengers to disembark, and Jerzy said a final goodbye to Paul and returned to shore.

Jerzy headed home, but when he arrived, he found the house empty.

Stasia and Aleksander had left for Michalin—a small summer resort area southeast of Warsaw. Stasia's family owned a villa there. Nestled amid a pine forest, it seemed far away from the rumors of a German invasion. Jerzy slept alone that night in Gdynia, but he slept well, knowing his wife and son were safe.

On August 24, 1939, the papers were full of news reports about the late night signing of the Molotov–Ribbentrop Pact. This treaty of non-aggression signed by the Soviet foreign minister Vyacheslav Molotov and the German foreign minister Joachim von Ribbentrop guaranteed "nonbelligerence" by Soviet and German forces. In other words, each side agreed not to ally itself with or aid an enemy of the other party. The treaty also included a secret protocol that divided territories of Romania, Poland, Lithuania, Latvia, Estonia, and Finland into German and Soviet "spheres of influence," which included "territorial and political rearrangements" of these countries. This was not good news for any part of Eastern Europe. War seemed inevitable and increasingly imminent.

Hitler, eager to create a pretext for war, had the Gestapo stage a bogus "border incident." On August 31, 1939, a small group of Nazi operatives dressed to look like "Polish aggressors" seized the German radio station *Sender Gleiwitz*. The "Poles" then broadcast nationalistic statements in Polish, thereby inciting fear in the local German population. In order to make the attack seem real, the Germans killed Franciszek Honiok, an unmarried forty-three-year-old Silesian-German farmer who was a known Polish sympathizer. Dressed to look like a saboteur, his body was presented to the police and press as proof of the attack. Hitler declared it a serious border incident requiring military force, thus justifying an all-out attack on Poland.

The German invasion of Poland began on September 1, 1939, from the north, south, and west. Just as quickly as the Germans invaded, the Polish forces, positioned near the borders, attempted to retreat to more defensible positions. News of the invasion spread quickly across Poland, and so did the German forces. On Wednesday, September 6, members

Nad rzekami Babilonu siedzieliśmy i płakaliśmy
(By the Rivers of Babylon We Sat and Wept) *(1938).*
Whereabouts of this painting and whether it survived World War II are unknown.

of the Polish government began to flee Warsaw to the south and east. On Friday, September 8, German ground forces reached Warsaw, having covered more than two hundred miles in just a single week, and within another week, all of Warsaw was surrounded.

It didn't take long for the scene outside the Rynecki apartment complex at 24 Krucza to transform from an urbane, well-mannered, and cultured city street into a war zone. As Poland's capital became the target of an unrestricted aerial bombardment by the German *Luftwaffe*, damage to the city was widespread. The *Luftwaffe* ruthlessly attacked hospitals, schools, market squares, and Warsaw's infrastructure, including water supply facilities. Poland's initial efforts to defend its airspace were modestly successful. The Polish antiaircraft defenses shot down a number of German bombers, and over the course of the campaign Polish fighters were surprisingly effective, shooting down more planes than they lost. But they were heavily outnumbered, and by the time the German troops arrived at the outskirts of Warsaw, few of the Polish planes could fly. The constant air attacks, joined soon by an incessant heavy artillery barrage, took an even greater toll on civilians than on the military defenders of the city.

"Help me, Perla. I want to move the paintings into the dining room."

"Why? What for? There's a war outside and you want me to move paintings? Have you lost your mind?"

"Fine. Don't help me. I'll do it myself."

"You can't do it by yourself. There are too many pieces," Perla said.

Moshe stood and stared at the works stacked around the room. He picked up and momentarily studied his work of chess players, as if thinking about the composition or the day he painted it, then put it back on the stack from which he'd just picked it up.

"Perla, I have to do something. I have to protect the paintings. I can't do anything about what's happening outside, but with the paintings I can at least feel like I'm doing something. . . ." Moshe's voice trailed off. He sat down and looked at the piles and stacks of drawings, sketches, unfinished pieces, canvases, watercolors, and notes—literally a lifetime of work. He put his head in his hands. There was a knock on the door.

"I'll get it," Perla said.

Moshe started rearranging the stacks of paintings. Nothing made sense. "Should I sort them by size? Maybe medium is better. . . . Or maybe in chronological order?" Moshe mumbled to himself. He lifted up another painting—a self-portrait and bride piece, 1918. So long ago, and yet the details of the wedding were still vivid in his mind. He could hear Perla at the door and the echo of footsteps in the hallway.

"Who is it, Perla?" Moshe called out.

"Jerzy, Stasia, and Aleksander are here," Perla said. Moshe put down the self-portrait and bride painting and came into the living room.

"He just started to tell me how they got here," Perla said.

"Please, Jerzy," Moshe said, "start over so I don't miss anything."

"All right," Jerzy began. "I left Gdynia a few days ago." He took a deep breath and began again, trying to keep the tension out of his voice. "There were German troops in the street. I thought it best to leave. I had a car, a German Opel—it belonged to a friend who fled Gdynia on a ship, the *Batory*, three weeks ago. You know Stasia's brother, Henry?" Moshe and Perla nodded their heads. "He came with me. He wore his Polish officer's uniform, and the army let us pass through all their checkpoints. We arrived in Michalin, at the summer cottage, late at night. After a few hours of sleep we woke up to German bombs. When the bombing stopped, we went outside to take a look at the damage in the neighborhood. What shocked me is someone had stolen the Opel off the street. Most of the homes were fine. It was no good to stay in Michalin—it's too isolated—but since we didn't have the car, and the railroad is out, we had to walk into Warsaw."

"You walked from Michalin? But what about my grandson?" Perla asked, looking at Aleksander. "He's not even three—that's too far for him."

"I carried him on my shoulders, and we would have gotten here sooner, but the railroad ties and sand under the tracks made for slow walking, and it was hotter than hell. We stopped a lot because I was exhausted. By the time we reached the Vistula and Kierbedzia bridge, all I wanted to do was come the last little bit to the apartment here, but the Polish soldiers were building a barricade to protect the approach from the east, and an officer stopped me and insisted I help. Who am I to refuse?"

Jerzy sat down and motioned for Stasia and Aleksander to join him on the couch.

Aleksander lay down in his mother's lap.

"He's tired," Stasia said.

"Of course, of course, let him rest," Perla told her daughter-in-law.

"May I have a glass of water?" Jerzy asked.

"Yes, come with me," Perla said.

As they walked through the dining room and into the kitchen, Jerzy paused. "What are you doing with all of Father's art?" he asked.

"I'm not really sure," Perla said. "Maybe he can tell you what he's thinking. He hasn't told me a thing."

"Dad?" Jerzy called out. "What are you doing with all of your art?"

"I don't know," Moshe called out as he walked into the dining room. "I just know I have to get the paintings out of here. Maybe if I split them up. Maybe if I ask some friends to help." It was a good question, and he didn't have a good answer. "But this is foolishness. People can't even figure out where to find food or if the trains are running, and I'm worried about my paintings." Moshe's voice trailed off.

"I think you're going to have to take everything out of frames. They're too bulky otherwise," Jerzy said.

"Yes, I've thought about that," Moshe said.

Jerzy set down his glass of water, picked up pliers, and walked over to the wall to remove a painting. He turned it over and started removing the staples and nails to release the canvas. When he finished, he rolled up the canvas and carefully laid it at his father's feet. Then he tiredly walked back to the wall to remove the next painting. His father joined him, and before long, the stacks of prints, sketches, and canvases were piled high, with even larger piles of empty frames nearby.

After several hours of removing pieces from frames, they were emotionally drained and physically exhausted. Well into the new day, they stopped for a few hours of rest, with about three quarters of the job completed. The next morning, they continued. The house was mostly quiet; even Aleksander was still recovering from the long journey, spending much of the morning in a state of exhausted slumber. Even after he awoke, he played quietly while the adults removed paintings from their frames. They stopped briefly twice to eat, but for Moshe it was too hard to stop; he couldn't bear not to finish. Moshe worked silently, and as he did, he thought about each piece—its history, where he had painted it, and the people he vividly remembered: a vegetable seller at the Kazimierz Dolny marketplace a few summers ago, old men reading the newspaper on a bench in Krasiński Park, his father's home for Pesach, and the shul, or temple, in Siedlce. On the table he kept a pad of paper. As he reviewed, sorted, and divided the collection, he made a list of which pieces went into which pile. It wasn't a terribly descriptive list, but he didn't know how much time they had left, and it just had to suffice. "It's just to help me remember what's where," he said to himself.

Late into the night Moshe finished sorting. By the time he was done, everyone else was sound asleep. Moshe himself was spent, but he found the energy to survey his work one last time. Each stack consisted of around one hundred pieces, and depending on whether he ultimately combined a few of the slightly smaller stacks, he was going to end up with somewhere between six and eight bundles. He could hardly believe there were more than eight hundred pieces. He had never stopped to count the works he'd completed over the years. When he looked back, he could account for the days, but he wasn't sure how the years had slipped by so quickly. In the morning he'd have to bundle up the packages and make those final decisions. He hoped Perla had something in the store he could use to wrap around and protect the paintings. Maybe some packaging paper or something sturdier would work. And twine. He needed twine to hold it all together. It seemed such an inadequate solution. He couldn't use the type of crates he used for local exhibitions, much less the safer kind he used when he sent his works to the Brussels International Exposition of 1935. They would take too much room and draw far too much attention if he tried to move them across the city, much less asked anyone to hide them. It certainly wasn't enough, but it just as certainly had to do. Sighing, he went to bed.

Perla woke before anyone else. She put out coffee and a small breakfast. Stasia and Aleksander were up next. They sat at the table and tried to eat.

"Eat, eat," Stasia told Aleksander as she placed some cheese and bread on the plate in front of him.

"Did you sleep okay?" Perla asked.

"Sleep?" Stasia replied. "Who can sleep?"

Perla nodded her head. She hadn't slept well either.

"It looks like Moshe finished dividing his paintings and sculptures last night. I think I'll retrieve some packaging material from our store. Come downstairs and help me collect a few items?" Perla asked Stasia.

Perla led the way downstairs. She rummaged around for a while, finding the things she needed. For a moment it all just seemed too much, and she briefly sat with her head in her hands. Looking at Perla, Stasia was struck with an overwhelming sense of déjà vu. After a moment, she realized how Perla's pose was strikingly similar to a portrait Moshe had painted perhaps ten years before.

In the portrait, Perla occupies the foreground, resting her head in her right hand, gazing outward. Her stare is deeply contemplative, lost in thought. In the foreground surrounding Perla is a panoply of round ornaments in a range of colors—orange, blue, white, gold—that glow and reflect the light in the store. On the right side of the painting are several masks, some of them haunting. One looks like a snake. Above it is a skull. And then a dark mask in orange with red eyes and bright red lips and even some sort of horns. In the lower background is a large white horse—not a rocking horse, but a toy a child might climb upon. Above the horse, hanging from the ceiling, is a large red teddy bear. The whimsical and unusual nature of the items around Perla suggest more a toy store than an art supply store. The store, of course, carried practical items as well—writing materials, books, and painting supplies for artists—but these were not featured in the painting.

Then, as now, Stasia noticed a tension and a dissonance between the bright-colored shapes and whimsical forms of items in the shop and the contemplative, deeply pensive countenance of Perla. A decade later, facing war rather than the vagaries and mundane challenges of life, Perla looked older and sadder than in the painting, making the contrast even starker, but the portrait had captured an almost ineffable quality of Perla's spirit, a stoicism and a fortitude, that could still be seen on her face.

Coming out of her reverie, Stasia looked at a toy horse in the corner of the store. Aleksander might like to play on it, but dragging it upstairs seemed both inappropriate and ridiculous. Perla stood up and handed Stasia a spool of twine. Its twisted strands felt rough to Stasia's fingertips.

"Just another minute," Perla said before disappearing into the back of the store. She returned with brown paper, set it down on her desk, and then searched through a jumbled pile of oversized papers and other materials from the nearby desktop for more packing materials. She carefully extracted the top half of the pile and handed it to Stasia. Stasia tucked the twine under her arm and shifted some of the larger pieces with her arms to make it less awkward as Perla picked up the rest.

"Ready?" Perla asked.

Stasia nodded and the two left the store and returned to the apartment. In the time they were gone, Moshe had gotten up and was in the kitchen drinking the last of the coffee and holding a pen over a pad of paper.

"Oh, good, you've found some packaging materials." He reached for the paper and twine Perla held out to him. "Help me start packaging the pieces? Some I've laid flat but others are rolled up into bundles. It just depends on the pieces."

Perla helped bind the paintings together into bundles. Stasia too.

"I've started a new list. It's the names of people we can ask to store the packages," Moshe said, savoring another sip of coffee.

"I can take a smaller package to Praga today," Perla said as she peered over Moshe's shoulder and pointed to one of the names on the list.

"Not by yourself, Perla," Moshe said. "Have Jerzy go with you. Meanwhile, I'll find a way to get the rest of the packages delivered to these other addresses. Hopefully, enough people will be home and willing to take the bundles. I'll explain it's just for a short while. Until things settle down. I'll retrieve the packages when it's safer. They'll be willing to help."

"We can only hope," Perla said.

"Yes," Moshe said. "We can only hope."

You could never truly get used to the sound. Day after day, constant fire from an endless array of artillery, from small mortars to giant rail-based howitzers, could be heard as the German military bombarded the city around the clock. German *Stukas* with their terrifying sirens dive-bombed the city, targeting everything with even the remotest potential military value, and often they missed, causing substantial damage to civilian areas. It was clear to Warsaw's citizens that the city was under siege and the end was just a matter of time.

Jerzy, Stasia, and Aleksander stayed with Moshe and Perla at the apartment on Krucza Street for several days. Eventually, the inevitable happened: a bomb dropped in their neighborhood and smashed the building. Fortunately, no one in the family was seriously hurt, but the damage was extensive; the apartment would have to be abandoned.

The Rynecki family moved into the cellar. Gas and electricity no longer served the building, and the water and sewer pipes were broken as well. The only drinking water came from an old well. Given how cloudy it looked, it was probably unsafe for the family to drink. Within a few days, they came near to the end of the food they had salvaged from the wreck of the apartment, and with fall approaching, the cellar grew cold at night.

Moshe, Perla, Jerzy, Stasia, and Aleksander needed food, blankets, milk, and other provisions. Stasia and Jerzy took turns foraging for food and other necessities in the bombed-out city, while Aleksander stayed behind with his grandparents, who tried to keep the almost three-year-old boy entertained and calm. Daily scavenging yielded less and less. They needed a better solution.

"Stasia, I've been thinking," Jerzy said late one afternoon.

Stasia looked at Jerzy expectantly.

"Do you remember the warehouse I told you about outside the city?" Jerzy asked.

"No," Stasia replied.

"Yes, yes, I told you I stored canned sprats there to sell this winter. Herman and I overestimated how many sprats the business needed. Rather than selling them and losing out on the value of the cans, we put them in storage."

"I'm sorry, I don't remember," Stasia said. She shook her head.

"Well, I suppose it doesn't matter if you remember. What's important is that I remember," Jerzy said. "And I'm going to go get them. There are thirty cases of fish. We planned to sell them in late October, but that doesn't make sense anymore. We need them for food and to give us something to trade."

Jerzy found a wagon, two horses, and a driver. It was easier than he had expected to leave Warsaw at six o'clock in the morning. No one paid much attention as the wagon made its way through the city's streets. For every person traveling east, there were two or three others moving south. One more wagon weaving its way through the chaos of the streets didn't arouse much interest. Almost ten hours later Jerzy returned, and as he began unloading the wagon at the Krucza Street apartment, a group of people gathered around to watch.

"We want whatever you've got," a man said.

"This is my property," Jerzy said.

"We're hungry! Help your neighbors," two people replied.

Jerzy looked at his parents, wife, and son, who helped unload the wagon. Then he looked at the growing crowd. He didn't want any trouble; he just wanted to unpack the sprats in relative peace and to have something for his family to eat. Things were not looking good. The appearance of the wagon at the building, combined with the shouting, had brought more curious onlookers who, upon learning there was food involved, circled tighter around the wagon. Jerzy feared things would soon get ugly, and he could see only one solution that would not end with violence and an empty wagon.

"Back off," Jerzy said, looking warily at the crowd. "If you're civil, I'll sell each of you one can."

From the back of the wagon Jerzy tried to organize the cans. The crowd pressed closer. Jerzy held out the first can and the woman closest to him held out a few zlotys. He took them and shoved them in his front right pocket. Then he reached for another can and held it out to a young man who offered him a few coins. Jerzy sighed. He certainly wasn't going to profit.

The selling continued and soon a soldier could be seen at the back of the throng. The crowd parted to let him through.

"Why are you out of uniform?" the soldier asked.

"I have my papers," Jerzy explained. "I haven't been called up yet."

"Sell me two cans of whatever it is you've got and I won't report you," the soldier said.

"But I have my papers," Jerzy said. "Besides, I'm only selling everyone one can."

"Two cans or I report you," the soldier said.

Jerzy grudgingly handed over two cans. Moshe, after he realized a crowd had formed, stacked as many cans as he could in a pocket he'd fashioned out of his shirt and carried them to the basement of the apartment house. He managed to make several trips while Jerzy sold the rest.

As Jerzy finished selling the last of the fish, he calculated an estimate in his head. It didn't look promising. They'd started with close to three thousand cans. Knowing the size of the crowd and watching how many trips Moshe had made into the cellar, he figured they had about two hundred cans left. "Well, at least we won't starve tonight," Jerzy muttered.

After the sprat incident, no one wanted to venture out. The few times any of them had gone looking about the city, they'd seen and learned bad news. Every day the situation worsened. Men, women, and children carried their belongings in sacks—forced to flee, but with nowhere to go, they camped out in the middle of the sidewalk. Looters took everything and anything. Trash piled up in the streets. Dead and dismembered horses lay in the roads. Things got so bad many people longed for the Germans to occupy the city. Entire blocks of apartment houses burned or smoldered. People lost their sense of civility seemingly almost overnight.

"It's chaotic," Jerzy told his father.

"Anarchy, really. When the Germans settle in, they'll straighten things out. They'll bring order to this mess," Moshe said.

But the Germans brought a superior military force. First came the closing of nonpermissible stores. Then orders for Polish citizens to surrender radios. Then weapons and gold were to be turned over. But there was initially, for the Poles, some improvement. The chaotic looting in the streets had been replaced by the more systematic and orderly German looting under the occupation. People were able to move about, and although no one had German marks, they could at least barter for goods.

Unfortunately, what little money Jerzy made selling the fish soon became worthless, as the zloty was being replaced—no one was willing to take the zloty, no one was sure what would ultimately replace the zloty, and no one had German marks. The two hundred cans of sprats Jerzy and Moshe had managed to save were exceptionally valuable. Jerzy was able to barter the sprats for milk, potatoes, bread, flour, vodka, and cigarettes.

During one such barter exchange a man told Jerzy to not worry too much.

"It'll all be over in a few weeks," he guessed.

"Not a chance," Jerzy told the other man. "Six years," he said, "and you can quote me on that."

Soon, the Germans began to tighten the screws on the enormous Jewish population in Warsaw. As was German custom, it was done in orderly phases, starting a week after the occupation with the establishment of the *Judenrat*, a Jewish council tasked with administering German orders. After that, there was a brief pause of two months, a calm before the storm. The first edict of the *Judenrat*, on November 23, 1939, required Warsaw Jews to identify themselves by wearing white armbands with the Star of David on them. Jewish schools were soon closed, and Jewish organizations dissolved. Jewish property was confiscated, and the men forced into labor.

This phase of confiscation and repression lasted about a year, before the screws were tightened again. In October 1940, an order went out that a Jewish ghetto would be established. Its 1.3 square miles would be packed with more than four hundred thousand Jews from Warsaw and surrounding areas. To prevent escape, it was surrounded by walls topped with barbed wire. Sealed off from the rest of the city, with a closely guarded entrance, the Jews inside were grossly overcrowded, with severely inadequate food and water supplies; as a result, disease and starvation ran rampant.

Jerzy refused to wear the Star of David. It seemed like a bad idea to willingly identify himself as Jewish and to make it easy for Germans to target him for the imagined transgression of being Jewish. And if wearing the Star of David seemed like a bad idea, willingly entering a walled-off ghetto where the Germans said he must go seemed like a horrific idea. To him it meant giving up—the end. Moshe knew it was a bad idea as well, but to Moshe his identity was his people. His entire adult life he had been telling the story of the Polish-Jewish people through his work. While he could potentially hide his identity, he couldn't stand the thought of abandoning his community. It seemed unfair to those who didn't have a choice. So while Jerzy thought it necessary, indeed critical, to hide his Jewish identity in order to save his life, Moshe thought it more important than life itself to remain with his people. Perla and Moshe went into the ghetto, Moshe carrying his paints and sketch pads. Stasia and Aleksander kept outside the ghetto with Jerzy.

As conditions continued to deteriorate, this was a tremendous source of conflict between father and son. More than a year after Moshe went into the ghetto, in 1942, Jerzy managed to reach Moshe by phone.

"I can get you out," Jerzy told his father during a heated conversation.

"I don't want to leave," Moshe said. "These are my people."

"There is no good ending to all of this," Jerzy said.

"I'll paint them," Moshe said. "The Germans are connoisseurs of the arts. They'll like it if I paint their portraits."

Jerzy shook his head even though his father couldn't see him over the telephone wire.

"Please, Father," he pleaded. "Let me get you out. If I don't get you out, it'll be the end of you."

"If you are right, my son, then let me go where my brothers and sisters go. And if it's death, so be it," Moshe said.

"Then, at least, let me get Mother out," Jerzy said.

"She'll have to make that decision herself," Moshe said.

Although it was a difficult decision, the situation in the ghetto was already grave, and Perla could see it was rapidly getting worse. In the end, as much as she loved Moshe, she wanted to survive, so she took her son's help to leave the ghetto. In 1942 Jerzy arranged her escape, and she spent the remainder of the war with a Polish Christian woman, Emilia Komarnicka, in Służewiec, a neighborhood in Warsaw's Mokotów district. Emilia's brother was the artist Marian Trzebiński. Komarnicka was her married name.

Perla's timing was fortunate. Soon after she escaped, most of the Jews in the ghetto were deported to Treblinka, and soon after that, most of those who remained were killed in the Warsaw Ghetto Uprising. Moshe managed to avoid the initial round of deportations, and survived the uprising as well. Sadly, after Perla escaped, neither Jerzy nor Perla ever spoke directly to Moshe again, although they would hear from him one more time.

FOUR

Defying Hitler

By the beginning of 1943, more than 10 percent of the Jews in the Warsaw Ghetto had died of starvation and disease, and three in four had been deported to Treblinka. After the massive deportations in the summer of 1942, there was a lull, but the Germans hadn't finished clearing the ghetto. In early 1943, Heinrich Himmler, the chief of the SS, ordered another eight thousand deportations, but the mentality in the ghetto had changed dramatically. By this time, word had gotten back there that the "resettlements" were to death camps and ended in execution. A Jewish resistance had formed. So when a small detachment of Nazis entered the ghetto to gather a group for deportation, they were ambushed by the Jewish resistance. The resistance fighters could strike quickly, then escape across rooftops or into cellars. The Germans moved much more warily, and weren't willing to follow into the cellars. Fighting lasted several days, with no progress, so the Germans withdrew from the ghetto. The victory galvanized the resistance, adding to their numbers and increasing their will to fight. Although they continued to arm, train, and fortify as best they could, some in the Jewish resistance thought they had stopped the deportations. Others thought the Germans would return in greater numbers.

On April 19, 1943, on the eve of Passover, units of the German regular army and the SS, supported by heavy armor, entered the Warsaw Ghetto. The operation was launched by Himmler in honor of Hitler's birthday, April 20. Under the command of SS General Jürgen Stroop, the soldiers were under orders to complete the deportation of the ghetto within the next three days.

Jewish insurgents again ambushed the SS units, firing upon the German troops with guns, Molotov cocktails, and hand grenades from windows, alleys, sewers, and bunkers. The Germans suffered losses including damage to several armored vehicles.

Ammunition for the Jewish defenders was in very short supply, and they had few guns. Despite the critical lack of weapons and supplies, the Jewish revolt maintained its vigor for several days, and on April 22, when the Nazi forces issued an ultimatum to surrender, the Jewish defenders declined. Shortly thereafter, the Nazis opted to systematically burn houses block by block, and to blow up basements and sewers. The combination of flames and thick, black smoke forced many of the survivors from their hiding places. While some Polish resistance forces battled the Germans outside the ghetto during this period, they ultimately failed to breach the ghetto walls. With the collapse of an organized defense, surviving fighters and the remaining Jewish civilians took cover wherever they could find it in the ruins. The Germans used dogs, smoke bombs, even flooding, to force people out.

In mid-May, General Jürgen Stroop personally pushed the demolition button to blow up the Great Synagogue of Warsaw on Tłomackie Street. Although sporadic resistance continued for several more weeks, ultimately the outcome was never in doubt. With few weapons and little ammunition, and resistance fighters on the edge of starvation, the ghetto uprising wasn't about a choice between life and death, but a choice to die fighting rather than be led peacefully to slaughter.

With the ghetto mostly destroyed, the burned-out homes and structures were demolished and the SS continued hunting down Jews hiding in the ruins and in the city. Tensions were always high for Jews with false papers living in Warsaw, but after the ghetto uprising, those families who had somehow successfully hidden in the larger Polish population, like the Ryneckis, were particularly on edge. In late May, two of Stasia's nephews, one five, the other ten, were arrested with the father of one of the boys, and then disappeared.

Just a few weeks later, Jerzy had a terrible scare when he went to visit his good friend John Kojder, with whom he had a number of business dealings during the war. Kojder, who didn't know Jerzy was Jewish, welcomed him into his home, but then excused himself to go take a shower. He'd had a long day and needed to clean up. Jerzy didn't mind. He sat in the living room and prepared to wait. While he was waiting for Kojder, the phone rang. Jerzy, for some inexplicable reason, reached over and answered the phone. There was a woman on the end of the line. It was his wife, Stasia.

"You have to come quickly. There's been a horrible mistake. You have to come get us. Hurry up. Aleksander is crying. I showed them my papers, but they won't let us go. I can't believe they let me call. Please. You must come quickly."

"Stasia?" Jerzy asked.

"Yes, yes, of course it's me."

"Where are you?" Jerzy asked.

"Aleksander and I were running errands in Mokotów [the southern district of Warsaw]. The Polish police brought us into the station. I told them we aren't Jewish. This is crazy. You must come get us," Stasia said.

"I'll be right there," Jerzy said. He hung up the phone and ran out the door.

It was late, bordering on curfew. But Jerzy wasn't far from the station and he knew if he didn't get to Stasia and Aleksander fast enough—well, he didn't even want to think about it. He ran toward the station, making only a brief stop at their apartment, where he picked up a fourteen-karat-gold cigarette box weighing two hundred grams (seven ounces) and also pocketed a small amount of money, in case he needed to bargain with the police.

Sweaty and stressed, Jerzy arrived at the station. Before he went inside he took a brief moment to steady himself.

"I'm here to collect my wife and son," he told the man behind the desk.

"Papers," the man said.

Jerzy looked over at Alex sitting on a bunk crying, Stasia sitting next to him trying to quiet the boy. Then he looked back at the man with his papers.

"You are not involved, we can see that, but she and the child are Jewish and we have to deliver them to the Gestapo," the policeman said. He looked up into Jerzy's eyes from his position behind the desk.

"Are you certain that's really necessary?" Jerzy asked as he placed the gold cigarette box on the desk and slid it toward the policeman.

The officer picked up the box and turned it over in his hands.

"Okay, but it is not enough." He leaned back in his chair. "And if we should let them go, there has to be a lot more money. And now. No delays." Jerzy nodded. "Before nightfall they'll be delivered," the Pole said.

Jerzy looked at Stasia and Aleksander, looked at the gold box, looked at the policeman, and then took a deep breath before spinning a bluff he hoped would help their dire situation.

"You better do what I tell you," Jerzy growled, "because in five minutes, if I don't show up downstairs with her and the kid, this whole complex will blow sky high. You are here surrounded by my colleagues from the Army of the People. I am not making jokes. This time you are trapped, not me."

The policeman looked at him with a stony expression, no reaction at all.

Jerzy placed every bill he had in his pocket on the desk. The policeman looked at the pile.

"Tomorrow, noon, the restaurant on the corner. You bring five thousand more and pay for lunch and drinks," the policeman said.

Jerzy nodded and turned toward Stasia and Aleksander. Together they ran out of the police station. It was now past curfew and, if caught, they could be executed. When they reached the apartment and shut the door behind them, they wept in fear as a family.

The next day Jerzy showed up at the restaurant for lunch with the policeman and handed over the money.

"You're a good man," the police officer told Jerzy. "No one will ever touch your family. Our word," he told him.

It was a promise Jerzy didn't believe for a second. Best case, he figured that they would soon come back for more, and the worst case was unthinkable. Since neither he nor Stasia felt safe, they decided to move again. This time they relocated to a relatively new development at Fort Mokotów. While Jerzy and his wife and son were settling into their new apartment, a postcard arrived from Moshe at the Warsaw address where Perla was hiding. It was hastily scrawled, but Perla was thrilled to find out Moshe was somehow still alive. On the postcard, Moshe wrote that he had arrived at a place outside Lublin called Majdanek and that he hoped to be able to paint soon. Perla held out a sliver of hope, since Moshe had miraculously survived both the initial deportations as well as the ghetto uprising. It seemed to be unbelievably good fortune. The majority of Jews in the ghetto had been sent to Treblinka, and the majority of those who survived had died in the ghetto uprising. So perhaps, surviving all this time, there was some hope for Moshe? Tragically, as Perla later learned, Majdanek was indeed a death camp, and Moshe was never heard from again.

Soon after Perla received this sliver of false hope, crushing news arrived at Jerzy's house in the form of a knock on his door. A woman stood at the door. He thought she looked like a friend of his sister's.

"Come in," he said quietly, looking past the woman to see which nosy neighbors might be watching.

"I have news," she said barely above a whisper.

"Is it Isia? What happened to my sister?" Jerzy asked.

The woman looked down at her shoes and tucked her long dark hair behind her ears. She cleared her throat. Jerzy didn't need to ask if it was bad. He knew it was bad.

"I'm sorry," she said, fighting back tears. "It was a few weeks ago, she was murdered at the entrance of the Warsaw Ghetto, in front of a slum house on Nalewki Street. He shot Isia first and me next, in the back of the neck. Isia fought for air, making noises. I got shot through the side of the neck, so I could still breathe. I kept quiet and survived. The murderer, he had one eye. He shot Isia the second time between her eyes."

"I'm glad you came to tell me. It would have been worse not knowing." Jerzy touched the woman at her elbow.

The woman wiped away her tears and nodded.

"I'll be on my way," she said as she walked toward the door. And like that, she was gone, and Jerzy had another hole in his life.

Jerzy didn't have time to mourn the murder of his sister or the deportation of his father. As a Jew living in Warsaw, he hid his identity to live, but his life was anything but normal. He had to move often, always keeping ahead of German authorities and Poles who might deliver him to the Gestapo. In keeping with his trading background before the war, he was involved in the black market, making money by taking small items from areas with greater supply to places where they would be more valuable, always looking for a bit of barter or a good deal. Of course, being a Jew moving across Poland meant a need for good papers, smooth talking, and a tremendous amount of chutzpah.

One of the biggest assets Jerzy managed to acquire during 1943 was high-quality papers, excellent forgeries made from the right paper and on the correct machines. Because of this, they were indistinguishable from official papers, and although they couldn't guarantee his safety, they provided a greater sense of self-confidence, which could make all the difference if you were stopped or had to get through a checkpoint.

His new papers said his name was Jan Trzaska. He learned to be and do everything as Jan. He knew his birthday, birthplace, current address, former address, relatives, names of employers. . . . The list went on and on. If he gave the wrong address at a registry office and someone investigated his fictitious landlords, he could get caught in a web of lies that would quickly snare him and ultimately his family. The risk of exposure was always at the back of his mind, so he expended tremendous effort on his cover identity.

Using these papers, he often took trips to Kraków, a city in the southern part of Poland. Although Kraków suffered some damage in the early days of the war, it had avoided the intensive bombing, artillery barrages, and open rebellion that had heavily damaged much of Warsaw. Both because its infrastructure remained intact and because the Nazi government set up its General Government in nearby Wawel Castle, it was a good city to visit to make deals on the black market.

On one visit to the Kraków marketplace with his friend Kojder, a man pointed at Jerzy and shouted, "A Jew!" Upon hearing the pronouncement, an official of the *Hitlerjugend* approached the two men to investigate the claim. Eventually Jerzy and Kojder visited the home of a Gestapo official to sort out the matter. When they did, they were led into the living room and told to wait. Then a large German shepherd was led into the room. The dog sniffed at Jerzy for a moment before settling at his feet. Jerzy patted the animal, and then it was quiet.

"You are not Jewish," the official said. "The dog would tear you apart if you were. He was trained to do it. Too bad some people sidetrack us with these false reports. These are mostly jealous Poles, and we have to check every case as it comes. I wish I didn't have the duty to do it to you. You are free to go, of course."

"Thank you, sir," Jerzy said, and then added, "Would you please write me a letter confirming my status as non-Jewish?"

"Of course," the official replied. "Come tomorrow to my office and you'll get one."

For Jerzy, any scrap of official paper might spell the difference between life and death. With his letter and his Jan Trzaska papers, he continued to make enough money for his family to eat, to pay for people to hide them, and ultimately to pay bribes. But as the war turned against the Germans, their level of suspicion increased, so every trip, every deal in a marketplace, every checkpoint was a greater risk. Remarkably, Jerzy's people skills and deal-making got him through five years of Nazi occupation. But in September 1944, his luck ran out.

"Your papers," the officer said.

"Yes, sir," he said, handing over his documents. Jerzy stood tall and did his best to look sharp and confident. While the officer took his papers to his desk to review them, he could hear cannon fire not too far away. Word on the street was that the Russians were just outside of Kraków, just east of the city. The actions of the officer seemed more subdued than Jerzy's prior encounters with the Gestapo. He could see the man carefully reading each of his documents.

"You seem to have someone else's documents here."

"Excuse me, sir?" he asked.

"You have two sets of documents here. You can't be two people. Who are you?"

Even as he prepared to reply, Jerzy's mind raced. Had he slipped up, had he made a fatal error? But he did his best to appear calm. "Jan Trzaska, sir. I'm Jan Trzaska."

"I see," the officer said. Then he held out a cigarette. "A smoke?"

"Thank you, yes. I'd like that."

The man lit the cigarette and handed it to him. Jerzy inhaled deeply, trying to calm his nerves. It was a chess game he was playing here. He needed to be one step in front of the questions. He needed to be Jan, to be always on his toes. No room for further mistakes.

"I can get you a cup of coffee as well, if you like," the man said. "Take a seat. You'll be here awhile."

"Coffee would be perfect," Jan said as he sat down.

"So tell me. Who are you?"

"I am a Pole and I am fighting for my country."

"Uh-huh. And why are you in Kraków?"

"I'm here on business," Jan said.

"But you live in Warsaw—is that correct?"

"Yes, yes, I live in Warsaw. I'm just here for a few days on business."

"And this business . . . ?"

Jan brushed an imaginary speck of dust from his high Italian riding boots, straightened out his leather coat, and looked the Gestapo man in the eye. "It is my business," he said.

As Jan spoke, the official looked up from his papers at the man sitting in his office. Such bravado surprised him. Most people who ended up in his office begged to be released, offered him bribes, and swore they were innocent.

Before there was time to ask another question, a second man came into the office. "We have orders to depart immediately," he said.

"It's your lucky day," the Gestapo man said to Jan. "I'm taking you with us to Prague."

The train ride from Kraków to Prague was surprisingly and suspiciously pleasant. Jerzy slept in a private compartment with an SS man who provided him with food and drink, let him take a nap, and offered him coffee, chocolates, and cigarettes. He was well rested upon his arrival in Prague, but what lay ahead was both terrifying and uncertain.

The Kraków Gestapo officers handed Jan off to the Prague staff. The questioning began again. For endless hours he had discussions with different officers, the same questions over and over, in more ways than he could count. He was hungry, but there was very little food. Occasionally they offered him a bowl of coffee-colored water. The interrogations kept going, over days and ultimately weeks. He was kept in a cell in between interrogations. Usually, around two p.m., there was a bowl of soup and a slice of bread the size of two fingers. Jan never said much of anything during the interrogations. He didn't say he was a spy, but he certainly didn't disavow their thoughts he might be one. He felt the uncertainty was the only thing keeping him alive. They thought he might know something, and his only chance of survival was to keep up that suspicion.

The officers in Prague didn't really know what to do with Jan. One of the colonels tried to convince him that he should return to Poland and organize resistance against the Communists.

"Go by parachute," the colonel said.

"I don't know how to use a parachute," Jan said.

"Then we will teach you," the colonel said, and smiled.

They ultimately did not have the time or resources to train Jan as an anticommunist insurgent, as the Red Army rapidly advanced from the east. Instead they sent him off to Pankrác Prison.

Pankrác Prison was one of the largest in the German occupied territories, holding more than two thousand prisoners. It was not an extermination center, though a substantial number of executions were carried out there later in the war. Conditions were better than some prisons in Nazi-occupied Poland, but overall they were unpleasant. Jerzy's assigned cell, number 19, was on the first floor. The cell was perhaps eight feet long and five or six feet wide. At the entrance was a toilet bowl that also provided the only available drinking water. Hanging directly off one wall were two very narrow bunks, stacked vertically. Jerzy had two cellmates, a Russian soldier caught in Czechoslovakia, not far from the Polish frontier, after he escaped from a German prisoner of war camp, and a Czech captain. They outranked him for the two mattresses, so Jerzy slept on the concrete floor. There was a tiny table and a single chair in the cell. A few nails were pounded into the walls for hanging clothes. And up high on the wall, just below the ceiling, was a very small window. Because it was twelve feet off the ground, inmates couldn't see out of it. The cell was generally bitterly cold or stiflingly hot.

Pankrác Prison was tremendously overcrowded and inmates were given very little food. A dark liquid, supposedly coffee, was served most mornings at 6 a.m., and in the afternoons, a thin soup and a small piece of bread the size of three fingers. Once a week, on Fridays, a spoonful of cooked blood instead of the soup was served. That was Jerzy's favorite, and he was not alone. One of the Czech prisoners went so far as to say that if he were ever freed, he would eat the blood every Friday of his life.

Every morning after coffee, rain or shine, there were outside exercises. Oftentimes guards beat inmates during these exercises and subsequent roll call. Jerzy did his best to avoid the beatings, but was not always successful. After a few months at the prison, he suffered his worst assault: beaten unconscious, he suffered a kick to the lower back so strong he limped for many months; the injury never fully healed.

Despite the conditions, Jerzy tried to make the best of prison, talking to people and learning what he could about the outside world. He and his Czech captain cellmate passed the time by teaching each other languages. He learned Czech from the captain and helped him learn German. In the unlikeliest of coincidences, he discovered his friend and fellow black marketer, John Kojder, was also at Pankrác Prison. John had been arrested for selling food rations on the black market.

John was looking out a window at the courtyard when he first saw Jerzy, but it wasn't easy to find a way to communicate. This was because, as a *Volksdeutsche* (a Nazi term for an ethnic German living outside the Reich, literally "German folk"), he would never be on the yard at the same time as non-German prisoners such as Jerzy. But one night a large transport of Hungarian Jews were delivered to Pankrác and placed in the prison's corridors. Immediately the older prisoners and the newly arrived prisoners began talking and exchanging news of the outside world. Amid these conversations, Jerzy and Kojder managed to establish a chain of prisoners willing to pass messages back and forth. Given their long friendship, Kojder tried to help, and was able on occasion to get Jerzy extra rations and sometimes information. Kojder was even able to find out and share that Jerzy and he would be part of a group soon to be transported out, to a place called Dachau.

One day in February, Jerzy noticed an enormous armada of five or six hundred American planes flying over Pankrác. He figured this meant the Allied forces must be very close. This was a message all prisoners understood without having to talk about it. It seemed to say to just hold on a little longer, to be patient. With that, they felt stronger, and it even reduced the ever present pangs of hunger. As if it was an omen of coming change, soon afterward, Jerzy was taken downtown to see the colonel. After offering him a piece of bread and a cigarette, the colonel told him to take a seat.

"After all our questioning, we believe your story."

Jan kept a solid eye lock with the colonel. He wanted to make certain he didn't flinch or give himself away.

"So," the colonel continued, "because you've told us the truth, we will send you to Dachau until the end of the war. You'll survive. Germany will win, and you'll go back to Poland then." The colonel shook Jan's hand.

Jerzy's journey to Dachau was in two parts. For a brief time he had the "luxury" of being packed into a cattle car on a train that took him from Prague for a distance of about ten miles. After that, the guards forced everyone out of the cattle car. Jerzy wasn't sure whether the track was out, or whether they were low on fuel, or needed the train for some other task, but the rest of the journey was made on foot. Certainly, it was easier to breathe than in the crowded car. Six SS men were assigned the task of transporting Jerzy, Kojder, and about two hundred others, mostly Czechs. Guarded around the clock with machine guns, the prisoners were forced to haul a small wagon used to pack the SS luggage, some food, a kettle to cook with, and a few tools, like picks and shovels. The SS men tried, although not too hard, to feed the inmates. With monotonous frequency, they warned the men that any attempt to escape would result in their death.

Time and distance blurred for Jerzy. Months spent in captivity meant he had almost no strength in reserve. Marching with little or no food for almost two months didn't help. By the beginning of May, Jerzy had lost over a third of his body weight. One way or another, he figured for him the war would be over soon. But on a day in early May, as he began to give up hope, he heard artillery fire. First sporadically, the next day more frequently, and then from multiple directions. As they walked, he could increasingly hear how close the front must be. Eventually, it sounded as if it was almost on top of them; the sounds of war came from everywhere. The end of the war suddenly seemed possible, but first he had to survive somehow in his weakened state until there was a chance at escape or salvation arrived from an Allied army. At the end of that day, which had been an exceptionally long day of walking, the SS picked a spot to stop for the night—a spot on the railroad tracks outside Rosenheim. Just like all the other nights, the SS guards trained the mounted machine guns on their prisoners. All night the inmates and the SS heard and saw fire bombings. In the morning, the prisoners started to talk among themselves, because it was clear the end was coming.

"I can smell freedom," someone said.

"So close, but so far," another said.

"They've been gathering their ammunition," said a third.

"They're going to wipe us out now?" asked a fourth.

A Czech who spoke German stood up and faced the SS. "You can't kill all of us," he told them. "And for those you do kill, you'll be tried for war crimes and be hung. Spare us and we will save you. Our word of honor."

The SS men listened. The men, a bit older, seemed open to discussions. They talked, the six of them, contemplating their choices, the inmates, their bullets, war, humanity. No one moved. Eventually they stopped speaking, and the prisoners weren't sure what the decision was. There was a long moment of quiet as the fate of the inmates rested in the hands of the armed SS. To Jerzy it seemed to stretch on forever, his life hanging in the balance. And then there was the sound of a car. After a moment, they could see it was an American jeep. It came from down the road. Just two men inside, two black men from different services—the inmates knew because they were wearing different uniforms and different helmets. It didn't look like they had rifles or machine guns. As the jeep pulled up close, the prisoners were all scared to death. The SS might just shoot the Americans and the prisoners, or the Americans might drive on by, and leave the prisoners to their fate.

The multilingual Czech stood up. "We need help. Don't leave. The Germans are going to shoot us all," the Czech called out in English as he stood up. But as soon as he spoke, the Germans threw their hands up in the air to surrender.

"C'mon," Kojder said, grabbing Jerzy's arm and pointing to a few of the Czechs who ran up the track bank and slid down to the other side.

"I can't run," Jerzy said.

"What do you mean you can't run? Run!" said Kojder.

Jerzy tried, but he was so weak. And everything was so quiet. A moment passed. Jerzy looked up into the sky. It was a brilliant day. The sunshine was beautiful. Jerzy wanted to move, but he couldn't.

"I'll carry you if I have to," Kojder said, and he did. He tried to put Jerzy's arm over his own shoulder and drag him away from the SS men and toward freedom. They didn't get far. Although Kojder was better fed and stronger, he was weak himself and he collapsed.

Suddenly Jerzy remembered a promise he had made himself a long time ago. Whoever saved him, he must kiss that person's hand in thanks. Wary of getting into the middle of the crowd, but determined to get to the jeep, Jerzy moved closer to the Americans. The two black American servicemen were still in the jeep. The vehicle was running. One of the servicemen held a handgun, a .45, close to his thigh. The other spoke with the English-speaking Czech, trying to explain something to him. It was too loud. Everyone was talking, moving, trying to figure out what would happen next. There was commotion and then a shot in the air. The American had fired his gun. Immediately a hush fell over the prisoners. The English-speaking Czech turned to the crowd, essentially taking control of the situation.

"The Americans," he said, "want nothing to do with us. They claim not to be from a fighting unit. They lost their way trying to get to Bad Aibling, the next little town, a few kilometers away. The SS men are ours. We can do with them what we want."

The Germans sat on the ground, some already stripped of their clothes. A few of the younger Czechs commandeered the machine guns to point at their former guards, now their prisoners.

"You promised us if we didn't kill you, you would spare our lives," one of the SS men told the Czechs.

Jerzy tried not to pay attention to the change of power, the shifting roles. He only wanted to get to the jeep, to kiss the hands of his liberators. But as he got closer, the Americans yelled something, and the jeep rolled backward and headed back down the road from where it had miraculously appeared. In a cloud of dust, the American liberators were gone.

"Kojder," Jerzy said, "let's get out of here. We don't have much in common with these Czechs."

Kojder and Jerzy stood together and made a concerted effort to walk down the same road the jeep had followed.

"Where do you think you're going?" a Czech called out to them.

"It's over," Jerzy said. "It's all over. We just want to go."

"You're not going anywhere," the Czech said. "We need you to be witnesses."

Jerzy and Kojder were forced to stand and watch. It didn't take long. The self-appointed Czech leader asked if anyone objected to hanging the Germans. Nobody answered. Some men fashioned a rope out of the Germans' pants and shirts. A small group of men overpowered the SS sergeant and pulled him to a telegraph pole. Not really knowing how to hang the sergeant, they more or less choked the man to death, rather than actually hanging him. They attached him to a spike on the pole and someone yelled, "He is dead." And then they started in on the next former guard. All six former SS guards were murdered this way. Jerzy watched, and got sick. He tried to vomit, but there was nothing in his stomach. And then it was over. It was suddenly all over.

Kojder and Jerzy started trudging along the rails. It would have been a modest walk for someone in good health, but it took them several hours to stagger into Bad Aibling, a small, clean little town with red crosses on all the roofs. In another amazing bit of good fortune, it was a hospital town that had been spared from bombing. The whole town was undamaged, and had food and medical supplies. The war, for Jerzy and Kojder, was finally over.

FIVE

Displaced

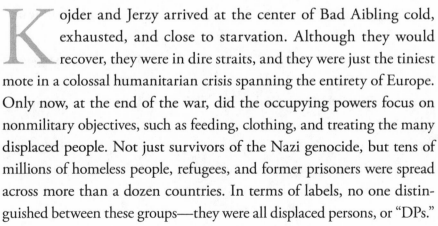

Kojder and Jerzy arrived at the center of Bad Aibling cold, exhausted, and close to starvation. Although they would recover, they were in dire straits, and they were just the tiniest mote in a colossal humanitarian crisis spanning the entirety of Europe. Only now, at the end of the war, did the occupying powers focus on nonmilitary objectives, such as feeding, clothing, and treating the many displaced people. Not just survivors of the Nazi genocide, but tens of millions of homeless people, refugees, and former prisoners were spread across more than a dozen countries. In terms of labels, no one distinguished between these groups—they were all displaced persons, or "DPs."

As the German Army was finally defeated, the scale of the problem slowly dawned on the Allied forces, as the tide of refugees became a torrential flood. Millions of people across Eastern Europe fled the advancing Soviet Army into Germany. Shortly after the war, millions more tried to return to their former homes, or were forcibly deported from countries that no longer wanted them. Changes on the map became very real on the ground. Poland itself moved more than one hundred miles to the west, taking substantial territory from Germany as partial compensation for the territory the Soviets had captured (and annexed) at the beginning of the war. In addition to the mass movement of refugees, many cities and towns were heavily damaged or, in some cases, virtually annihilated—making their surviving residents essentially homeless refugees as well. Military officials, unprepared for the vast numbers and the daunting list of their needs, struggled and often failed to provide basic necessities.

Of course Jerzy and Kojder only knew they desperately needed food and shelter.

They were remarkably fortunate to have stumbled upon Bad Aibling, one of the few places in newly occupied Germany that had enough of both. It had been a spa town before the war, and it had been converted by the U.S. Army into a hospital to treat the wounded, a detention camp for prisoners of war, and a refugee camp. Jerzy and Kojder were relieved to learn they could recover in a place where there was food, clean water, and a sense of order amid the chaos.

Jerzy settled into camp as a refugee, a DP, fairly easily. He got along well with the camp staff and, as a quick study with languages, rapidly picked up English. As a result of his facility with languages, Jerzy was asked by his new American friends to assist as a translator, to help communicate with the influx of displaced persons arriving at the camp. He was particularly useful for helping out with Polish-speaking refugees. As the number of refugees in camp climbed, there just weren't enough staff members to handle all of their needs. One way of reducing staffing responsibilities, as well as improving services to and communication with the DPs, was to enlist their aid. A number of committees were formed from the ranks of the DPs, one for each of the major nationalities in the camp. Jerzy was appointed as the head of the Polish Committee.

While Jerzy was working with the camp staff and other members of the committee, he, like many other DPs, was desperate to find his family. Fortunately, there were lists of displaced persons—one for each of the DP camps, as well as lists for cities and towns with large DP populations. These lists, produced by the United Nations Relief and Rehabilitation Administration (UNRRA) and the International Refugee Organization (IRO), shared names and locations of DPs spread across Europe—it was a way for people to search for and reconnect with family and loved ones. Unfortunately, there were hundreds of lists, and the lists were constantly growing and changing. With the flood of DPs arriving at camps, by the time a version was completed for a given camp, the list was likely already obsolete. Worse, with more than ten million non-German DPs in Germany alone, there was no real way to have a "master" list: even if it had been possible to compile quickly and accurately, the document itself would have filled tens of thousands of pages. Still, there was hope. Every day Jerzy pored over the lists that the camp received, hoping to find his wife, son, and mother.

Remarkably, after just two months of searching, in July 1945 he found Stasia and Aleksander on a list; it said they were in Linden. Because of his good relations with camp staff and his status as head of the Polish Committee, he was able to get both a U.S. Army staff car and the paperwork to make a trip to Linden possible. On a continent still very much in shambles, where most refugees were fortunate to get enough food to eat, and where gasoline supplies were controlled entirely by the military, this was a remarkable feat.

The paperwork was a certificate, typed on Polish Committee Expeditionary Forces Military Government letterhead, which certified that "Mr. Dr. Trzaska-Rynecki Jerzy, Chief of the Polish Committee, ex–political prisoner of the Concentration Camp SD Prag, is travelling to Linden for the purpose of looking for his deported family. All Civilian and Military Authorities are kindly required to aid and assist the holder of the present." Signed by the Leader of the Polish Center, and endorsed by MMLA (UNRRA) team 710, it also included an attached note, stating that "this man is well-known to us, and has done very good work in relation to the Polish question in Bad Aibling. Please assist Dr. Trzaska-Rynecki in every way possible," signed by First Lieutenant R. Genot, who was in the Medical Corps of the U.S. Third Army.

Jerzy maneuvered the olive drab army staff car with its polished white star on the side of the door out of the Bad Aibling DP camp and headed down the open road, thinking about how long it had been since he had seen his family. It was now July 1945. He had been arrested in the Kraków marketplace and sent to Pankrác Prison in September 1944, ten months ago. Aleksander was eight years old. His birthday was three months away—in October. They would celebrate early, Jerzy thought. He smiled for the first time in a long time, and accelerated the car just a little bit more. He wanted to get there quickly—to see their faces and to embrace them.

The journey itself took longer than expected; some of the roads were in poor condition, and he had to pull to the side for several military convoys. But from Jerzy's perspective, the trip, although long, was uneventful. He managed to get to the camp before sunset, and was pointed in the right direction by the camp staff upon his arrival.

A woman screamed. Not a scream of fear or pain, but a screeching, astonished sort of scream. After a moment, Jerzy realized it might be someone calling his name, but he wasn't certain. He turned to look, and saw a boy running toward him.

"Father!" Aleksander shouted, running as fast as he could, and then collided into his father. Jerzy leaned over to hug him, tears streaming down his face.

"It's over," Jerzy said both to his son and to himself.

"I was sure you'd been shot," Stasia said.

"I'm lucky to be alive," Jerzy said.

"I didn't know what to do," Stasia said, fighting back tears.

Jerzy nodded.

"I thought you were dead," Stasia said.

"It's okay, Stasia," Jerzy said. "I'm here. We are a family again."

Jerzy stayed the night with his family, and the next morning there was very little to pack for the return trip. The drive back was full of long and awkward silences. The night before, everyone had talked, sometimes all at once, so glad, so amazed to find one another, and to all be alive. But over the long drive back, the war, the friends and relatives still lost or dead, the past year of separation hung over all of them. Jerzy talked a bit about the arrest in Kraków and his time at the Prague prison. It seemed somewhat cathartic for him to talk about it. But Stasia wanted to forget it all as fast as possible. She said a word or two and then just started crying. She stared out the window.

"Will you tell me about it later?" Jerzy asked.

"What for? It doesn't matter," Stasia said.

"But I want to know," Jerzy said.

"It doesn't bring back my brother or my sisters and their families," Stasia said. "It doesn't change anything."

Jerzy nodded his head.

"But you want to hear it anyway," Stasia said.

"I do," Jerzy said. "I want to know."

Stasia sighed.

"The last home we stayed at in Warsaw, before the uprising, was with the Stefański family in the Żoliborz district. We were with Franciszka [Stasia's sister-in-law] and Halina [Franciszka's daughter]. That neighborhood was a stronghold for the resistance, and managed to avoid the devastation in most of Warsaw. But even though the neighborhood suffered less than the rest of Warsaw in the uprising, when capitulation happened, the surrender, we were sent south. The Germans took us all on the street and put us in a coal wagon. Can you imagine? Coal! Aleksander and I were so dirty. We had no place to sit down. No chair, nothing, just like how animals—cows!—are transported. We arrived in Kraków, all black from the coal, with Franciszka and Halina, but after that we were separated. Aleksander and I were sent to live with a peasant woman. I had to cook for her standing in front of a brick wood-burning stove every day. I scrubbed potatoes and carrots. I made soup. It was all food for men in the field, although sometimes they let us eat a bit," Stasia said.

"At least you and Aleksander had a place to sleep. Something to eat," Jerzy said.

"Yes," Stasia replied. "It was okay for a while, almost enough to eat, but then the war grew close again and it got worse, when the Red Army was coming. We had to flee. I can't even tell you how lucky we are to still be alive."

"What happened?" Jerzy asked.

"I don't want to talk about it. If I never have to think about it again, it would still be too soon." Stasia was relieved for the nightmare to finally be over, ecstatic to see Jerzy again, but worried she would never be free of the shadows of dark memories and nightmares in her sleep.

After a very long silence, Stasia decided to change the subject. "What's it like at Bad Aibling?" she asked.

"It's okay. There is enough food, and shelter for now. But we need to figure out where to go next."

Stasia looked down at her hands in her lap. "Won't we go back to Poland?" she asked.

"Back to what?" Jerzy asked. "Who's left? What's left? I'll tell you what's left. Nothing."

Stasia bit her lip. Her thoughts were jumbled and she wasn't sure what to say. She had so many bad memories, but it felt so strange to be without a home.

Jerzy took her silence as dissent, so he continued. "And the Poles . . ." Jerzy took his right hand off the steering wheel and batted it in the air. "You want to move back and live next door to your fellow patriots who took money from the Gestapo for turning over Jews, children, women, young and old? They turned in our families. I don't think I can forgive the Poles. Some helped, but for money, nearly always for money. No one ever did it for free or out of the goodness of their heart. Not one!"

Jerzy looked over at Stasia. She nodded. How could she disagree? Jerzy continued. "So while I've been looking for you, I've been thinking of where to go." He paused. "I've been thinking we should go to Italy."

"But Dad, I don't speak Italian," Aleksander said. "I've never even been to school."

"We will learn Italian, and you'll go to school."

"And how will we get to Italy?" Stasia asked.

"I've been working at the DP camp. I've saved a little money. If I can save a little more, I'll find a car to buy. We'll drive."

After arriving back at Bad Aibling, Stasia and Aleksander settled in while they planned and prepared in hopes of moving to Italy. Over the two months Jerzy had been at Bad Aibling, the camp had become more confusing and more chaotic. Not only were there more arrivals almost every day, from many different nationalities and with a broad array of cultures and languages; there were also the thousands of German POWs in the camp next door. Trying to get families back together and eventually find places for the DPs to go on a permanent basis, as well as processing and repatriating the POWs, was extraordinarily difficult.

Shortly after he reunited with his family, Jerzy's friend Kojder and another man he'd met at the camp, Günther Ebeling, were also reunited with their wives and children. One night the men sat to talk about the supplies in camp, which were getting increasingly scarce as the number of DPs increased.

"We should see if there are any canned goods or other supplies at the nearby railway station," Ebeling suggested.

"Don't you think that's already been tried?" Jerzy asked.

"Probably, but it's worth a look," Kojder said.

Jerzy shrugged. "Well, if nothing else, it'll make a nice walk," he said.

The next day the three men set out for the station. Jerzy took

Aleksander along, thinking it might be nice for him to get out of the camp for a bit. The walk itself was short and fairly uneventful. When they arrived at the station, Kojder and Ebeling went inside. Jerzy waited outside with his son.

"Can I go pick some flowers?" Aleksander asked, pointing at the wildflowers growing in the space around the station.

"For Mom?" Jerzy asked.

Aleksander nodded.

As Aleksander gathered flowers near the edge of the lawn for Stasia, a man approached. Hearing footsteps, Jerzy turned, and saw a tall, formidable man walk toward him. The man seemed overdressed for the summer day. As he came nearer, Jerzy realized he was dressed in a German officer's uniform and that his hands were shoved into his coat pockets. This made Jerzy exceedingly nervous.

"What are you doing here at the station?" the German asked Jerzy.

Jerzy tried to smile and look nonthreatening. "Sir, we are hungry and looking for supplies." After a moment's consideration, the man pulled a pistol out of his jacket and brought it to bear on Jerzy. As Jerzy looked into the barrel of the pistol, it seemed enormous. Jerzy was terrified he might be gunned down in front of his eight-year-old son. Just in time, Ebeling called out from the roof of the station, *"Seien Sie vorsichtig, ich habe auch eine Waffe!"* ["Watch out! I too have a weapon!"]

The German officer looked up at the roof, then back down at Jerzy. He paused for a moment, then slowly lowered his pistol. Jerzy backed away toward Aleksander while he continued to look at the German officer. When he got close to his son, he grabbed his hand very tightly and moved as quickly as the boy could run back toward the camp. Aleksander cried from the pressure of Jerzy's grip, but Jerzy was too scared to relax his hand until the German officer was far out of sight. Jerzy, drenched in sweat, started shaking, felt as if he would cry, and at the same time stifled a nearly overpowering urge to laugh. The irony was absurd—he was convinced his life was over as he looked down the barrel of the German's pistol—a fraction of an inch, an unmeasurable moment from death. He had somehow escaped that fate, yet again. But the thought of living through five years of occupation and hiding, a year in prison, a forced march to a death camp, finally making it through and finding his family, and then to be shot? After the war was over? It was ludicrous.

Jerzy continued to work at the DP camp, and in his free time, he went out into the German countryside searching for a car to buy. Meanwhile, Stasia wrote to her uncle—her mother's brother, Louis Weicensang—in Texas. She wanted him to know she'd survived the war. She also hoped he could help her family. Her mother had sent money to Louis's family during the Great Depression. Before the war, Stasia's father ran a successful furniture business, so they had been fortunate enough to be able to help their American relatives get back on their feet. Stasia hoped her American relatives might be able to help the few surviving Polish relatives. Unfortunately, due to the patchwork nature of postal service in war-ravaged Europe, and the low priority of civilian mail, Stasia didn't hear back until many months later.

While Jerzy was hopeful Stasia's relatives would eventually help, he wasn't going to wait to leave Bad Aibling. In the rural area surrounding the town, he found a farmer who had stored an old BMW in his barn, under bales of hay, for the duration of the war. The farmer was delighted to sell it and get a bit of money. Surprisingly, in the immediate aftermath of the war, cars had less value than might have been expected. Certainly working vehicles in Germany were hard to find, but once found, they needed gas, and gas was almost impossible for most civilians to obtain. In addition, for many people, there was nowhere to go. Jerzy was able to get some gas through his connections at the camp, and some paint as well. He painted the car U.S. Army green. Unlike gas or cars, U.S. Army paint was easy to come by. It obviously wasn't a military car, but at a distance or in poor light it might just pass. Once they had the car, a tank of gas, some modest supplies, and their scant possessions, they set off, first southwest toward Innsbruck, and then across the Brenner Pass into Italy.

While Jerzy, Stasia, and Aleksander headed to Italy, and away from Poland, Perla (Jerzy's mother, Moshe's widow) headed back to Warsaw, or what was left of it. Warsaw had truly suffered during the war. Between the initial attack on the city in 1939, the Warsaw Ghetto Uprising in 1943, the Warsaw Uprising in 1944, and Hitler's orders for demolition teams to destroy the city block by block after the uprising, more than 85 percent of the city had been destroyed by the time the Soviet Army captured it in January 1945.

Gazing out at a sea of rubble, several Polish politicians proposed abandoning Warsaw as Poland's capital. Perhaps, they opined, the city could be left as a monument, a vast and eerie wasteland, as a reminder of what was lost. But the remaining inhabitants weren't interested in political statements or relocating. They had lost their homes, schools, and factories, but to them Warsaw was still home in the larger sense of the word, and for most of them, there was really nowhere else to go. So they began to clear the rubble and rebuild. Perhaps sensing a fresh start would be good for his eventual plans of a Communist government, Josef Stalin supported the rebuilding project. An Office for the Reconstruction of the Capital was formed, which sought not only to build a new city, but to reconstruct its historical streets, buildings, and monuments, all as it had stood before the war.

As word of the city's rebirth began to circulate, more of Warsaw's former inhabitants came back. A little more than six months after the war ended, Perla, along with her cousin Sophie Binstock, was among those who returned. But they did not come to participate in the rebuilding efforts; they came to find Moshe's paintings.

Perla knew from the list Moshe had given her where the bundles had been hidden, but many of the locations had been completely destroyed. In some places the buildings were gone, as if they had never been; there Perla could tell there was no hope of finding a bundle. Other locations were stacks of rubble, and she searched with little hope. A few sites appeared slightly more promising, with buildings partially standing or even mostly intact, but still she found nothing. It seemed hopeless. The last place Perla and Sophie checked was Praga. A district of Warsaw on the eastern shore of the Vistula River, Praga was hard to get to from the rest of Warsaw because so many of the bridges were still down; only one bridge was available to cross. Praga sat directly across the river from Warsaw's Old Town and was home to the Warsaw Zoo as well as the National Spirit Monopoly, which was the vodka factory. When they finally found their way across the Vistula, Stasia was surprised to see Praga relatively unscathed.

"It's surreal, Sophie," Perla said, pointing at the red brick industrial buildings, their facades pockmarked by wartime bullets. "All these buildings are still standing."

"And look," Sophie replied, gesturing to the entrance to Ząbkowska Street. "The main gate is almost completely unscathed."

"I wouldn't believe it if I didn't see it with my own two eyes," Perla said.

Perla and Sophie walked westward toward Praski Park and the zoo, looking up at the still standing buildings. After a few moments of walking, Perla paused and looked around.

"I have to orient myself, Sophie. It's been so long since I came this way," Perla said.

"Do you really think the house will still be standing, Perla? And the art still there?" Sophie asked.

Perla reflected for a moment. "I don't know, but I have to hope so. There has to be something of Moshe that survived."

They continued walking toward the address Perla remembered as the residence where she'd left the bundle more than five years ago. A few turns and fifteen minutes later, Perla stopped again, this time suddenly. There was no traffic; no one walked the neighborhood. The entire scene was eerily quiet.

"What is it, Perla?" Sophie asked.

Perla couldn't speak. She just pointed. Sophie followed the direction of Perla's gesture to the house across the street.

As they crossed the street, Perla tightly grabbed Sophie's hand.

"Do you think anyone is home?" Sophie asked.

"I don't care if they are or not," Perla said.

"Still, let me knock on the door," Sophie said.

Perla stood on the sidewalk while Sophie climbed the steps up to the entrance to knock at the front door. First, she offered a polite knock, but there was no answer. After a long while, Sophie tried a louder series of knocks, but there was still no sound, no sign of movement inside. Sophie knocked a final time on the front door and again waited in vain. "I guess they aren't home," she said. After a moment, she tried the door, but it was locked.

The two women looked around briefly; then Perla started back down the steps.

"Down here, Sophie," she called as she hurried down another, smaller set of steps toward a side door below street level. "Maybe we can get in this way."

There was a catch as Perla twisted the knob, and Perla was suddenly overcome with worry they wouldn't be able to check, that the occupants might not be back for weeks or more, that they might never know whether anything survived. After the briefest moment and some jiggling of the doorknob, she felt the latch retract. "Yes!" Perla exclaimed, barely able to contain her excitement as she gently pushed the door open and went into the gloomy cellar.

The light from the doorway seemed to get lost in the large, shadowy space, making only a faint impression on the floor nearest the door, so she and Sophie waited a few steps inside for their eyes to adjust to the darkness.

As she started to make out the far wall, Perla took another few steps forward and heard a modest sound, a crackling and scuffing noise from underfoot. She felt something faint in contact with her shoe, so she bent over and tried to discern what she stood on. She grasped and then carefully picked up a large piece of paper, and held it toward the light as she unfolded it into a larger, rectangular shape.

"Sophie . . . !" Perla exclaimed.

"What is it?" Sophie asked.

"Look," Perla replied, her hands shaking as she held the paper out toward Sophie. "It's me. It's the piece he painted of me in the store."

"It's damaged down the middle," Sophie said.

"So it is," Perla replied, seeing the heavy crease in the paper.

Sophie's eyes adjusted to the cellar's low light, and she saw more papers on the floor. She reached for one that at first appeared blank. As she picked it up, she realized it was merely upside down, the image facing Perla as she picked it up.

"Someone tore out a piece in the middle of that one," Perla said.

"I can see that," Sophie said, "but why?"

"I don't suppose it matters," Perla said, shrugging her shoulders. "We're lucky any of them are here."

As their eyes continued to adjust, they could see that the cellar floor was nearly covered with layers of discarded papers, the paintings strewn haphazardly among them. With Sophie's help, Perla began sorting and organizing the mess, picking out the art and making careful stacks. There were so many memories, so many familiar works: here a portrait of a girl in a sailor outfit on top of one of a student studying, there an old man sitting with a cane. Then came women in the park with children, a wedding, seamstresses . . . From the chaotic disarray of the dusky cellar, they pulled out a cascade, a dark and slightly damaged cornucopia of Moshe's works, some pieces miraculously undamaged, but some suffering grievous wounds—torn-off corners, creases in multiple directions, missing chunks and sections.

Sophie helped gather the paintings off the floor and counted them as they collected the works. Six years of war to destroy a people, a community, and just twenty minutes to stack together what remained of Moshe's lifework. Nearly 120 paintings were stacked as neatly as possible. In one way, it was a tremendous find; with more than 85 percent of Warsaw in ruins, it was truly a miracle that anything had survived the devastation. At the same time, the pile of paintings, some seriously damaged, looked forlorn indeed next to Perla's memory of the much larger stacks Moshe had made at the start of the war; then there had been more than 800. But it was something, and it was all she had left of Moshe. Perla stood for several moments to contain her grief before she bundled up the stacked art. Afterward, she delicately tucked the paintings under her arm and stepped back outside. They carefully closed the door behind them, and stood blinking in the sunlight, letting their eyes adjust once more before they walked away.

"I'm going to take them to Jerzy," Perla said. "It's what Moshe would have wanted."

"Where is Jerzy?" Sophie asked.

"He, Stasia, and Aleksander are in Rome," Perla answered.

SIX

Italy

It wasn't until Jerzy, whom I knew as Grandpa George, died in 1992 that I realized how little of my family's history I knew. I understood that Dad and my grandparents were Holocaust survivors who'd lived in Warsaw throughout the war, on false papers. I also was aware they'd lived in Italy after the war. But the details I had were, at best, fuzzy: just the tiniest of snapshots and fragments of my family's story. I knew even less about what happened to my great-grandfather and his paintings. When Grandpa George died I began pushing Dad for details.

"So when exactly did Perla come to Rome?" I asked.

"That's so long ago . . . ," Dad said.

"There are photos from her visit. You're even wearing a suit."

"We used to get packages—clothes, food, money—from my mother's relatives. Money was exceedingly tight. My father tried to make money with a smoked fish business but it didn't work out."

"Then there was a cigar business?"

Left: Stasia, Aleksander, and Perla.
Right: Aleksander's school photo at Collegio Mondragone.

Dad nodded. "My dad partnered with a man importing cigars. It seemed promising but then his partner died in a plane crash and after that the business fell apart."

"How long did you live in Italy?"

"We arrived after the war; late '45 or maybe the middle of 1946. We were in Italy until we left on the USS *Marine Jumper* in November 1949. I was in school, Collegio Mondragone, for most of that time."

"A boarding school, right?"

"Yes, and when my dad took me to school I told him I couldn't go because I didn't know Italian. His advice was that I better learn it. I eventually did, and by the time I left I had caught up with my peers. The Jesuit priests gave me a solid education."

"Did you think you were going to stay in Italy?"

"For the long term? No. The people in Italy were kind to us, but there were not enough business opportunities. We had plans to go to Argentina."

"Really?"

"Yes, but my dad never really liked the idea. Besides, things worked out for coming to America."

Collegio Mondragone class photo. Aleksander is in the first row of standing boys, second from the far left, his hands behind his back.

"But you don't really know how."

"Not really. But I do have something for you that might help. I'll bring it into the office tomorrow."

And that was how I ended up on the floor of my office reading a stack of letters from a Chicago relative, Charles Weicensang. Charles was Stasia's cousin, or as he called her, Stelly. By the time I was born she was Grandma Stella.

Over the course of two and a half years starting in early 1946 Charles wrote several times a month to family he barely knew. The letters Dad gave me were mostly from Charles to my grandparents, although copies of some of Grandpa's letters were in the stack too. At first I read the letters haphazardly—spot reading sections when words or phrases grabbed my attention. But it quickly became apparent that reading the letters in chronological order would make a lot more sense. And when I did organize them by date, I could tell, even from the mostly one-sided conversation I had from Charles's letters, that my grandparents understood that getting to the United States wasn't going to be easy, that they didn't want to stay in Italy, and that they definitely weren't moving back to Poland.

Dad, it turned out, was right about Argentina. I found both their application and approved paperwork complete with fingerprints and passport photos. But the possibility of going to Argentina held little appeal for Grandpa George. Its government had a history of being difficult and restrictive for small businesses. For a serial entrepreneur like Grandpa, that was a major sticking point, especially as he experienced firsthand how hard it was to make a fresh start in Italy. Grandma was even more reticent about moving to Argentina. She wanted to go to America to be closer to relatives. My grandparents were hardly unique in their desire to go to the United States. Given a choice, it was where most DPs wanted to go. After the war, it had the highest standard of living in the world. But getting into the U.S. was notoriously difficult.

In April 1946 Charles believed their odds of getting in were slim to none. He told them, "I wish that I could offer you some ray of hope about coming to the United States but honestly, I don't believe that such a thing is possible in the immediate future."

As my grandparents mulled over cousin Charles's words, nations around the world struggled to cope with the vast multitudes of DPs. Surely something needed to be done. But refugees presented ethnic, religious, and economic challenges Allied forces and xenophobic potential host countries were unprepared and often unwilling to address.

Despite Charles's own pessimistic outlook about the potential for immigration, two months later, in early June, Charles and his brother, Harold, committed to help their cousins with the U.S. immigration application. The details and paperwork required were extensive and the

Brothers Charles (left) *and Harold Weicensang.*

review process would be lengthy, but between food packages, clothing, and other goodies sent to the Ryneckis in Italy, everything seemed manageable.

As immigration to America began to feel more plausible, my grandmother focused on how her son's successes at Collegio Mondragone might translate into opportunities in the United States. In one letter she went so far as to ask cousin Charles if he might open an account to help provide for Aleksander's future schooling. Charles's answer was a softened no. He explained that public education was free and cautioned her that while he had resources to assist her, he was not endlessly wealthy. "America as such, is not the land of golden streets, nor does money grow on trees. Jobs are hard to find, difficult to hold, and the cost of living does not leave much spread between one's income and outgo," Charles warned.

Meanwhile, Perla was still in Lodz, less than a hundred miles from

Warsaw. Being in Poland was hard; it reminded her too much of what she had lost. Even cousin Sophie, who helped her recover the Rynecki bundle of art in Praga, tried to emigrate to the United States or Israel. Perla considered moving to Italy to be with her son, but she knew Jerzy wouldn't be staying there. She also knew that immigration restrictions meant that if she followed him to Italy, she would likely end up stuck there when he managed to find a more permanent home. She thought about going to her relatives in Le Mans, but emigration to France was also difficult.

Perla suspected it would be many years before she could leave Poland permanently. She worried what might happen to the paintings if her own situation remained unresolved. After thinking about the problem for months, she decided to focus first on getting the paintings to Jerzy in Italy for safekeeping. Of course, it was not as simple as tucking the art into a suitcase and heading for Rome. Instead, she had to contend with a burgeoning bureaucracy established to prevent the looting of cultural works from Poland.

Poland suffered great losses to its cultural heritage—between Nazi Germany and the Soviet Union, an estimated half a million art objects went missing from Poland's institutions—and the Polish Ministry of Culture and Art was understandably anxious to prevent further theft of its treasures.

In April 1947, Perla prepared a list of Moshe's work for the ministry; she needed them to approve the list in order to take the art out of Poland. The document identified each work with a number, subject description, and medium. The typed list included painting descriptions such as *"w jeszybocie"* ["the yeshiva"], *"Autoportret"* ["Self-Portrait"], and *"W Ogrodzie"* ["In the Garden"]. The pieces were mostly watercolors, but there were a few ink drawings and oils as well. Professor Dr. Jan Kachwatowicz, the codirector of the Warsaw Reconstruction Office and the lead conservator, reviewed the document, signed, and stamped it. With permission to take the art out of Poland, Perla planned a trip to Rome.

Around the same time, my grandparents received a particularly disconcerting letter from Charles informing them that his brother, Harold, their official immigration sponsor, had, tragically, died nine months earlier in an eleven-floor fall from his apartment building onto the roof of an adjacent garage building. Charles had kept the news from them because it was incredibly difficult to share and he was still sorting out the details himself. The death was thought to have been the result of an accidental late-night slip. Any undertones of a possible suicide were not discussed.

Harold's death was a shock—not only as a tragedy in itself for his family, but also because it might derail any chance for immigration. Charles anticipated Stella's concern and wrote to her. "I urge you not to discuss this situation with anyone. I rather feel that the papers which have been filed will be valid, provided nothing is done to disturb the circumstances." Charles urged them to keep it a secret, in hopes they could emigrate without refiling paperwork. Ultimately, it didn't even matter, because the application process took so long they were forced to refile anyway, which, as they feared, stretched the process out even further. This time their sponsor was a branch of Stella's family living in Texas who could guarantee a job and a place to live.

While they continued waiting, my grandparents attempted to find work, but locating employment was practically impossible. Given their status as Jewish refugees, they were at the bottom of all hiring priorities. If there were jobs, native Italians were given preferential treatment.

My grandparents' inability to secure work weighed heavily on their minds. They also worried that Charles saw them as uneducated Eastern European shtetl Jews who would continue to be a burden once arriving on America's shores. Grandpa George wrote to Charles, "We know perfectly that in the U.S. gold also does not lie in the street but anyone willing can find the work. You know that besides our old mother, who is living in Poland, we have no one in the world. And that is why, although we are sorry to bother and burden you—we really do not see any other way and it seems to us that you could be our last chance of rescue."

My grandparents' lives were in limbo, and at the end of 1947, it was unclear when, if ever, they might be able to immigrate to the United States. They maintained a brave front, but things were difficult and money was tight. And despite Grandpa George's pride, and his desire to hold everything together, he wrote a desperate letter to Charles bemoaning his "bitter hardship" and expressing panic at his inability to care for his wife and son. My heart ached as I read Grandpa George's urgent cry for help:

> *It's our last alarm-bell for salvation. Really I do not know what will become of us if you refuse a helpful hand. If we should have to wait another such period until the time reaches for our emigration visa, we are facing the same danger as some recent years ago.*

Charles worked, as best he could, to help meet the family's constant need for food, clothing, and shelter. If he ever had any thoughts about abandoning them to their own devices, he never expressed it in any of his letters. By March of 1948, the cousins reached a two-year letter-writing anniversary. Charles and the extended network of U.S. cousins combined their resources to send a large check. My grandparents were grateful for the funds and careful with the money, but even then, it just wouldn't last long.

Charles, eager to help make my grandparents financially independent, cast about for another way to raise needed capital. What eventually occurred to him was the possibility of selling Moshe's artwork. Charles wondered if Grandpa George might consider selling some of the works Perla brought to Italy. "I wonder if it would not be an idea to send one or two of them to see whether they can be disposed of here in the United States. That is of course, if the pictures are worth their commercial value to you. You, of course, know more than I do as to whether or not you want to dispose of your paintings," he wrote.

For Grandpa George, the survival of the paintings was nothing short of a miracle. With the paintings he had a small connection to the past, to everything he had lost in the war. He tried to explain to Charles as best he could how important the paintings were, and Charles, in part, seemed to understand. He wrote to my grandmother:

> *I have every appreciation for George's respectful attitude towards his father's work, and can understand why he does not care to offer the paintings for sale. I may say quite frankly that I didn't know the character of the work, and it was for this reason that I thought the paintings could be transferred into money for their commercial value alone.*

The topic, for now, was dropped. For the next several months, the letters focused almost entirely on navigating the bureaucratic maze necessary to complete the Rynecki family immigration. It was at this point that Grandpa George took over letter writing, in part because of his strong grasp of English. Charles, impressed with his command of the language, praised him for his efforts.

In the summer of 1948 Congress passed the Displaced Persons Act of 1948, authorizing two hundred thousand DPs to enter the United States. President Truman was not thrilled with the bill. On the positive side, it allowed more DPs into the United States. Unfortunately, it strongly discriminated against those, mostly Jews, who arrived in Germany, Austria, or Italy after December 22, 1945, the cutoff date the bill used for immigration acceptability. Truman said the bill was incredibly intolerant in its exclusion of so many, but acknowledged that if he refused to sign the bill there would be no legislation to help the displaced population, at that point still numbering around a million people. "I have signed this bill," he told the world, "in spite of its many defects, in order not to delay further the beginning of a resettlement program and in the expectation that the necessary remedial action will follow when the Congress reconvenes." Fortunately for Dad and his parents, they'd arrived in Italy prior to the cutoff, so although there was a long road ahead, their prospects were noticeably brighter after the passage of the bill. Still, to actually immigrate they had to answer a seemingly endless series of questions, generally multiple times, wait, then complete additional forms and paperwork, then wait some more. They were not yet, Charles noted at the end of 1948, at "the end of the road." He implored them to hold on tight. "Please do not lose heart," Charles wrote, "and please believe that whatever can be done will be done, and that if there is any way in which we can make your life easier and help you get out of Rome to another place, we shall certainly utilize every effort."

Yet even with the prospect of immigration to the United States, Charles urged Grandpa George to consider other options. At the top of the list was the possibility of heading to Australia or Israel. Australia seemed somewhat appealing, but because Grandpa George noted a financial requirement to possess one thousand Australian pounds to even be considered for immigration, it was out of the question. As for Israel, this held no appeal at all. "I'm not suitable to work on fields and for other business one requires a certain amount of money," Grandpa told Charles.

Grandpa George felt some guilt about rejecting Charles's suggestion he consider Australia and Israel. He knew his financial and emotional condition were trying and draining on Charles. "I do not know if our survival has had any sense. Would it have been better if we were between the other 6,000,000 victims of our family?" he wrote.

Following liberation, survivors were forced to contend with the everyday responsibilities of their new lives. While it was a moment they'd dreamed about for years, its reality was much harsher than they'd imagined. Grandpa had been fortunate the war ended before he arrived at Dachau, but that didn't stop the sense of guilt that he survived when so many others didn't. For him the guilt of survival was added to the guilt and stress he felt at being unable to provide for his family. The combination often overwhelmed him. Still, he got up every day and continued to look for ways to make some money and put food on the table.

From thousands of miles away, on a continent physically unscarred and emotionally distant from the war, Charles tried to provide emotional support for his distraught Polish cousins. In late December he replied. "Naturally we are all very distressed to learn that your circumstances are not improving. It is, of course, with the deepest sympathy that I tell you how very sorry we all are."

In January 1949, as Charles continued to search for other ways to rally funds for the Rynecki family, the letters turned again to the Moshe Rynecki paintings. Jerzy, despondent with his business frustrations, began to consider that selling a few of the paintings might ease their financial woes. But even now he had conditions. He would send only a few works. He held back paintings he considered seminal or critical to his father's career, that were unique in form and style, or the loss of which he thought might threaten an eventual exhibit.

The art market was on the rebound at the time. According to a 1948 summary in *ARTnews* magazine, "for the first time since total war had slackened into sporadic war, dominant exhibitions, ideas, and personalities passed from one country to another and hard-to-find old masters reappeared in America to enrich further U.S. museums. All this combined to build confidence in art as a world commodity and a medium for the communication of ideas." Both art museums and private collectors in the United States were ready and eager to make notable acquisitions.

George duly sent along a few works, which arrived safely in Chicago. Charles let Grandpa know that once they cleared customs he would carefully attend to them.

> *I shall be very glad to see what can be done with them commercially, and if it is at all possible, you may be sure that I will lend every effort towards disposing of them at the best possible price. I am frank to say*

however, that the market for pictures of this type is very limited in Chicago, and it seems to me that New York would be a more proper place in which to dispose of them.

To thank him for his generosity in one of the only ways available to him, Grandpa told Charles one of the paintings was to be a gift. Charles, grateful and understanding of the importance of the gesture, wrote to him, "I appreciate your giving me one as a gift very much indeed, and I am sure that it will be a valued treasure."

Charles had an expert examine the paintings, and despite the robust art market it soon became clear the works weren't commercially valuable. Although the U.S. art market was active and engaged in the late 1940s, art collectors were captivated by the works of such artists as Rembrandt, Goya, Cézanne, and Winslow Homer. The reality was that while the Rynecki works had high sentimental value, the subject matter—Polish Jews from the interwar period—was of little or no interest to U.S. buyers.

Charles retracted his original suggestion that selling the paintings might help financially. He wrote to Grandpa George:

The paintings arrived by air express, and I have them in my possession. I am afraid that they have very little if any commercial value, inasmuch as I have talked with two or three art connoisseurs, who tell me that pictures of this type might have deep, personal sentimental value, but very little value commercially, except that they might be loaned to Jewish Clubs, synagogues and temples on a no-charge basis from time to time.

I do believe, and I am told that your father exhibits excellent work in his paintings, but I am afraid that they have infinitely more value to you than they have to anyone else . . . I am holding the paintings in my possession pending your arrival, at which time I will turn them back to you. I hope I do not hurt your feelings in saying that the paintings have no resale value, but facts are facts, and what may be important to one, has little if any value to another.

Grandpa George appeared to take the bad news in stride. In part, he was just relieved he wouldn't have to sell them. By the time he wrote back to Charles, he was fairly dismissive of the whole experience: "As to the paintings I fully agree with everything you said and I appreciate all your deeds on behalf [of me] as much [as] your touching [and] kind words."

Charles also seemed to absorb the news without much difficulty; it was just one more setback. After learning the paintings wouldn't yield the financial windfall they'd hoped for, they all turned back to the problem of getting the Ryneckis to America.

By March 1949, the family was thrilled to find out that they had finally been approved, and they began to plan for departure. Almost immediately, their plan was imperiled when Aleksander was thought to have tuberculosis. A series of doctor visits led to a hard-to-obtain X-ray, which confirmed he only had bronchitis. Unfortunately, this resulted in yet another delay. In August 1949 the family finally began to move, first by heading to Bagnoli, to what Grandpa George called a "transit concentration camp" outside of Naples. Time at the camp was mandated by U.S. immigration services to complete even more paperwork and undergo further medical examinations. Despite the fact they now had their long-awaited visas, they were back to the waiting game again. They were stuck at Bagnoli, and the conditions were, at least according to Grandpa George, exceptionally unpleasant. He wrote to Charles, "The living conditions [are] awful beyond description, let's hope for a short stay in this ~~hell~~ prisonlike place. It is a pity to be so badly treated just before our final leave. Yet our greatest worry is . . . we will be surely out of money." Charles responded by sending more money. In late September, after more than a month there, Grandpa George used a portion of the funds to move the family out of the DP camp and into their own space in town.

In early November the family finally got a good piece of news about their impending departure. While earlier refugees had been forced to travel from the camp to Germany to board ship for the United States, the November departure would leave directly from Naples. It was, in fact, the first U.S. displaced persons ship to sail to New York directly from an Italian port. That same week a Jewish newspaper ran a story with the title "Refugee Ship Leaves Italy for U.S. Carrying 673 Jewish Displaced Persons." The article reported that on board were "673 Jews who waited for more than four years to secure passage to the U.S. The contingent brings to 917 the number of Jews who left Italy under terms of the Displaced Persons Act of 1948. . . . An additional 2,000 Jews now in Italy have registered for emigration to America."

Grandpa George, ecstatic to be aboard the ship and headed to America, found work in the ship's laundry facilities. He made his first American dollar and vowed never to spend it. As the ship got farther from Europe's shores and closer to America, he convinced many of the other Jewish passengers to pool their resources and send President Truman a thank-you-note telegram. "844 Displaced Persons from Italy on USAT 'Marine Jumper' thank you Mr. President and the people of the United States for giving them the possibility to emigrate to your free country."

On November 21, 1949, the SS *Marine Jumper* arrived in New York. On the official "Manifest of in-Bound Passengers (Aliens)," Jerzy was number 614, Stanisława was number 615, and Aleksander was number 616. They were finally in America.

After arriving in the U.S., they settled in Denison, Texas, where Sidney Karchmer, their sponsor, lived. Grandpa George worked for Sidney, a dealer and broker in scrap iron and metals, for two years, but then grew antsy. Although he greatly appreciated all the Weicensang family had

A far cry from Dachau: news coverage of the Rynecki family's arrival in Texas.

provided—a place to land in America, a job, support, and family—he never felt like Texas was where he belonged. He had ambitions he believed he could fulfill more quickly elsewhere. Grandpa George decided they would "Go West" to California. Grandma Stella moved out first, taking the train to San Francisco and ultimately securing a job making hats. Grandpa and Dad followed shortly thereafter, driving from Texas. They lived in San Francisco for a short while, until Grandpa secured a job in Eureka, a town on the far northern reaches of the California coast, about three hundred miles north of San Francisco. At first Grandpa worked for someone else in the scrap metal business, but eventually he bought out the owner and ran it himself.

At the same time, my father, Alex, was growing up, completing high school in Eureka, California, and college at the University of Nevada at Reno, where he got a degree in Engineering. Wanting to avoid the draft, he eventually voluntarily enlisted with the navy, where he was trained as a salvage engineer, a job he turned into a career after his service ended. In the mid-1960s he met Fern Bershodsky, a Minnesotan whose parents emigrated from Poland and Russia in the 1920s. After a relatively brief courtship Alex proposed. "People our age [thirties] don't get engaged," Fern said and so they married with little fanfare. Three years

Alex in the U.S. Navy.

later, in 1969, they welcomed a baby girl into the family. That baby girl was, of course, me.

I grew up surrounded by my great-grandfather's art. It silently hung on the walls of both my parents' and my grandparents' homes. An only child, I was unusually serious and mature. I had friends, but preferred the company of books and adults. After middle school I went to the relatively unusual Urban High School of San Francisco, located in the Haight-Ashbury neighborhood, which focused on instilling a desire to learn and developing critical thinking skills. Then it was off to Bates College, a liberal arts school almost three thousand miles away in Maine. Mom teased me that I took a string and stretched it across the map to find the school farthest from home but still in the United States. Like many students, I wasn't initially clear on a course of study. I briefly experimented with English and Political Science, but ultimately found a good fit for my interests as a Rhetoric major. After graduation, I contemplated law school, ultimately taking a job with Williams & Connolly, a Washington, D.C., law firm, to get a better sense of the practice of law. My experience at Williams & Connolly steered me away from law, but I was still working there and mulling over graduate school and career options when my grandpa passed away in 1992.

Grandpa's death had a profound impact on my choice of study and my interest in both my family history and the broader history of the Holocaust. By the following spring, when the United States Holocaust Memorial Museum (USHMM) opened its doors to the public, I not only wanted to go, I was desperate to go.

SEVEN

Legacy

Entering the United States Holocaust Memorial Museum (USHMM) from Fourteenth Street, just off the Washington, D.C., Mall, I walked along a hallway on the main floor to reach the elevator; the exhibition starts on the top floor. The museum tells twelve years of history in thirty-six thousand square feet of exhibit space spread over three floors—beginning with Hitler's rise to power in 1933, then introducing events such as *Kristallnacht* in 1938 and the German Nazi invasion of Poland in 1939, presenting the Nazis' establishment of a police state, and explaining the Final Solution in detail. It includes a model of Auschwitz-Birkenau, demonstrating the ghastly reality of the gas chambers and ovens used for the genocide and the subsequent disposal of remains. The museum is not for the faint of heart. Emergency exits exist for those who are overwhelmed and need to leave quickly. I must admit the museum was a terribly difficult experience for me, and I seriously considered using the exits more than once.

The USHMM has a number of displays of personal effects—clothing, wedding rings, toothbrushes, eyeglasses, instruments, books, and leather goods—that belonged to those individuals murdered by the Nazis. These displays symbolize the enormous scope of the atrocities, and serve as a reminder of the Nazis' systematic, industrial approach to murder and the plunder of personal effects. I was both irresistibly drawn to and greatly repelled by one such display, a long and deep rectangular bin holding four thousand pairs of shoes of those who were murdered at the Majdanek concentration camp. The shoes on display at the museum are only a small subset of the original mounds, hundreds of thousands of pairs, discovered at the Nazi camp by liberating troops. I stood and stared at the shoes for an extraordinarily long time. I tried to look at each shoe—whose shoe was it: Was it a woman's shoe, a child's shoe, a man's shoe? And what was it for: Was it a dress shoe? A summer shoe? A practical work shoe? What I really wanted to know, more than anything else, was if one of the shoes belonged to my great-grandfather who perished at Majdanek. I knew how unlikely it would be for one of his shoes to be in the display, and yet I stared, transfixed—searching for a clue, a sign, somehow a message through time for something that once belonged to Moshe. I can't explain how real Moshe's murder felt at that moment, as time seemed to stop. I stood there, unable to move away from the exhibit, yet at the same time I wanted to run screaming from the nearness of his death.

The other exhibit that deeply affected me was a railcar used to transport Jews to the camps. Looking at the car made me sick to my stomach. I had read about deportations. I knew how the Nazis stuffed people into cars in such great numbers they couldn't breathe or find their own space. I knew many had died in the transports and how those who made it to their destinations often went straight into the gas chambers. But here was a real car. An actual car used for transport. As part of the exhibit you can actually walk through the car, and I didn't think I could do it. I felt claustrophobic at the thought. I was deeply grateful there was a bypass ramp, but as I passed, I touched the outside of the car. Perhaps this car, or one much like it, was used to transport my grandmother's sisters and their children to their deaths. Did they try to escape? Did they die on the railcar? Staring at the car was pure anguish. Again, it was a long time before I could move on. Eventually, shaken, I made it through the entire museum.

As I left, and even in the days following, I couldn't help but speculate about what had happened to my family members during the Holocaust, and the speculation haunted me. Despite how deeply the exhibit had affected me, I learned nothing about my family specifically, and the desire to know more began to burn ever more brightly within me.

At the same time, I had a perspective on the broader community destroyed by the Holocaust that wasn't strongly communicated by the U.S. Holocaust Memorial Museum. In order to give a bit of context, I need to say that I love museums in general, and particularly art museums. I like to see famous works and lesser known pieces and play the game of "if I could take one thing home from the museum, I'd get . . ." But when I thought about the Holocaust Memorial Museum there was nothing I wanted to bring home. Instead, it seemed that in the museum's focus on the genocide, there was little about the culture and communities that had been so nearly annihilated as well. There was a piece missing that could give greater depth and context to the losses of the Holocaust: the story of the Jewish community before the war. I felt its absence particularly acutely because I had grown up surrounded by dozens of depictions of a vibrant and thriving Polish-Jewish community, which were the heart of Moshe's work. The paintings were also survivors themselves, a tiny fraction of the original collection. Their scars and rips spoke to the good fortune required for them to survive. To me it seemed that their stories needed to be told; that they could bear witness in their own way. I felt an overwhelming urge to share Moshe's work.

I vowed I would return to the museum to meet with the curatorial staff. I was certain they would want to know of my great-grandfather's paintings and would want to exhibit his art. I called the museum and was eventually put in touch with Jacek Nowakowski, the director of the curatorial department. I told him a bit about my great-grandfather's artwork and asked if I could meet him in person. Mr. Nowakowski kindly agreed to do so.

I was thrilled to return to the museum with an appointment. Taking an active role in sharing my family's history rather than passively experiencing history on display felt powerful. I'd been emotionally drained as a visitor to the museum, but upon my return I felt optimistic. I was hopeful my great-grandfather's art could offer visitors a positive entry point into discussions of Polish-Jewish history, Jewish art and culture, Judaism, and ultimately, the Holocaust. It was, I thought, a perfect fit for the museum. So to say I arrived in Mr. Nowakowski's office full of confidence and delight to share my idea would be an understatement.

"Come in, come in," Mr. Nowakowski told me. "Please, take a seat," he said, and pointed to the chair across from his desk.

"Thank you for meeting with me," I said.

"Of course. What can I do for you?" he asked.

"It's my great-grandfather's art," I said. "I told you a bit about it on the phone."

"Right," he said, and then paused, as he waited for me to continue.

"Well, I was thinking you could put it on display here at the museum."

Mr. Nowakowski looked at me; again he waited for more.

"My great-grandfather's work once showed at the Judah L. Magnes Museum in Berkeley, California. He painted scenes of the Polish-Jewish community from the interwar period," I said, and pulled out the abbreviated catalog that had been put together for the 1981 exhibition and passed it to him across the desk.

"Right, you mentioned that on the phone," he said as he reached for the materials.

"I was thinking you could exhibit his paintings here," I said for the second time. "My family could arrange a special loan. It would be another way for visitors to understand what was lost in the Holocaust."

Mr. Nowakowski flipped through the catalog—more a booklet, I thought—as I watched him turn the pages rather quickly.

"Your great-grandfather's work is interesting," Mr. Nowakowski said as he stood from his desk and walked toward a bookcase behind me. "I've seen your great-grandfather's works before. I saw several of them on display in an exhibit in Poland," he told me.

"Really?" I asked. "Are you sure?"

Mr. Nowakowski turned the pages of the book he'd taken off the shelf. "Here," he said, and pointed at a piece in his book. "This is his work, right?" he asked.

I took the book from his hand and stared. I could hardly believe it. How was it possible there were paintings by my great-grandfather I'd never seen before? But there was no disputing the evidence on the page in front of me. These paintings were obviously the work of my great-grandfather. I recognized the style immediately. No doubt about it. After a moment, I felt myself exhale, which made me realize I had been holding my breath. My attention jumped between the different images on the page, my eyes unable to fixate on any one image. I didn't know any of these pieces, and yet there was something hauntingly familiar about every single one. I loved them right away. But of course I would; they were my great-grandfather's work.

"I appreciate your coming in to see me," Mr. Nowakowski said as he reached for his book. I wasn't ready for him to take it away, but I had clearly stayed longer than he'd expected. This was his signal to wrap things up.

"And an exhibit?" I asked, trying to linger and stay just a little bit longer.

"I'm sorry," Mr. Nowakwoski said. "I'm really afraid it just won't be possible. But if you ever want to gift the paintings to the museum, we'd be delighted to have them. We could make them accessible to researchers."

I looked at Mr. Nowakowski, unsure what to say. This wasn't going at all how I'd imagined. I'd thought he'd want to see the whole collection. That we'd look at the calendar and pick a date for the exhibit. Now I realized exactly how overblown my optimism had been. All the confidence I'd had when I entered the museum dissipated. I was a recent college graduate. I'd only just visited the museum for the first time myself to get a better sense of Holocaust history. Who was I to march into his office and ask for an exhibition? Clearly I hadn't thought this all through.

"Thank you so much for your time," I said. And then I stood and left his office. It was anticlimactic and tremendously disappointing.

I visited Mr. Nowakowski in the late spring of 1993. I had already applied to graduate school at that point, and I began studying at UC Davis in the field of Rhetoric and Speech Communication in the fall. I'd gotten over the idea of an exhibit at the United States Holocaust Memorial Museum, but Grandpa George's memoir and Moshe's paintings continued to trouble me. If the museum wouldn't display them, I'd find another way to tell their story. In the meantime, I focused my energy on graduate school and, to be entirely honest, on a fellow graduate student, Steve Knowlton, whom I ultimately married four years later. Just as I'm certain Mr. Nowakowski didn't quite know what to make of my request, my graduate school advisers weren't sure what to make of my need to incorporate Grandpa George's memoir and my great-grandfather's art into my master's thesis.

By contrast, Steve never thought my obsession was odd; in fact, he was quite supportive. One night early on in my first semester at Davis, I stayed up late watching *Europa Europa*, the true story of a Jewish boy separated from his family in the early days of the Holocaust and his harrowing experience hiding in plain sight in the heart of the Nazi world as a "war hero" and member of the Hitler Youth. When the film was over, Steve happened to call. At the time, I was sobbing from the powerful emotionality of the film, and Steve was worried about me. Concerned about my state of mind, but not knowing me well enough to come to my apartment, Steve insisted we meet. It may have been the first time he offered a shoulder to lean on, but it was a shoulder I increasingly leaned on over the years. Ultimately, between Steve's emotional support and my advisers' academic encouragement, I explored a wide variety of Holocaust-related stories, ultimately finding a real resonance in learning about the children of Holocaust survivors. I started with Helen Epstein's *Children of the Holocaust: Conversations with Sons and Daughters of Survivors* and was ultimately most inspired by Art Spiegelman's *Maus* books.

Spiegelman is the son of survivors, and the *Maus* story line is in large part about his struggle to understand his father's past and how it relates to his own identity. The narrative is unusual and was both unique and groundbreaking at the time. *Maus* is a graphic novel in which Spiegelman represents Jews as mice and Nazis as cats. It tells his parents' Holocaust narrative while simultaneously trying to understand his relationship to their history. Despite the original controversy surrounding the book, volume one was widely read and won the Pulitzer Prize. For me it was transformative, radically changing the way I viewed my own story. I was so moved that I wrote to Spiegelman, explaining that I had never met another child of Holocaust survivors. I told him how his books touched me and how grateful I was to understand others' struggles with the weight of their families' Holocaust legacies. He graciously responded with a *Maus* postcard. "Yes. The legacy is a baffling one," he wrote. Indeed. I was only beginning to understand what he meant.

While academic advisers offered sage advice and invaluable guidance in focusing and understanding my topic, Steve was instrumental in helping me translate my ideas into words on paper. Still, my thesis had the kind of absurdly technical title, so commonly found adorning theses and technical articles, that obfuscates more than it clarifies for most audiences. The title of my thesis was *Emerging Constitutive*

Rhetorics: Maus' Re-Interpellation of the Second Generation. Quite simply, it was about the role and voice of children of survivors in Holocaust literature. Perhaps *The Role and Voice of the Children of Holocaust Survivors* didn't seem pretentious enough to me to merit a degree, and I did get my master's, and headed east to Penn State to pursue a doctorate in Speech Communication. Steve was about two hundred miles away at the University of Pennsylvania pursuing his own studies. I planned to research and write about the representation of Jews in television and movies. Over the course of the first year, the fact that Steve and I were three hours apart (while only I had a car), the drudgery of school, and a massive winter snowstorm that buried my car for more than two weeks were very difficult. The following summer, Steve proposed and I accepted. At that point we realized that the prospect of a long-distance marriage was just too hard, so we decided to quit our graduate programs and return to California.

For a number of years I worked as a corporate communications specialist, until my company cut back on my hours and eventually let me go. My next career move was to work with Dad and Mom in the family commercial real estate management business. Our office suite consisted of three small rooms in a building we owned in Marin County, just north of the Golden Gate Bridge. While I studied for my real estate broker's license, I helped out with tenant leases, kept abreast of property maintenance issues, and worked on possible property development plans. Glad to be out of graduate school, but sad to have set aside my focus on Grandpa George's memoir, I began to chronicle my relationship to my great-grandfather's art and legacy. I also renewed my efforts to get his paintings exhibited. While passionate about my goal, I was repeatedly unsuccessful in my attempts to secure a museum exhibition. After a number of fits and starts, the first real step forward came in 1999, seven years after Grandpa George died, when Dad had my great-grandfather's paintings professionally photographed.

Dad and I carefully placed the unframed painting on the easel. The photographer peered through the viewfinder of his camera on the tripod a few feet away. We looked expectantly at him, waiting for feedback on its placement.

"A little to the left," he said, and motioned for us to adjust the painting.

Dad slowly inched the painting, of a piano player, toward me. It was a work I hadn't seen in a while. A man, in a dark full-length winter coat with its collar turned up high and nestled tightly against his neck, is playing the piano. The angle my great-grandfather depicted gives viewers the privileged position of seeing both the pianist and the keyboard. Although the pianist is seated on a small, round four-legged stool, his body appears to be in motion. His back curves forward, drawing attention to his hands on the keyboard, fingers perched, but clearly in motion, on top of the white keys. There is little else to tell about the pianist or the room where he plays. It seems it's in a home—the arm of a couch abuts the edge of the piano. There are no telltale clues to reveal who this man is or where he is playing. The painting isn't dated; it's not even signed.

The photographer snapped several shots, adjusting the aperture and bracketing the image to capture the same image with multiple exposure levels, to produce a range of images, from relatively light to relatively dark. Since we were in my parents' home and not a studio, the lighting was a bit fickle. The photographer couldn't alter the ambient light levels easily, so he instead compensated with the camera. He hoped that when the slides were developed, we could find one nearly ideal shot of each painting, which we would then have scanned and burned to a CD to maintain a digital image of the work.

"You know," the photographer said as we prepared to put the pianist

Pianist *(undated).*

away and put a different painting on the easel, "maybe you want to make a website with these paintings."

Dad looked up expectantly.

"They're such great paintings," the photographer said. "Maybe it would be a nice way to share them with other people."

"An online gallery?" Dad asked, and looked at me.

I wasn't quite sure where this was headed. I looked at the paintings, the photographer, and my father, and I had a palpable sense that they were waiting for my pronouncement on the matter.

After a long silence, I gave in to the tension. I blurted out, "I have a friend who taught herself HTML. She said it's easy to learn."

"Great," Dad said. "Look into it."

Although I had some apprehension about the potential size and scope of the project, I soon began to build the first website to display my great-grandfather's work. By the spring of 1999 I had finished and www.rynecki.org went live. It was a simple, bare-bones design, in large part due to my inexperience with HTML and lack of graphic design instincts. The available Web technology of 1999 was also fairly limited. As a result, the site was divided into simple components: visitors could see photos of paintings, read a brief biography, and learn the works were on display at the Judah L. Magnes Museum in Berkeley from November 1981 to January 1982. I even quoted the exhibition catalog.

Despite its shortcomings and less than stellar layout, Dad and I were excited about the website, and every day we checked the statistics of visitors to the site and page views. Over the next few months I sent emails to art museums, Holocaust museums, and anyone else I thought might be interested in my great-grandfather's body of work. I also asked many other sites to link to my "virtual art museum." Some did, others didn't. In the very earliest days of the Internet, these links were the primary way visitors stumbled onto the site, as well as the primary way search engines at the time ranked results. Generally, the more links you had, the more people visited your site.

And then I got bold. I wrote a letter to Elie Wiesel, the Holocaust survivor and Nobel Prize winner. I told him I was the daughter and granddaughter of Holocaust survivors. I explained that my great-grandfather was a Warsaw-based artist who painted the Polish-Jewish community in the interwar period and that he perished in the Holocaust. I mentioned that the goal of the website was to share the art with the world, and I asked for his help. Soon afterward, I received a letter in reply.

"I am moved by your commitment to the work of your great-grandfather, and therefore wish I could help you, but I know nothing about 'virtual' museums. I do not use the Internet at all and therefore, I am not familiar with 'websites,'" Wiesel wrote. He suggested I contact various Holocaust museums and centers that had opened across the United States. "If the paintings have been exhibited at the Magnes Museum in Berkeley, surely these other venues would have some interest." I was exhilarated that Wiesel replied, but crushed that he didn't offer more assistance or guidance. Steve tried to console me. For me the letter represented a failure to move the project forward. Steve saw it for something else—the story's power to elicit a response.

Ultimately, I framed Wiesel's letter and hung it on my office wall, as an inspiration. But I was still stuck on the problem of how to get people to view the website. If no one looked at the art in a virtual gallery, then it was no different than hiding the paintings in a closet: seldom seen and unknown.

While I brooded about how to drive traffic to the website, a number of people managed to find and explore its content. Unfortunately, I had little information about who they were or why they had come. Occasionally I received emails asking where someone might see the work in person. Sometimes people wanted to know if the paintings were for sale. Others requested prints. But the most interesting email arrived just about a year after the site went live, from an AOL account. The subject line, "To Ms. Elizabeth Rynecki," was from a Katherina and Maciej Rauch-Grodecki, in Queens, New York. Their email said they had found my website by accident, but they knew my great-grandfather's work quite well. They didn't tell me how they knew his work. "Judging from the previously seen work of the Artist," they wrote, "we didn't expect such a variety of subjects, emotions, and approaches to the people he captured in his paintings. It was a surprise to see such bright, bravely used colors." The email closed with a phone number and asked me to call. Intrigued, I picked up the phone and dialed their number.

The phone rang, but a recorded phone company message announced, "This phone number does not accept private calls." I was stumped. Dad and I wrote an email to Katherina and told her we had tried to call, but that we couldn't get through. Katherina wrote back. She was sorry. She had a service that did not accept calls from private numbers and to bypass it we needed to first dial *82. She closed her email with a sentence I found rather mysterious. She told me that when we talked she would give me "more detailed information about saving your [great] Grandfather's paintings." I had no idea what she was talking about, but I had a faint hope that her family had found one of Moshe's bundles after the war.

After many tries I finally got through to Katherina. She told me she thought that before the war her husband's family had had some sort of connection to my great-grandfather, but she didn't know the whole story. She promised to ask her mother-in-law for details and to take photos of the paintings to send me. I was thrilled by the prospect of seeing paintings I had never seen before.

In April, about six weeks later, with no sign of the promised information and photos, I wrote Katherina and gently reminded her of the promise to take photographs of the Moshe Rynecki paintings in their home and to send them to me. I offered to display them on our website in a special "works owned by others" gallery. Another three weeks passed before Katherina replied to my email. She apologized for her long absence and delayed reply. She had been in Florida for several weeks and then gone to Poland. The pile of mail in her home and the emails in her inbox were overflowing. She was looking for a job. "Please give me some time," she said imploringly. And then she promised, "And of course, I will send you the photos of his paintings as I have promised."

April turned into May and then into June. I tried to be patient. In late June I wrote to see if Katherina was enjoying her summer and inquired about the status of the letter from her Polish mother-in-law, and about the possibility of obtaining photographs of the Rynecki paintings in her home.

A month later, in July, Katherina responded. She had health problems. She had gone to Poland. They had house guests. Her cousin had just arrived at JFK and was staying with them for several weeks and she needed to go clean up supper and make the bed. Four paragraphs into the email she announced she had finally acquired a scanner and that while this was GOOD NEWS (she wrote it in all caps), she didn't know how to operate it but promised, "I am much closer to fulfilling my promise: sending you images of Mr. Rynecki's pictures."

In September Katherina wrote to me again. Again she apologized for not sending me photographs. She had gone to Poland in August for business. She flew British Airways and thought they were the best. She spent a few nights in London with a friend. And then her closing sentence sank me: "As you can imagine, I didn't have a chance to become friends with the scanner yet."

After eight months, I felt extremely frustrated. I still didn't have photographs of the paintings she had of my great-grandfather's work, and I had less hope with each passing day. Nor did I have a letter from her mother-in-law to explain how she knew my family and how she had my great-grandfather's paintings in her possession. Trying to put aside my sadness, I shelved the idea that I would ever see photographs of the Rynecki works Katherina had in her home.

Over the next year or so I fiddled with the website, but not much happened on my project, and as important as it was, it took a backseat to some very personally exciting news. Steve and I were thrilled to learn in October of 2001 that we would soon be parents. In what seemed to be the blink of an eye, in June of 2002, I gave birth to my first son, Tyler. Between incipient baby brain and working in the family commercial real estate business, it became more and more difficult for me to focus on the art project. Both the overall project and the website languished. Twenty months after Tyler was born I gave birth to a second son, Owen, in February of 2004, which made the focus on my immediate family unit that much more intense. Being a mother of two young boys was an unbelievably exhilarating, awesome, and draining experience. Balancing marriage, motherhood, and career left me with little time to focus on my great-grandfather's art legacy.

By April 2004, I was a working mother with a two-month-old and a twenty-two-month-old, and I had pretty much given up on ever seeing photographs of Katherina's Rynecki paintings; they were no longer even remotely on my radar. That, of course, was precisely when photos of some of the paintings arrived in my life. They arrived in the form of an email from Katherina's husband, Maciej. Maciej's email was brief and to the point. "I have in my collection six paintings done by M. Rynecki. If you are interested to buy some of them, please contact me."

Initially I was outraged at the suggestion that my family buy the paintings. I ranted to Dad about the audacity Maciej had to hit us up for buying the works when what he really should do was package them up and ship them to us. But I also had to admit, despite my outrage, that I didn't know the provenance of the pieces he had, since the mysterious letter from the mother-in-law explaining their relationship to the Rynecki family had never materialized. Perhaps my great-grandfather had given the pieces away or sold them. I couldn't be sure, so I told Maciej we were interested in learning more. Given my previous inability to acquire images of the paintings, I offered to send a disposable camera so Maciej might take photographs of the paintings for me. This time I was not waiting for anyone to learn how to use a scanner. A few days later Maciej replied and informed me he already had digital photos and asked where to send them.

In early May 2004 an envelope arrived from Maciej. It contained poor-quality color computer printouts of two paintings. One showed a market scene with vendors selling fruit and vegetables. A clothesline ran through a courtyard, garments blowing in the wind just over marketplace stalls. My great-grandfather's signature was visible in the lower right-hand corner. The second showed two men in a workspace with what appeared to be a large loom in the foreground. The loosely woven threads draped under, over, and across the machine. Again, the telltale MRynecki signature was visible in the lower right-hand corner of the painting.

Despite the limited quality of the photos, I was excited to see the pieces. I could tell immediately that these were works painted by my great-grandfather. While I had never seen these exact scenes, the style was intimately familiar. They were not portraits of individuals, but group scenes, slices of time from the Polish-Jewish community. And despite issues with color balance and bleeding caused by the printer, the colors and color palette resonated with me as true to my great-grandfather's style. Finally, I recognized my great-grandfather's trademark signature, with the "M" and the "R" united together across the top, and the line of the "i" at the end of the name forming a long tail, which curled left and underlined the signature as a whole. I was disappointed that Maciej had sent only two prints instead of all six, but at the same time I was surprised and happy to see any at all.

I walked into Dad's office.

"You got a minute?" I asked.

"For you? Always."

"The pictures arrived from New York," I said, and tossed the printouts on Dad's desk.

Dad adjusted the images on his desk. He liked everything neat and orderly.

"Where's a magnifying glass?" Dad asked.

I walked into Mom's office and searched the office supply cabinet. On the third shelf I found a magnifying glass still stored in the cardboard box it came in when it was purchased. I removed it and returned to Dad's office.

Dad took the magnifying glass and placed it above the signature in the photo of the painting. He squinted through the lens and tried to read the signature. He looked up.

"What do you think?" he asked.

"It looks like his signature."

Dad nodded.

I pointed to the people in the painting. "Notice how the features on the faces are stylized and suggestive rather than detailed. That is exactly his style."

Dad turned the two sheets over. On the backside of both was written: "2 X 13 Watercolor. Good condition. Framed."

"He wants us to buy them?" Dad asked.

"That's what his email said."

"And should we?" Dad asked.

"Buy them?" I balked. "It makes me so mad."

"Don't get so emotional," Dad told me. "It's a business transaction. He wants to sell them. The question is if we are a willing buyer, and if so, what to offer."

"I guess I'm a willing buyer. I haven't a clue what they're worth."

We sat in a pretty intense, but still somehow companionable, silence, staring at the printouts for a long while, as if by being examined in just the right way, or seen from just the right angle, they would magically yield more information. As if we could somehow divine their past. Dad seemed to be considering their value, while I was instead focused on the mystery of how these paintings had ended up with a couple in New York. I wondered what Grandpa George would have thought of seeing the works and being asked to buy them. We had never been in this position before, so we were a bit stumped.

"We should ask someone who knows how to value art," Dad said. "I'll call an appraiser."

"Right now?" I asked.

"No time like the present," Dad said.

We first contacted some auction houses to get the names of reputable appraisers. The appraiser we decided on was based on a referral from Bonhams & Butterfields. An auction house originally known in San Francisco as Butterfield & Butterfield, it had been sold to the British auctioneer Bonhams. The appraiser asked my father numerous questions about the artist and the art. The appraiser wasn't terribly interested in style, history, or what was depicted. Ultimately, he told us that the best way to value the works of lesser known artists was to search for records of prior sales.

"But we've never sold anything," Dad said.

"Not a problem," the appraiser said. "I'll just take a look on artprice.com." Dad waited while the appraiser tapped on his computer keyboard.

"Here we are," the appraiser said. "Two Rynecki paintings sold at New York Sotheby's in 1993. *Café Scene* and *The Accordionist*, both dated 1934, had a combined hammer price of seventeen hundred dollars."

Dad reached for a pen and a yellow legal-sized pad of paper and quickly wrote it all down. We stared at each other. This was no ordinary bit of news. It was absolutely stunning. Who had sold Rynecki paintings? Where had these two paintings been before they'd come to market in 1993? Where had they hung? Who had loved them and why were they selling them? Was it Maciej and Katherina who sold them? Were they unhappy with the auction house results and now trying to sell pieces directly to us to avoid the auction house fees and commission?

"The most important part," the appraiser continued, "is the size of the pieces. Apparently the two works were identical in size. It says thirty-seven by fifty-one centimeters."

"And now what?" Dad asked.

"Well, that's easy," the appraiser said. "You take the size of the painting and the auction price, and you calculate the price per square inch." Dad and I looked at each other.

"Price per square inch?"

"Yes," the appraiser said. "You know the size of the work you're being offered, right?"

"I do."

"Well, then, you just do the math. That'll give you a pretty good valuation of the work," the appraiser said.

"Thank you for your time," Dad said, and then hung up the phone.

Dad tore off the top sheet of paper from the yellow pad and set it aside. He always liked an entirely clean sheet of paper when he was thinking. Then he turned on his calculator, a classic Hewlett-Packard model that used reverse Polish notation. I found it beyond confusing because you put in all of the numbers and then the mathematical operation you wanted to do with them. Dad loved it. Maybe, I thought, you needed to speak Polish to know how to use it.

"Thirty-seven by fifty-one centimeters. That's fourteen and five-eighths by twenty-one inches," he said. "So fourteen point six-twenty-five times twenty-one is three hundred and seven and one-eighth square inches. Right?" he asked.

I hated when Dad asked me math questions. I was intimidated by the numbers and his facility with them. I nodded my head in agreement without cross-checking his work. If I told him I didn't know and that it would take me a while to make the computations myself, he would lose patience with me and we would end up arguing about my mathematical ineptitude instead of figuring out what to offer Maciej.

"So if two pieces sold for seventeen hundred dollars," he said as he entered the figures into his calculator, "and they are the same size, we can take half the price, or eight hundred and fifty dollars, and divide by the area of one painting. That means it would be two dollars and seventy-six cents per square inch."

I stared at the piece of paper, willing what we should offer to magically appear. Dad kept writing.

"Say, two dollars and eighty cents per square inch if we round it up, and the paintings we want to buy are two hundred and sixty square inches each," Dad said and punched the figures and order of operations into the calculator. "I can practically do it in my head," he said.

I could not do the math in my head, so I looked at him expectantly. As was his custom, rather than telling me the answer, he turned the calculator toward me, so I could see it for myself. I thought he assumed I had estimated it in my head and this was just for confirmation. In any event, the answer was right there on the LCD screen: $728 per painting.

I didn't really object to calculating a price per square inch, but I looked at the photo of the painting and I looked at the price on the calculator, and I suddenly had a very bad feeling about where this was headed. I had no idea why Maciej wanted to sell these two pieces, but I strongly suspected he would not be pleased with a price based on a mathematical equation, regardless of how it was related to market value. In contacting us, his expectation was likely that what he had was quite valuable and that as the artist's descendants, we would pay a premium for the paintings. More about pride of ownership than a business transaction, in other words. I cringed when I wrote Maciej with an offer and a request for photos of the other Rynecki paintings in his home. And then I waited.

A letter arrived a week later. It was written to Dad. It was worse than I had anticipated. Not only did Maciej not like the offer, but our offer deeply offended him. He was really angry.

> *As you know I have sent you photos of only two of my paintings.*
>
> *I have considered selling them, but only those two, and for a fair price.*
>
> *As for your request: I am not sending you photos of the other Rynecki's paintings, because they are not for sale at the present time. They are extremely interesting, probably the best work Rynecki had done, but I am not ready to show them to the world just yet.*
>
> *Your information about the Sotheby's art auction in the early nineties is maybe accurate, but it is obvious that the prices paid then have a very little to do with today's art market.*
>
> *First of all it was more than 10 years ago.*
>
> *Also it was exceptionally bad year for the art. For example: during the same auction most of the paintings of the valuable famous artists like Picasso, Dali and Pissaro were sold for much below the appraisal value. On the other hand the paintings of Rynecki were sold for a bigger amount than intially asked.*
>
> *And please note, those were the very first paintings of this artist sold officially in USA.*
>
> *Only then people have the first opportunity to learn about the existence of Moshe Rynecki.*
>
> *Things have changed since then. More and more people are interested in Jewish painters from that era, including Moshe Rynecki.*

The paintings of M. Rynecki do not appear often at the auction or galleries for maybe a very simple reason:

Besides the Jewish Historical Museum in Warsaw, perhaps the only two people who have them are you and I?

And right now we are not selling. Not for the proposed price.

I am sorry, but to calculate the art of such a wonderful painter as Moshe Rynecki, who died in the Holocaust, "by square inch," and in lower rate than many today's below the average paintings, is for me unconceivable.

I got several offers for my paintings during last years, from people who might have no sentimental reasons, but artistic ones. Every offer was significantly higher in dollars than yours. But I didn't want to sell just to anybody.

As a Polish man, born in Warsaw, who's father fought in the World War II and shed blood in the Warsaw Uprising, and who's family lost several family members, I have also sentimental attachment to the paintings of Moshe Rynecki.

To prove it: I am willing to pay you twice as much for any of your painting.

This is a serious offer.

Or maybe you would consider exchange two paintings?

You would get those two paintings you have seen, and I will get two of yours?

It would be interesting to refresh our collections, wouldn't it?

Sincerely,
Maciek

Dad looked at me. He put the letter down. "I guess he didn't like our offer," he said.

"That's putting it mildly," I said.

"Well, we tried."

"Want to take him up on his offer to trade pieces?"

"Absolutely not," Dad said. "The pieces we have were discovered together at the end of the war. I am not breaking up the collection into further fragments."

"What am I supposed to do?" I asked.

"We made a legitimate offer, he didn't like it. I'm not offering more, and I am certainly not trading pieces with him," Dad said. "There's nothing else to do."

"So I'm just supposed to put all of the correspondence into a file folder and forget about it?"

Dad looked at me but didn't say anything.

I stood up and walked out of Dad's office and back to my own. I was angry, but not at Dad. Yes, his offer based on a price per square inch had been crazy, but it also was the valuation advice given to us by an appraiser who knew more about art pricing than we did. But I was cross about the whole thing less because we hadn't successfully obtained the paintings than because Maciej refused to send photos of the other four Rynecki pieces in his possession. Witholding information about my great-grandfather seemed downright cruel. I wished there was something I could do about it, but what exactly I wasn't sure.

"Knock, knock," Mom said, from my doorway. "How'd it go?"

I fingered the pieces of paper Maciej sent us before answering. It seemed strange for Mom to ask. She had probably heard most of the conversation from her own desk. On the other hand, it was incredibly classy of her to give me an opportunity to tell her what happened instead of rushing to judgment about what she'd overheard.

"Not very well," I finally said.

"Meaning?"

"Meaning our offer was too low and Maciej is angry."

"You think you should have offered more?"

"I guess."

"Dad didn't want to offer more?"

"Exactly."

"So now what?"

"Nothing."

"Nothing?"

"Well, what would you suggest?"

Mom shrugged and tugged at her earrings and then took them off. Sometimes late in the day, they began to bother her. She paused, idly toying with the earrings now in the palm of her hand. Finally she spoke. "I have no idea. It seems like you've hit a dead end with Maciej."

"It seems like I've hit a lot of dead ends."

"You mean the Jewish Historical Institute."

I nodded, thinking back on an email exchange I'd had more than four years ago, an email exchange inspired by my visit to the United States Holocaust Memorial Museum.

EIGHT

Cultural Assets—Lost Art

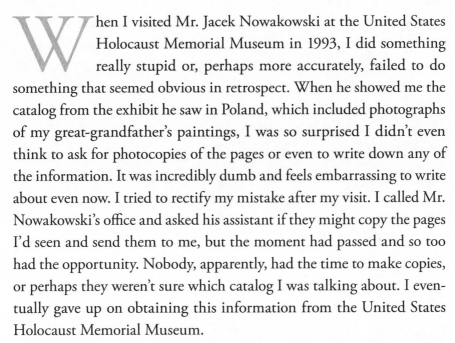

When I visited Mr. Jacek Nowakowski at the United States Holocaust Memorial Museum in 1993, I did something really stupid or, perhaps more accurately, failed to do something that seemed obvious in retrospect. When he showed me the catalog from the exhibit he saw in Poland, which included photographs of my great-grandfather's paintings, I was so surprised I didn't even think to ask for photocopies of the pages or even to write down any of the information. It was incredibly dumb and feels embarrassing to write about even now. I tried to rectify my mistake after my visit. I called Mr. Nowakowski's office and asked his assistant if they might copy the pages I'd seen and send them to me, but the moment had passed and so too had the opportunity. Nobody, apparently, had the time to make copies, or perhaps they weren't sure which catalog I was talking about. I eventually gave up on obtaining this information from the United States Holocaust Memorial Museum.

But then in 2000, shortly after I'd built the Moshe Rynecki: Portrait of a Life in Art website, I had a renewed and invigorated need to get my hands on that catalog. I wrote to a man named Sam Gruber, who ran a Jewish heritage website. Sam advised me to write to a woman named Lena Bergman. Lena in turn forwarded my email to Renata Piątkowska. Renata, it seemed, was currently employed at POLIN Museum of the History of Polish Jews, but she had formerly worked at the Jewish Historical Institute. Her reply absolutely stunned me. "In the collection of the Museum [the Jewish Historical Institute]," Renata wrote, "are 52 works by your great-grandfather." My mind absolutely boggled at the number. Fifty-two pieces! It was astounding. When I finally recovered my wits, I was able to read Renata's next sentence. She explained that over the prior few decades the museum had seen a growth in interest in the history and culture of Polish Jews. This, Renata said, was why my great-grandfather's pieces had appeared in several exhibitions, most notably the Kraków exhibition, *Polish Jews*, put together by Polish art historian Marek Rostworowski, which included twenty-two Rynecki paintings. Rostworowski, Renata explained, was well-known in Poland and quite a fan of my great-grandfather's art. If I wanted to know more about the works held by the Jewish Historical Institute, she said, I really should write to Magdalena Tarnowska, the current head of the institute.

I tried to absorb all the details in Renata's email, but was still completely gobsmacked that a museum in Warsaw was in possession of fifty-two of my great-grandfather's paintings. Grandpa George thought everything had been destroyed in the war, and yet there were *fifty-two* fully intact pieces in Warsaw. I needed pictures immediately, or preferably yesterday.

In 2000 I exchanged emails with Magdalena and requested photographs. She informed me there were forty-four watercolors and eight black-and-white works. She offered to send photographs, but at a substantial price—the price quoted at that time would have more than paid for me to fly to Poland and hire a professional photographer to boot. I was excited we could get photographs, but disappointed they wouldn't just give them to me—they most certainly already had documentation of what was in their collection—or at least send them to me at cost. I desperately wanted to see the paintings, but I struggled with a lot of negative feelings: I truly believed the institute should try to help me, the heir of the artist, at least to see the works. Asking for photographs seemed like a reasonable request. Asking them politely to either send us images they almost certainly had already (at least for the works they had previously exhibited) or take snapshots at cost didn't seem unfair. Steve and I had recently purchased a house in the San Francisco Bay Area, and because we were feeling exceptionally house poor, paying the institute's price was not feasible. After stewing for a while, I reluctantly approached Dad about Magdalena's email and the price. His response was almost exactly what I'd predicted.

"It's substantially more than we paid to photograph our collection here in California. That was more than twice as many pieces, and all we're asking for is snapshots, not a CD or professional prints," Dad said.

"True, but it's the only way they'll give us photographs," I said.

"Offer to send them film and to print the negatives here in the States. It'll be cheaper," Dad suggested.

"I can try."

"They see America and they think big money," Dad said. "I'm not paying what they're asking."

I sighed and wrote back to Magdalena offering Dad's suggestion.

Magdalena didn't like my proposal. "I am sorry, but your proposal is unacceptable," she wrote. "The cost will be the same. The cost depends on how much work a photographer must do."

I passed the message on to Dad. He felt the cost was exorbitant. In particularly ungenerous moments I felt like the museum was holding the works hostage, but at some level I was aware that they needed money to pay their expenses. I resolved to find another way to get pictures of the paintings, and I did, eventually, although not of all the pieces. Six years later I discovered photos of eight of the fifty-two pieces. I learned about them serendipitously, when I was working on a slightly different part of the project.

In 2006 I retained Marlena Rosłan, a Polish-speaking friend of a friend, to do a bit of translation work for me. I needed an excerpt translated from the book *Pamiętnik malarza* [*Diary of a Painter*] in which Marian Trzebiński, a Warsaw-based artist, wrote about my great-grandfather. When Marlena completed the work, she spent a bit of time checking facts to ensure the translation was correct in context. In so doing, she happened upon eight Rynecki paintings included on the pages of a Polish stock photography website called Lookgalleria. Marlena wondered if I was familiar with the website and the paintings. I was not. One of the eight was a particularly insightful and interesting discovery—a self-portrait.

The self-portrait was a watercolor in which my great-grandfather showed himself from about midshoulder up. He was wearing a white button-down shirt with a blue pinstripe. His hair was short, his countenance clean shaven. A watchband was visible on his right wrist. The landscape-format painting showed him mostly in profile, but not entirely because I could see both sides of his face. The right part of the canvas was filled with wide, abstract paintbrush strokes in hues of purple, blue, and green. He must have been resting his arm on a table because he had his chin in his hand. The four fingers of his right hand fanned out across the right side of his face, the pinky resting against the side of his nose. His shirt was very cosmopolitan in style, in dramatic contrast to the more traditional depictions he made of the Jewish community as a whole. I took an immediate liking to the painting. There are no known photographs of Moshe, so the discovery of another self-portrait was incredibly exciting. It gave me just a bit more insight into his life.

I wrote Marlena the most ridiculous, over-the-top, gushing email, trying to convey all my emotions about her discovery: "OOOOHHHHH MY GOSH!!!! Marlena—a bazillion and one thank yous!" I wrote. I was embarrassed at my exuberance, but how else could I communicate even a fraction of the feelings—the pent-up hope of finding his work, the uncertainty about what survived, and the surprise of what each found work depicted, what new thing it showed, of the community and about Moshe? It was just so exciting to find a link to the past and get a bonus glimpse of my great-grandfather. I returned to the Lookgalleria website to find out if I could order prints of the photographs. I also wrote the company to ask who owned the paintings and where the paintings were located. Marcin, the man with whom I exchanged emails, told me he didn't know anything about the paintings themselves. He explained that his photo library represented the photographers and their photography copyrights only, that all other rights belonged to the owners of the paintings, and "unfortunately, we do not know who the owners are. As far as we know, some time ago these photographs were published in a book about Jewish paintings in Poland." I ordered prints, the biggest ones available. Marcin told me I could get them thirty by forty centimeters, or about twelve inches by sixteen inches. I ordered one of each image.

A few weeks later a large brown paper package wrapped in twine arrived at my house. I carefully untied the string and unwrapped the bundle. I gently pulled out the photos one at a time, and set them on a table to study them. It couldn't be the same as seeing a painting in person, but it was much better than squinting at pixels on my computer monitor. I loved each of the eight paintings, but one felt particularly haunting. It was a portrait of a girl—perhaps she was a preteen or a teenager. I didn't know who she was—a relative? a neighbor? a girl he saw in the street? Her top had a square collar with some color variations, but with no distinct pattern. I couldn't tell if it was a shirt or a dress. She had shoulder-length brown hair parted in the middle. She was staring right at me. Her gaze was not at all playful, even though she looked like a young girl who ought to be laughing. She seemed hyperaware that Moshe was painting her. In the space surrounding her portrait, Moshe painted wide brownish-red strokes. The effect was that I felt more and more directed to stare at her face. I couldn't look at it for

W Knajpie (In the Pub) *(undated). Held by the Jewish Historical Institute.*

too long. There was something troubling about her gaze, or maybe it was just because I knew too much history—I knew the Holocaust was coming and it seemed quite unlikely she survived.

A year later, still trying to answer the riddle of who possessed these paintings, I learned that my cousin Aliza Knox (from Mom's side of the family) was traveling from Singapore (where she lived and worked) to Warsaw for work. She offered to visit the Jewish Historical Institute to see if she could see the fifty-two Rynecki works in their collection. I was ecstatic about her offer and immediately accepted.

Before Aliza's trip to Warsaw, her friend, a Warsaw resident, contacted the museum and scheduled an appointment to see the museum's Rynecki holdings. Aliza enthusiastically emailed me the news and promised to photograph my great-grandfather's works.

Aliza believed some paintings would be on display and the rest would be brought out for her to review in private. Instead, when Aliza arrived at the museum, the staff was surprised at her arrival and unprepared to show her the Rynecki paintings. The paintings, they explained, were in an off-site warehouse. In an effort to modestly accommodate my cousin, the museum staff offered her a seat in their office, where they showed her black-and-white photographs of the Rynecki works in the institute's collection.

Aliza, not so pleased at the snafu, and knowing how badly I wanted to see the Rynecki pieces, snapped pictures of the black-and-white photographs. She photographed nine black-and-white photographs and seven index cards with her camera phone before the museum staff insisted she stop.

When Aliza's photographs arrived in my email inbox, I felt a strange mix of joy and anger. I felt a great deal of joy, because Aliza's photographs showed paintings I had never seen. But also anger, because the museum clearly already had in their files precisely the kind of photographs I wanted, and didn't want to share them, even to the extent of letting someone take pictures of them.

I tried to decipher the Polish on the index cards by typing the words into Google Translate. Although automated translation has improved over time, it generally gives only a general sense of what is said. In this case, it was enough to understand that the cards weren't much more than basic descriptions of the paintings' content. "Old, bent woman distributes gifts to children in Cheder. In the lower right corner: MRynecki." Date of the painting, size, and year acquired were also listed. The cards didn't say how the pieces had been obtained—whether they were a purchase or if they were gifts to the museum. They certainly didn't say anything about provenance, which would have been essentially who possessed the painting prior to the museum's acquisition, and how the institute itself acquired the work from that previous owner.

Aliza, frustrated by her experience, told her story to a number of people. One of her friends told her I should speak to Jonathan Petropoulous at Claremont McKenna College in Claremont, California, a professor of history with a particular interest in the fate of art looted during World

War II. It was not the first time I'd heard of Petropoulous. A contact at the USC Shoah Foundation had also suggested I speak with him. I called his office, left voice mail messages, and sent emails, but I never received a reply. Unfortunately, it appeared this was another dead end.

While questions about the Rynecki works that were at the Jewish Historical Institute went unresolved, I decided to push forward on another front—finding more interactive ways to share my great-grandfather's paintings with others. My initial plan centered on using the services of a relatively new company that was getting a lot of attention, YouTube. My thought was to put together some sort of art education and history mashup. I spoke to friends who worked professionally as video producers and documentary film editors, and they all told me the same thing: you have too much material for a short YouTube piece. Almost universally, it was suggested that I had a multilayered story which needed to be fleshed out more thoroughly. Perhaps a documentary was a better fit.

With grand visions of documentary filmmaking dancing in my head, in the summer of 2008 I hired Johnny Symons and S. Leo Chiang, both accomplished documentary makers, to film an interview between myself and my father. I wasn't yet sure how I would use the footage, but I would ask Dad about his Second World War memories and we would talk about the Moshe Rynecki art, with the idea that at a later date we could use the footage in a documentary. For now the goal was simply "to get the footage in the can."

The interview with my father was formal. Far too formal. We both sat stiffly on couches adjacent to each other, shy and guarded at the prospect of speaking to each other, in large part due to the boom mic and camera recording our every word and gesture. While I struggled to relax and to help my father feel at ease in front of the camera, I flashed back to a prior interview. Many years earlier I had interviewed Grandma Stella with a portable tape recorder about her Holocaust story of survival. She wanted to tell her story, but only to me. She had no interest in contacting the Shoah Foundation's survivor testimony program. Telling the story to a stranger was too hard for her, but she thought she could tell me the story—the two of us comfortably ensconced in her bedroom to discuss her memories. But even as we recorded her interview, I knew I was making horrible mistakes. The equipment I used was of poor quality, and when I later played back the tape it was difficult to discern my questions and her answers. But beyond the technical gaffes, it was my lack of knowledge about life in Poland under the Nazis that made the interview so much less than it could have been. For example, when Grandma said things about her sister's belief in the Nazi idea of sending the Jewish population to Madagascar or she talked about a *Volksdeutscher* she knew that sometimes helped her, I didn't understand, which made it hard to ask appropriate follow-up questions. Of course Grandma, like any other normal person recalling a traumatic time from a long time before, told the story in fits and starts, and out of chronological order. The difficulty of speaking about events from the past meant small details and even sometimes important events were hazy. Finally, the most intense memories were skimmed over because they were too emotional and made her cry. In the moment, I felt paralyzed, afraid to ask clarifying questions that might further upset Grandma. It was possible I could have pressed further, but one thing she said stopped me in my tracks. "People ask me about the war and I tell them, and then I don't sleep for weeks, but they go about their day and forget about it," she said. I wanted to know what happened, but I couldn't bear to see the pain on her face, so I tiptoed around her history, and failed to ask for details which might have made her testimony richer and more informative.

I didn't want to repeat any of these mistakes with Dad, but I had done little to improve my interviewing skills in the intervening years, and now I had two new problems. First, I felt immense pressure to nail every question and statement because our film time was very limited. In addition, Dad was very uncomfortable with the camera's presence in his personal space. While most people try to simply ignore the camera and go about what they would normally say and do, Dad tried ignoring the camera by looking past it. This made him appear disinterested and disconnected. I tried to make the questions more personal and emotional in nature to elicit natural responses. I asked things like "Do you remember being scared?" Dad answered everything in a third-person historic perspective: "Recollections from the early war years are difficult. I have memories of frequent moves from place to place and the carrying of food with us on these moves. I continue to dislike leftovers to this day, recalling the ongoing eating of scraps of food from one meal to the next. My father and mother diligently attempted to keep the family fed; it was an ongoing challenge and I do remember many times of hunger." I could tell there were feelings there, buried deeply somewhere underneath the responses, but the camera's presence dissuaded him from bringing them to the forefront. He told his own history in a detached manner, as if it had happened to a distant relative. Even when discussing the Warsaw Uprising in 1944, when he was older and might remember a bit more, his responses remained at arm's length. "After the Germans gained control of the city, Hitler ordered the city destroyed. It is estimated that over 85 percent of Warsaw was destroyed during and after the Warsaw Uprising. I remember turmoil in the streets, dead horses, and trenches cut into the streets to allow passing from one side to the other. I was nearly eight years old and the circumstances made an impression of great impact on me." Even though it made an impact on him, I couldn't elicit a personal description. The reality was that he had never shared these details with me as a kid, and he wasn't about to suddenly open up and be vulnerable now, especially on camera. Dad told his Holocaust story as best he could, but his guarded responses made the footage feel flat.

After a few hours of Dad answering questions, we took a break and went to lunch at a nearby Chinese restaurant. Everyone was hungry and needed a filming hiatus. The break also gave a chance for both Dad and the film crew to get to know one another personally. Over eggplant tofu and Singapore noodles Dad asked Johnny and Leo about their own projects, where they had gone to film school, and the state of the documentary film market. When asked about his own interests, he shared readings about the Peloponnesian War, opined about his favorite operas, raved about a recent play he and Mom had attended, and talked about his passion for sailing. The crew was charmed.

"We need," Johnny said, "to find a way to bring that personality out on film."

After fortune cookies were read, we returned to the house to commence more filming. Since the seated interview hadn't yielded great results, we cast about for a better idea.

"Maybe," Johnny suggested, "you should stand in front of the paintings and talk about them."

I liked his idea, so I spread the Lookgalleria photographs on the dining room table. We could stand and point at them, talk about them, and be more engaged with each other. Besides, it would de-emphasize the Holocaust story and instead focus our energies on the artwork, a topic much more palatable for both of us. As an afterthought, I put the photos Aliza had taken at the Jewish Historical Institute on one corner of the table. Leo signaled he was ready to film, and I stared at the photos spread before me, trying to think of what to ask Dad.

"Oh my God," I said, pointing at Aliza's black-and-white photo of chess players, "I just realized this photo is the same as the chess player painting in the photo from Lookgalleria." Dad and I stared at the black-and-white snapshot, then walked around the table to get a good look at the larger, higher-quality Lookgalleria photograph. It was an artistic riddle and challenge: were these two different photographs of the same painting, a painting we'd never seen in person?

I was pretty sure they were of the same painting, but I waited for Dad to peer closely at each of the photographs. He took his time.

"They're the same piece," Dad confirmed.

"All the paintings in these photographs," I said, gesturing at the

Lookgalleria photographs, "must be held by the Jewish Historical Institute." It was proof, solid evidence, linking the photographs for sale on Lookgalleria with the Jewish Historical Institute. This was absolutely enormous because up until now it had seemed that there might be another institution (or person) with my great-grandfather's paintings.

Maybe in retrospect it's easy to assemble the puzzle pieces and follow all the clues, but generally I get little pieces in drabs and dribbles over a period of many years, and sometimes it is difficult to connect the dots between the various clues. But now two pieces clicked together. Now I knew with absolute certainty that the paintings were at the Jewish Historical Institute. Now that I knew I had color photographs of eight of the fifty-two Rynecki paintings held by the Jewish Historical Institute, I wanted to see equally high-quality photographs of their other forty-four pieces. And to be honest, part of me wanted not just to see the paintings, but to have them packed up and shipped to my family.

As I stared at the photographs, it became crystal clear to me that finding my great-grandfather's paintings was about more than discovering their existence. I knew I had to recover them. Because I was the daughter and granddaughter of Holocaust survivors, it was a moral imperative I had to fulfill. For me, the paintings had become more than just a record of the past—they were an actual, physical link to the past. The paintings I grew up with were objects my great-grandfather actually touched. The brushstrokes on the canvas were an extension of his very being. I wanted the paintings back. They didn't just belong to my family; they were family. I would, I decided, recover the paintings and, in doing so, bring justice to my family and attention to my great-grandfather's lost art legacy.

Around the time of the interview, I exchanged emails with Chris Marinello, then the executive director and general counsel for an organization called the Art Loss Register (ALR). ALR is a company that maintains a database of lost and stolen art, antiquities, and collectibles. The idea is that if you own something valuable, you register it with ALR to discourage its possible theft. Criminals, theoretically aware of the database, are more likely to avoid works that might be traceable, thus raising the risk of their detection and making it more difficult for them to sell the stolen art. The database is then supposed to be a go-to resource for collectors, the art world, insurance companies, and law enforcement agencies as a central clearinghouse of art ownership information.

In theory, you should register art when you buy it. But ALR, aware that many people come to them after a loss, allows for registration of items subsequent to a loss or theft. For a relatively small fee—I think it was fifteen dollars per item—I could register the lost paintings of my great-grandfather's body of work with ALR. ALR would then keep the items on their database at no charge for as long as I'd like. Then, if and when the paintings were successfully recovered, I would become liable for additional fees. That fee was "calculated at 20 percent (plus VAT) of the net benefit to the claimant at the successful conclusion of the process." As I understood it, if ALR, *or anyone else*, were to recover the Rynecki paintings, we would owe to ALR 20 percent of the value of each painting recovered. It's understandable that ALR needs to cover their expenses, but I found it quite disappointing.

I downloaded the forms and started reviewing the required information. I quickly realized that my instinctive mantra—"Moshe painted it, someone else has it, it's mine; give it back!"—wasn't going to fit so well on a form. I also realized that I didn't know much about the world of art losses and claims in general, much less how it applied to Holocaust-era art losses. I decided I needed to learn more. Dad and I started searching for more information and started filing the results in a folder entitled simply "art loss."

What I found held little promise. One document we got from the Conference on Jewish Material Claims Against Germany, Inc. (the Claims Conference) painted a grim picture of Poland. Their website stated, "There is currently no legislation governing the restitution of private property." Furthermore, the Claims Conference explained, the Polish government had "so far rejected the validity of any class-action lawsuit filed in the United States for the return of property seized from Polish Jews during or after World War II." While we considered filing an individual claim through private lawsuit in Polish courts, the procedures were both complex and time-consuming, as well as expensive. "Because of the difficult procedures for the restitution of property in Eastern Europe, it is advisable to obtain legal counsel," the article warned.

Dad and I knew attorneys, some who had had involvement with the world of looted Holocaust-era art restitution, but none who were experts. After further searching, I eventually found an article on Bloomberg .com about the Max Stern estate. Max Stern was a Jewish gallery owner in Germany before the war. Forced by the Nazis to sell his paintings, he fled Germany after the forced sale and liquidation of his gallery, and eventually settled in Canada, where he rebuilt his business. The article mentioned that attorney Thomas Kline was involved in restitution efforts. I wrote an email to Kline, explained how I'd gotten his name, and told him my family's story. "I am writing to you to find out what sorts of rights we might have to these paintings. It is our understanding that it is extremely difficult to recover stolen art from Poland. If we were to hire you, what sort of chance might we have of recovering these paintings and what sort of costs might we be looking at paying?"

A few days later Tom and I spoke by phone. He was very polite and offered words of wisdom in the arena of looted Holocaust-era art recovery. I took notes and nodded my head, even though he couldn't see me. He clearly had a great deal of experience. I slowly began to grasp just how large an undertaking we were looking at and how little I understood.

"And how much do you charge?" I asked.

"I work on a contingency basis," Tom said. "My fee is a percentage of the value of the work after it's recovered."

"I see." I thought he would be none too pleased to hear about the price-per-inch negotiation with Maciej and Katherina. The fact of the matter was, in any reasonable number of paintings, there wasn't enough value to interest a good attorney. A restitution case often required hundreds or more hours of attorney time, which, for a multimillion-dollar work or set of works, made sense if the attorney was paid a substantial percentage. On the other hand, even if the works were recovered, the claimant ended up owing a large percentage—often a third or more of the market value. Unless the claimant was already wealthy, recovery itself then often forced the sale of the recovered works. While sad, and in many cases tragic, our problem was the opposite: even fifty paintings combined wouldn't be worth enough to pay for a reputable attorney's time. I found this disheartening. For me the recovery of the paintings was not at all about the value of the works; it was about rescuing my great-grandfather's art.

I realized that if we wished to retain Kline's services, all of our expenses would have to be paid out-of-pocket, and they would escalate quite rapidly, and there really wasn't an upper limit on what they could end up being. If that wasn't discouraging enough, Kline said I'd need to put together documentation, a list really, detailing all the missing pieces. "The idea," I explained in an email to my father, "is to try to create a provenance that shows/proves that the art was stolen/taken from our family." Finally, Kline didn't like to do this kind of work. Since the case didn't seem promising for a variety of reasons, he suggested three agencies who might be able to help. The first was the Polish Culture Ministry in Warsaw, but he couldn't give me advice about them since he represented them. The second was the Holocaust Claims Processing Office in New York. The third was the Art Loss Register. I already knew about ALR, so I began with the Holocaust Claims Processing Office (HCPO).

Established in 1997, the HCPO is an advocate for Holocaust victims and their heirs, seeking the return of stolen assets. The HCPO works, as stated on their website, "as a bridge between claimants and the various international compensation organizations and/or the current holder(s) of the asset be it a bank account, insurance policy or artwork. Claimants pay no fee for the HCPO's services, nor does the HCPO take a percentage of the value of the assets recovered." They have, the website declares, been involved in the resolution of cases involving more than fifty-six works of art that were lost, stolen, or sold under duress between 1933 and 1945.

Tom Kline was able to give me the name Anna Rubin as a contact at the HCPO, so I wrote her an email, telling her my story, and attached a document for her perusal titled "list of paintings held by others version 2." A few days later I was on the phone with another woman in the HCPO office, Rebecca Friedman, one of their investigative attorneys.

"So who is the claimant?" Rebecca asked.

"Well, I guess my dad, but me too."

"Your great-grandfather," Rebecca asked, "how many children did he have?"

"Two. Jerzy and Bronisława. Bronisława was murdered in the war," I said. "Jerzy was my Grandpa George."

"Might there be any other heirs or claimants?"

"I don't think so."

"I'm just trying to establish that there aren't any competing claims."

"No competing claims. Just Dad and me."

"Okay, so really the next in line is your father," Rebecca said. "He's really the claimant. But you can pursue it on his behalf if he's okay with that," she said.

"Yes, he's fine with that."

"Okay, let's talk about the art itself. Do you have any photographs of the paintings? Or lists?"

I laughed.

"Rebecca, my dad and his parents barely made it out of Poland with their lives. The fact that they were able to rescue a bundle of paintings was a miracle. No, there's no list."

"Mmhmm," Rebecca said. "Okay, well, how about documents?" she asked. "Maybe there are receipts, records of insurance policies, or paperwork from a gallery that represented your great-grandfather's work. Anything that shows ownership history for the paintings you say are yours."

"Rebecca," I said, "I don't want to sound rude, but this is ridiculous. There was a war. Warsaw was almost totally destroyed. I don't have anything like paperwork, photographs, or insurance papers showing proof of ownership."

"I understand," she said. "How about witnesses?"

"Grandpa George died in 1992. My grandmother in 1998. Dad was too little to remember details about the paintings," I said.

"But then how do you know what's missing?" she asked.

"Well, my great-grandfather was the artist. He painted a lot. I can tell you the style and show you the classic signature he put on a majority of his paintings. I know some pieces are held by a museum in Poland. Since Grandpa George said in his memoir that his father never sold anything, my claim is for anything he painted," I said.

"I hate to be the bearer of bad news," Rebecca said, "but the fact that he was the painter doesn't really help your case. In fact, it weakens it."

"What do you mean?" I asked, somewhat taken aback.

"Because he was an artist, he might have exhibited and then sold or gifted works. It's not like a gallery owner where the paintings were his inventory. His career was as an artist, and artists generally don't keep their artwork. They don't make money unless they sell their works. So unless you have proof the works weren't sold, your case is tougher."

"Oh," I said. I didn't know what else to say and felt incredibly deflated.

"I'm sorry," Rebecca said.

She sounded sincerely contrite. I visualized Rebecca sitting in New York, case files stacked on her desk, the floor, and into the hallway. Her job was to do what she could to fix the injustices of Holocaust looting. She dealt with people like me all day every day: elderly survivors with difficult-to-resolve claims as well as heirs of survivors trying to right the wrongs of a past they had learned about from their parents. But I guessed she'd seen weak provenance too many times—no sales receipts, no verifiable owner history, no photos of the stolen paintings, no inventory lists. I took a deep breath, hoping to steady my voice. This was my lost art legacy, my great-grandfather's life's work. I felt like crying, but I didn't want Rebecca to think I'd given up.

"So is there anything you can do for me?" I asked.

"The Holocaust Claims Processing Office takes a nonlitigious approach to art claims," she said. "If any information surfaces that helps your case, we're happy to be of assistance."

"That seems doubtful," I said and thought about how easy it would be to give up and forget about the whole issue. But as I spoke those words in my mind, something in me clicked and I thought about how Grandpa George and my great-grandfather were counting on me. I could dig deeper, work harder, and make something happen. Maybe, even without documentation, I could still make a difference; do something to honor the memory of Grandpa George and Moshe.

NINE

A Loan Request

In the summer of 2010 I received an email from Renata Piątkowska, the coordinator for the Core Exhibition Planning Team for POLIN Museum of the History of Polish Jews in Warsaw, Poland. The new museum, a 45,000-square-foot institution dedicated to the more than thousand-year history of Polish Jews, was set to open in two years, in 2012. At the museum, housed in a brand-new, not yet completed, glass-walled building facing the Warsaw Ghetto monument, visitors would experience the world of Polish-Jewish culture and history through a wide range of media, documents, and artifacts.

One part of the museum, a whole gallery in fact, would focus on the nineteenth century and the legal and social changes Jews experienced with the partition of the former Polish/Lithuanian Commonwealth. This particular exhibit planned to deal with the challenges brought about by modernity and how it altered the Jewish community. The museum, Renata explained, wanted to borrow one of my great-grandfather's paintings to include in an exhibit about weddings.

Specifically, she wondered if my family might loan *The Wedding* (*The First Dance*) (1919) for an exhibit that presented the traditional Jewish wedding process—from matchmaking to the wedding itself. The display case included *Jewish Wedding* by Maurycy Gottlieb, *Wedding Procession with the Bride* by Wincenty Smokowski, and *Jewish Bride* by Leopold Pilichowski from the National Museum in Warsaw and the Israel Museum in Jerusalem, as well as an original prayer book, a *tsimbl* (an instrument related to the dulcimer), a nineteenth-century wedding canopy (a chuppah), a wedding band, and wedding gifts from other collections. My great-grandfather's painting was to complete the wedding process wall as a representation of the wedding feast. It was, Renata assured me, "one of the most interesting exhibits in this Gallery—and one of the most important ones indeed." The painting would be part of "an extraordinary opportunity not only to make our audiences aware of the ceremony's course and its accompanying customs but also to show the wedding in a broader context of the century's modernization-related changes." The museum wished to borrow the painting for twelve months.

I politely replied to Renata, thanked her for her description of the museum and proposed exhibition, and said I would need to discuss the matter with my father, who was presently away on travel. As soon as I'd written an email reply to Renata, I picked up the phone and called Dad.

"You're not going to believe this," I said.

"What's that?" Dad asked.

"There's a museum in Poland that wants to borrow one of our paintings, the one of the wedding dance."

"No," Dad said.

"No, as in no you don't want to talk about it right now?"

"No, I'm not loaning a painting to a museum in Poland."

"Do you even want to talk about it?"

"No."

"But I can't just tell them no."

"Why not? It's our painting. The answer is no."

"But there are other paintings in Poland," I said. "I don't want to burn any bridges. I still haven't seen those paintings. If I tell her no, I might never get to see them."

"The Jewish Historical Institute won't show you the paintings they've already got, and you're ready to send a painting into Poland? Besides, with everything we've learned so far about Poland and issues of art restitution, we might never get the painting back if we loan it."

I understood Dad's reluctance but wasn't quite ready for such a firm no myself. In part I understood the draw of the exhibit, and it was an appealing theme. Similarly, one of my goals was to share my great-grandfather's artwork. I was also in the middle of putting together my documentary film and was concerned that if I said no to POLIN Museum of the History of Polish Jews, the Jewish Historical Institute would use that as a reason to never show me the Rynecki paintings in their collection. While I wasn't exactly sure of the relationship between the two museums, the world of Polish-Jewish museums had to be a small one, and it seemed very likely word would get out. As a result, I opted to think about it before replying. At the same time, I figured I could get more information. I wrote explaining that I had never been involved in painting loans, that I was not familiar with all the various elements in such an agreement, and that I needed answers to a list of questions (I wanted to know who would pack the painting; how it would be exhibited; who would pay for packing, shipping, and insurance; and the details of a contract for the requested loan). I told Renata that Dad and I needed these answers to have a more informed discussion about the request (this was perhaps iffy, since I already knew Dad didn't want to share, but I didn't want to seem negative about my father, and I did want to know the answers to the questions). I sent my email in June, and received a reply four months later, in October. The reply said that they were quite sorry for the delay in answering my questions; the museum staff had been engaged in the "very intensive (and exciting) stage of completing the design of the exhibition." They answered the questions, but unfortunately their answers were not nearly as informative as I'd hoped. My last question, really the most significant question of all, said I understood the original request for the loan was for twelve months, but that I wanted clarity. I wrote, "Are you actually hoping it would stay longer? If so, how long would the museum want it on display?" I suspected the answer to my question before I even asked. Their answer confirmed my worries, and made me even more nervous. They said they would be "very grateful if we could use it for three years."

Of course, there were many fabulous reasons for my family to lend my great-grandfather's painting. It would provide exposure for his work to museum visitors, while it also offered insight into a beautiful Jewish community destroyed by the war and hinted at the life of a Jewish artist in prewar Poland. Further, it created an opportunity for museum guests to engage in discussion about Jewish life, culture, religion, and community. With added exposure it could stimulate further interest in my great-grandfather's oeuvre of work and his life story—and perhaps even lead to additional discoveries for my project.

At the same time, three years was an awfully long time to send the painting six thousand miles away where we couldn't keep an eye on it. In addition, I'd had negative experiences with the Jewish Historical Institute. It wasn't at all fair to blame my problems on POLIN Museum of the History of Polish Jews, but it made me wary. And of course, before the exhibit even started, the request had ballooned from one year to three years. But those fears and worries all paled in comparison to the one mentioned by my father when I first brought the subject up. My final fear was that even if we agreed to loan the painting, the Polish Ministry of Culture and National Heritage might seize it, saying it was a stolen Polish cultural artifact, and then refuse to return it. This might sound absurd, but it didn't seem entirely far-fetched in light of the case of Dina Babbitt.

Dina Babbitt, an artist, was an inmate at Auschwitz. Chosen by Dr. Josef Mengele (a German officer and physician stationed at Auschwitz, notorious for selecting victims for his ghastly and often deadly experiments), Babbitt was given a choice: paint portraits of Romani prisoners, with special focus on skin coloration, or go to the gas chambers. In return for her paintings, Mengele agreed to spare her life and her mother's life. Babbitt survived the Holocaust and eventually settled in California. In the 1970s, several of her portraits were discovered outside the Auschwitz camp. The pieces were then sold to the Auschwitz-Birkenau State Museum, which later located Babbitt and asked her to come identify her work. She did so and then asked the museum to give her the pieces. The museum refused, saying, as the *New York Times* described it, "the paintings' historical and educational value superseded her right of ownership."

The Babbitt story did not instill confidence in what might happen if I shipped Rynecki paintings from California to Poland. Perhaps I was being a bit paranoid about the possibility of the Rynecki art being seized, but the history of art litigation suggested that if the Polish government or the museum curators changed their minds or policies in the intervening years, we might have a difficult path to recovering the painting, if it could be done at all. Another example that came to mind was Egon Schiele's 1912 oil painting *Portrait of Wally*.

The *Portrait of Wally* had once been owned by Lea Bondi Jaray, an Austrian gallery owner in the interwar period. Her gallery was forcibly taken over by the Nazis when Austria was annexed to Germany in 1938. Jaray lost control of all the works in her gallery to the Nazis, but still held pieces in a private collection in her apartment.

Unfortunately, as she prepared to flee Austria, Friedrich Welz, an art dealer, visited her home and insisted Jaray turn over the Schiele painting to him. Concerned Welz might make their escape out of Austria difficult, Jaray's husband thought it best if she left the work with Welz. After the war, the United States Army seized Welz and the paintings in his possession, and turned them over to the Austrian government. The United States mistakenly listed the *Portrait of Wally* as belonging to a Heinrich Reiger, who perished at Theresienstadt concentration camp. The Austrian government then gave the works to the Reiger heirs, and the Austrian National Gallery eventually purchased the works from them.

Jaray eventually discovered *Portrait of Wally* was in the Austrian National Gallery, and she tried to recover the piece, unfortunately to no avail. She eventually enlisted Rudolf Leopold, an Austrian art collector, to help her. Instead of helping Jaray, Leopold arranged the purchase of the painting for his own personal collection. Upon Leopold's death, his entire collection was sold back to the Austrian government, and Jaray died without recovering the painting. In late 1997 the Leopold collection loaned Schiele's work to the Museum of Modern Art (MoMA) in New York City. While it was on display, the *New York Times* published a story about the painting and the Jaray connection. Because of the *New York Times* story, Jaray's heirs contacted the New York district attorney, who issued a subpoena forbidding the painting's return to Austria. Litigation of the piece ensued, with the heirs fighting for the work. After thirteen years of this, an agreement was finally reached—nineteen million dollars would be paid to Jaray's heirs, which would settle all outstanding claims on the painting, and the work would return to Austria.

Clearly the circumstances of this case were much more complex, but the fact that, like many art recovery cases, it resulted in a legal battle lasting many years made me very nervous. So after much discussion and considerable internal anguish I politely explained to Renata that my family had concluded we would not be able to loan them the requested piece. I said I was sorry to disappoint them and suggested they instead borrow either a work from the fifty-two pieces at the Jewish Historical Institute or, perhaps, *The Wedding (The Gift of Bread)* (1919), held by the Magnes Collection of Jewish Art and Life (University of California at Berkeley).

Renata's reply was polite, but I sensed she was angry. She said the design for the exhibit was finished and the precise list of objects she wanted shown in the wall display was complete. At this juncture there was no room for change. Besides, she didn't like the suggestion of borrowing the piece held by the Magnes because the scene did not fit their vision for the display. She said she understood my family's decision, but asked us to please reconsider. And then she said they would still like to show the painting, even if it wasn't possible to show the original. If we were willing to provide a high-quality digital image of the piece, they would print it and place a photograph of the work on display instead. That, I thought, was the perfect solution, and I went about getting a very high-resolution digital file for their curatorial team.

Around the time that Renata and I were exchanging emails about the exhibition at POLIN Museum of the History of Polish Jews, I learned about an exhibit coming to the San Francisco Contemporary Jewish Museum. The exhibit, *Reclaimed: Paintings from the Collection of Jacques Goudstikker*, would open at the end of October. The exhibit showcased the legacy of Goudstikker, the leading Jewish art dealer in Amsterdam, whose vast collection of more than fourteen hundred paintings (many of them sixteenth-century Italian religious works and seventeenth-century Dutch portraits, still lifes, and landscapes) were looted by Hermann Göring in 1940. Goudstikker died while escaping the Nazis, in a freak accident aboard the ship on which he fled Amsterdam; he fell into an open hold on a dark night. Over the years, his daughter-in-law and granddaughter had, with the help of their attorney, recovered a number of the pieces. In addition to showing the reclaimed art, the exhibit shared the heirs' ongoing legal efforts. I wanted to learn more about those efforts because of the parallel nature of our two stories. I was particularly eager to attend a lunchtime talk offered by the museum, *Delayed Justice: Restitution of Looted Art*, by George McNeely, senior vice president of business development at Christie's auction house. I was most interested in the promised question and answer period.

I waited until almost the end of the Q&A to ask my question—essentially, how I could get more information from Sotheby's about the 1993 auction of two of my great-grandfather's paintings. I wanted to know how I might learn the provenance of the pieces (and whether the auction house had conducted such research), how to obtain photos of the paintings sold, and if it might be possible to be put in touch with both the seller and buyer of the works. As the head of development for Christie's, Mr. McNeely couldn't speak to Sotheby's internal workings, but he did tell me that there were certainly privacy issues, and while I could certainly ask Sotheby's for archival records and photos, since the two Rynecki paintings sold for such a small amount I shouldn't be surprised if the auction house did not have any photographs. Although McNeely's answer didn't really help me, asking it had the unintended consequence of making my story known to everyone at the talk. At the conclusion of the event, Carla Shapreau introduced herself to me.

A lecturer at UC Berkeley's Law School, Carla's special area of interest and expertise, she explained, was art and cultural property law. In particular, she was interested in anything related to music and the Second World War—sheet music, looted instruments, and musicians blacklisted from music groups because of their Jewish heritage. Carla and I exchanged contact information and eventually arranged to have lunch together with Richard Buxbaum, a legal professor at the UC Berkeley Law School, to talk about Holocaust-era art claims in general and my story in particular.

My lunch with Professor Buxbaum and Carla Shapreau in late November 2010 was at the Women's Faculty Club on the UC Berkeley campus. We took a small table toward the back of the dining room, and after we ordered, I began my story. Both Professor Buxbaum and Carla stopped me occasionally to ask clarifying questions—where were the paintings? how many did my family own? what sort of provenance research had I done?—and I did my best to answer each of them. But then they shifted their line of questioning.

"So have you spoken with attorneys about the strength of your claim for each of the looted pieces?" Buxbaum asked.

"We've talked to attorneys . . . ," I said, trailing off.

"And?" Buxbaum asked.

"And, I don't know," I said.

"What do the attorneys tell you?" Carla asked.

"I'm not sure they really tell me anything." Carla and Buxbaum looked at me expectantly, as if waiting for me to say more. "Some will talk to me, but then they brush me off for a variety of reasons. If they talk to me, they ask where the paintings are located and what they're worth. When I tell them museums in Poland and in private collections and that they aren't worth a lot, they usually become quiet and cut the conversation short."

"What are the paintings worth?" Carla asked.

"Not much. Two sold at Sotheby's for seventeen hundred dollars in the nineties."

"Have you retained an attorney to file a claim?" Buxbaum asked.

"No."

"Do you know how the paintings were stolen?" he asked.

"Not exactly. I know my great-grandfather bundled up and hid the collection in and around the city of Warsaw and that after the war his widow, Perla, recovered only a small percentage of the original body of work."

"Is there evidence of Nazi looting or of a sale made under duress?" Buxbaum asked.

"I don't exactly think Hitler or his henchmen personally stole my great-grandfather's paintings," I said, feeling defensive, "but their actions in Poland meant my family lost everything. Besides, it's still Holocaust-era looted art, and isn't that fact an important part of the story?"

"Yes," Buxbaum said. "And this is obviously very personal to you, but if you want to be a successful claimant, you need to think about the case in terms of the legal issues and the potential strength, or weakness, of your case."

"They destroyed my family, their way of life. It's amazing my dad and his parents made it out of Poland alive," I said, feeling frustrated. "My great-grandfather was murdered. That the paintings were never returned to my family after the war is an injustice."

Carla and Buxbaum listened intently while I vented.

"It should be easy," I said. "When you have something that's not yours, you return it. When did that concept get so complicated?"

"You can always file a claim," Carla said. "Don't ever forget that every single painting has a different provenance, a different history."

"An attorney's job is also to counsel you on the realities of your case," Buxbaum said.

"And?" I asked.

"One can always sue and go to court," Buxbaum said. "But at the end of the day you also have to pick a fight you can win. What's the big picture? Your goal?"

"My goal?" I asked and felt a bit confused. Wasn't my goal to get the paintings back?

"Attorney's hours add up quickly," Buxbaum said. "And these sorts of fights can be lengthy and may not end in your favor. Why are the paintings important to you? If you retain an attorney and your case ends up in front of a judge, a jury, or an arbitrator, and a compromise is necessary, what is it that you want?"

"I want lots of things," I said, fumbling to find my words. "I want to see the paintings. I want people who have his work to know a story that's been neglected. I don't want my great-grandfather's art to wither in people's attics, lost and forgotten. I want to rescue my great-grandfather's art legacy and give his work the attention it deserves."

"Have you considered," Buxbaum asked, "that perhaps instead of acting as a claimant, you might act as a historian?"

"A historian?" I asked, furrowing my eyebrows, unclear on the question.

"A claimant is one who files legal action for return of stolen items," Buxbaum said.

"Right," I said.

"You said one of your goals is to see the paintings and to know their history. Perhaps you don't want to go down the path of lengthy lawsuits with at best uncertain results. Maybe instead you want to research the lost art, visit the work you've located, and have the satisfaction of knowing more about the paintings as a whole rather than suing for the return of the individual pieces."

I pushed around the vegetables on my plate. "You're asking me to set aside my family's rights," I finally said.

"Never," Carla said. "But it is probably true that if you file claims, collectors may be unwilling to give you access."

"A lawsuit isn't the easiest way to build bridges," Buxbaum said.

"So you're suggesting that being a historian might give me opportunities to see the art in ways that being a claimant might not."

Carla and Buxbaum nodded.

Over the days that followed, while I tried to mentally process my conversation with the two of them, I followed up on attorney Tom Kline's recommendation to write the Polish embassy and ask for help with finding my great-grandfather's paintings in Poland. The reply was short and curt: "The Ministry of Foreign Affairs regrets that it will be unable to assist you in Poland. Its mandate does not allow it to act within Poland. The staff recommends that you retain the service of an attorney within Poland to investigate the provenance of the paintings and to pursue legal remedies if appropriate. If you need a recommendation for a lawyer in Poland I will provide you with it." Frankly, I felt like banging my head against a wall. If they weren't able to help me, I'd at least thought they might make a referral to another organization or branch of government that was more appropriate—that I would at least get a step closer to information. But it was just another frustrating dead end.

Looting has always been a part of war, but the extent to which the Nazis stole art and cultural artifacts was on a scale previously unseen. It was meticulously planned and carefully executed. Even before Germany invaded Poland in September 1939, the Nazi government had amassed enormous debt to pay for its military buildup. To help fund the conflict, the Third Reich eyed the assets of German Jews. They coveted cash, of course, but also business assets, stocks, bonds, real estate, personal assets, and art. The Nazi Party first squeezed funds out of Jewish families with the flight tax, levied against those leaving the country. They seized or "Aryanized" businesses for both those who fled and those who stayed. Rules were put in place to prevent Jews from liquidating assets before they could be seized. Deprived of a way to make a living, and faced with tax assessments they couldn't afford, many wealthier Jewish families had little choice but to sell for a fraction of their actual value whatever valuables had not been seized. Buyers knew the sellers were desperate. Sometimes those buyers were art dealers negotiating on behalf of the Nazi regime. Others, like Hildebrand Gurlitt—whose son Cornelius Gurlitt was discovered in March 2012 to have twelve hundred paintings the provenance of which was questionable—were art dealers who took advantage of access made possible by Nazi persecution. While the sales were "legal," they were made under duress, and clearly not made at market value.

Over the past decade, several well-publicized cases have brought a measure of justice to victimized families, who were able to reclaim at least a portion of the works that were stolen or acquired through forced sales. I am filled with joy for those who were successfully reunited with what was wrongly taken from them. I am also grateful for the attention these stories have given my own. But I sink a bit every time I am asked about my own personal experiences with Nazi-looted art, because I'm frequently asked when I will have my great-grandfather's paintings held by others returned to my family—as if it's as simple as filling out a bit of paperwork and waiting for the items to be shipped to my doorstep.

The Nazis took anything of value if it was possible to move it, regardless of whether it was nailed down or not—everything from entire libraries (they systematically looted libraries from Belarus and Belgium to Lithuania and the Netherlands), to bells (they wanted them for their copper and tin, to be used by the German military) and even headstones or tombstones, which were used as construction materials for walls, buildings, and roads. On the art side, many of the highly valued pieces they stole were destined for the *Führermuseum*, a museum complex and cultural center to be built in Linz, Austria, Hitler's hometown.

Once families fled or were murdered, the Nazi regime stole their personal effects too. In France, the Nazis ran a collection point for a program they called *Möbel-Aktion* (Furniture Action) or "*M-Aktion*," a plan to loot the now vacant dwellings of French, Belgian, and Dutch Jewish victims forced out and deported by Nazi orders. The Nazis packed up household goods and furniture for eventual use in the eastern occupied territories. They packed up dining room tables, couches, dinner place settings, children's toys, chairs, and more. Lynn H. Nicholas notes in *The Rape of Europa* that so much was taken that "the Union of Parisian movers was forced to supply some 150 trucks and 1,200 workers a day for the operation," and in the end "the ERR [*Einsatzstab Reichsleiter Rosenberg*, under Nazi Alfred Rosenberg] raided 71,619 dwellings, and shipped off more than 1,079,373 cubic meters of goods in 29,436 railroad cars."

In 1943, well before the war actually ended, the U.S. Military established a program known as the Monuments, Fine Arts, and Archives (MFAA) Commission. Later called the Venus Fixers by the GIs and then known as Monuments Men—although it should be noted that the commission included women too—this group of art historians, museum curators, and art professors was tasked with recovering and returning the looted art and cultural treasures stolen during the war. Some items, like the *Adoration of the Lamb* by Jan van Eyck, discovered in the Altaussee salt mine, were packaged up and returned to Belgium in an official ceremony presided over by Belgian royalty. Other items were returned, but to owners whose right to the works was questionable. One such well-known case was that of the Klimt paintings held by the Bloch-Bauer family.

In March 1938, shortly after Germany's annexation of Austria, Ferdinand Bloch-Bauer fled Vienna. Eventually ending up in neutral Switzerland, he was helpless when the Nazis seized his corporate assets as well as the personal assets left behind when he fled. This included his art collection, which contained the famous Gustav Klimt painting of Bloch-Bauer's wife, *Portrait of Adele Bloch-Bauer I*, better known as the *Lady in Gold*, or sometimes as "Austria's *Mona Lisa*." This painting, along with four others, eventually ended up in Austria's Belvedere museum. Ferdinand Bloch-Bauer died in Zurich in 1945. His niece, Maria Altmann, eventually sued for the return of the paintings. The museum's attorneys argued that the museum had every right to the works. Adele's will specified that she wanted the paintings donated to the Austrian government upon her husband's death. Maria Altmann's attorney, E. Randol Schoenberg, argued that Adele would never have wanted the paintings left to the government, had she lived to see Nazi Germany annex Austria in 1938 as well as watch her husband forced to flee for his life. After a protracted legal battle, Maria Altmann was eventually awarded ownership. In 2006 Altmann sold *Portrait of Adele Bloch-Bauer I* to cosmetics heir Ronald Lauder for a supposed $135 million. The painting is now on permanent display in the Neue Galerie in New York City.

While Allied forces worked to recover Nazi-looted art, Perla struggled to locate my great-grandfather's bundles hidden in and around the city of Warsaw. She found only the bundle Moshe had hidden in the Praga district of Warsaw. She assumed the others had been either stolen or destroyed, but it was hard to know precisely what happened after they were hidden.

The war was frightening and chaotic, and life afterward unruly and messy. I knew my great-grandfather's request of his friends to hold on to and protect his art until he returned was a tremendously big favor to ask. I was sure there were those who early on didn't have a problem with storing the art for him. But my guess was that at some juncture, over the course of the war, or perhaps in its immediate aftermath, those who still held his paintings or who ended up with them struggled with what to do with the bundles. In many, or perhaps most, cases those who had the paintings at the beginning of the war were forced to flee, and in some of those cases the works may have been left behind. If those entrusted with my great-grandfather's art remained in Warsaw with the paintings, they would have had essentially two choices. The first would have been to wait until a member of the Rynecki family showed up on their doorstep to collect the bundle; the second, to assume that no Ryneckis had survived and to keep, give away, or sell the art. A justification for keeping it or even selling it would not have been so hard to rationalize; they had saved it, the artist was gone, no heirs had come to claim it, and they hoped for some measure of compensation for having taken the risk of hiding the art throughout the duration of the war. It would be even easier to rationalize for those who happened upon an apparently abandoned bundle, whether in a bombed-out building or in discarded luggage or other belongings. Of course this is all speculation: while I know several bundles must have survived the war, I have never found anyone who stored one, or whose ancestors stored one, during the war.

Of course, as much as I wanted to assume all of my great-grandfather's surviving works were from the hidden bundles, information that his pieces might have been acquired under entirely legitimate circumstances—purchased legally by collectors before the war at an art gallery or art show—began to surface in my research. Specifically, I uncovered evidence of prices quoted for works he tried to sell in the interwar period. I had no idea how many sold, or who purchased the works. While some collectors may have bought Rynecki pieces before the war, it seemed impossible to know which pieces had been looted from the hidden bundles and which had been legitimately acquired.

This wasn't just an issue for Moshe's work. After the war, vast numbers of claims were affected by lack of information or proof of provenance. Individuals, organizations, and governments struggled with issues of how to determine the legitimacy of claims and what to do about restitution. While blame for the Holocaust was easy and straightforward—it has been placed quite squarely on the shoulders of the Nazi regime—there were numerous gray areas in the looting of art, and culprits didn't always wear Nazi uniforms. It was a difficult time, and many people did things that were questionable, or worse, in hopes of making their lives better or just in the effort to survive. But of course the messiness of real life didn't make the return and restitution process any easier, and ultimately many people wished the whole issue would just go away. Laws were passed, proclamations made, and moral pleas lodged. As a result, resolving the unjust dealings and wrongful takings during the Second World War is a never-ending and often seemingly hopeless task.

After lengthy negotiations, in 1988 the Washington Principles were signed by forty-four governments, endorsing eleven principles for handling Nazi-looted art. These nonbinding principles were guidelines to suggest morally appropriate ways to deal with looted art. The first principle was simple and straightforward: "art that had been confiscated by the Nazis and not subsequently restituted should be identified." But even this basic imperative—to make archives and records accessible to researchers, and to have museums comb through their holdings and conduct provenance research—has been exceptionally difficult and met with varying degrees of resistance. The Washington Principles also stated that when artwork was identified as having been confiscated by the Nazis, that information should be made public so prewar owners and their heirs could lay claim to the pieces. This seemed like an obvious thing to do, but the question about how to inform the public lingered. A looted Picasso, Klimt, or Da Vinci elicited great interest from the press and resulted in news stories and the tracking down of the proper heir, but not all looted items were from famous artists, and sometimes heirs didn't know enough about what belonged to their family before the war to step forward and lay claim to the items.

The last principle stated that every effort should be made by nations "to develop national processes to implement these principles, particularly as they relate to alternative dispute resolution mechanisms for resolving ownership issues." Again, a basic and straightforward suggestion, but few nations followed through on their promise to address these issues.

When I learned about the Washington Principles, I was both buoyed and dismayed. These principles gave direction about how to best address looted art issues from the time period in which my great-grandfather's works went missing. But for my particular situation, there were two problems.

The first problem related to the stance of the Polish government. Poland was one of the forty-four nations that signed the Washington Principles, but to say that Poland is not particularly friendly or encouraging to looted art claims is a fairly generous summary. To be fair, Poland had enormous numbers of its own works stolen from museums and libraries in the Second World War, by Nazi Germany, Stalin's Soviet Union, and Poland's own population. Since 1992, the Polish Ministry of Culture has worked hard to document its own cultural heritage losses, estimated at about half a million art objects. The Polish government has had some success in its own recovery efforts. In 2014, the United States government's Homeland Security Investigations was involved in the return of the oil-on-copper painting *St. Philip Baptizing a Servant of Queen Kandaki*. In October 2015, a 1728 oil painting by Krzysztof Lubieniecki that had been looted twice—first from Poland's National Museum by the Nazis, then from liberated Austria by a U.S. serviceman—was returned to Poland. Then in November 2015, *Bust of the Goddess Diana*, a late-eighteenth-century work by Jean-Antoine Houdon, looted from the Royal Łazienki Palace in Warsaw by the Nazis, was discovered for consignment at a Viennese auction house and returned to Poland following an amicable resolution. Given the sheer number of missing works, recovering them one at a time is a noble but essentially impossible task, but one which the Polish government has pursued diligently.

Unfortunately, while the Polish government makes substantial efforts to recover their own cultural heritage, heirs who have sought looted assets located on Polish soil have had a tough time with their own cases. The Babbitt case mentioned earlier was, perhaps, a bit unusual in that the artwork had been created under dire circumstances inside Auschwitz during the war. It was not work produced before the war and looted in the course of the war. But this distinction hardly mattered, because in April 2011 the Polish government announced they were suspending work on a law designed to address the historical claims of families who lost property during the Nazi occupation and under Communism. The reason for the postponement, as reported by various news outlets, was that it would add too much of a financial burden to public debt. Government spokesman Paweł Graś was quoted as saying that if the law took effect, the state would have to immediately pay out twenty billion zlotys ($7.3 billion) to former property owners. The Polish government said this obligation was impossible to meet.

Sadly, or perhaps optimistically, the Holocaust Claims Processing Office has, on their website, a colorful flow chart of the claims process in an assortment of blue, red, orange, pink, and green boxes. In essence, the chart shows how different organizations and entities function and work with one another to resolve claims from around the world. To the side of the chart are three white boxes, each with a dotted line around its edges. One box is for Poland, one for Serbia, and one for Romania. The "dotted frames indicate future processes," it says on the chart. Poland is the only country in the European Union that has failed to establish a program to address the issue of Holocaust (and Communist-era) looted property. One can only hope there will be a future process.

In addition to my seemingly hopeless situation with getting the Polish government to return looted art found within its borders, I had another problem. The Washington Principles, and later the Terezin Declaration in 2009, were written to address looted art held in public institutions. There is no legislation I know of that is binding upon individuals. In other words, while the spirit of the Washington Principles and the Terezin Declaration offers moral guidelines for individual collectors in possession of my great-grandfather's lost pieces, there is nothing that compels private individuals to give Moshe's art back to my family.

After a great deal of thought, I realized I needed to take Professor Buxbaum's words to heart. I had learned attorneys were not interested in my case, in part because it wasn't going to be lucrative. Worse, I had no documentation of my family's provenance, and I couldn't prove which pieces Moshe had hidden in the bundles, versus sold, or given away. Even if I found proof for particular works, Poland had little interest in cooperating with outside claimants. So any claims process was likely to be lengthy and almost certain to end poorly. I ultimately had to admit that perhaps the professor and Carla were right; pursuing my great-grandfather's paintings as a historian rather than as a claimant might open more doors. But I didn't want to just be a historian. A historian gathers information to document the past or learn about a particular era or culture. I wanted to be a historical advocate for my great-grandfather's work, to give voice to the family story and my great-grandfather's legacy. In order to do that, I would willingly set aside questions of legal ownership in exchange for access to the works themselves and whatever history the collectors might possess.

Once, after explaining my choices to a friend, she asked, "But don't you want the paintings back?"

Yes, yes, I did. But I would place that moral weight and responsibility onto those with my great-grandfather's works, and I would instead claim his legacy and rescue his story. Of course, if anyone had a Rynecki work and was willing to return it, I would be delighted to accept it with open arms.

TEN

Gifting Moshe's Paintings

Neither Holocaust survivors nor their heirs can bring back those who perished; that is an injustice that can never be redeemed. But that is not to say that there is nothing to be done to help survivors and heirs of those who perished. One way to help is to fight for the return of plundered property. There are many organizations and agencies involved in pursuing Holocaust-era looted art claims, such as the Conference on Jewish Material Claims Against Germany (the Claims Conference), the World Jewish Restitution Organization (WJRO), and the Holocaust Claims Processing Office. Heirs can also hire private law firms specializing in art and museum law. There are also art organizations that focus on provenance research and recovery of fine art and antiquities. But even with the assistance of these organizations and experts, rescuing stolen art is almost always difficult, costly, and prolonged.

While Maria Altmann was successful in reclaiming her family's Klimt pieces from the Belvedere museum in Austria, not every significant case has a happy ending or even an ending in sight. Marei Von Saher sued the Norton Simon Museum in 2007 for the return of Cranach the Elder's *Adam* and *Eve* paintings. The family and the museum have a difference of opinion not only on the law, but also on the facts of what happened. The case was dismissed twice in federal district court, only to be reinstated by the Ninth Circuit Court of Appeals. The two sides insist they will continue to pursue all legal options. So far, nearly a decade after the initial filing of the case, the trial hasn't even started yet. It is *tentatively* scheduled to begin in 2016, shortly before publication of this book.

In other cases, the work is recovered but the heirs disagree on what should be done with the art. If the work has substantial value, heirs who want to retain it are often forced to sell as the only way to divide the inheritance. In the high-profile case of Cornelius Gurlitt, German tax investigators found a stash of art in his home in 2012 (although the public didn't learn about it until 2013 when the German weekly *Focus* reported the discovery) that ultimately presented heirs with these difficult choices. Cornelius, the son of art dealer to the Nazis Hildebrand Gurlitt, had a hoard of more than twelve hundred paintings in his apartment. Many of the pieces had questionable provenance. One of the paintings recovered was *Two Riders on a Beach* by Max Liebermann, which before the war belonged to David Friedmann. By the time the work was discovered, the living heir who distinctly remembered the painting hanging in the family home had been blind for a decade. When the piece was found in the Gurlitt stash, the rightful heirs and their attorneys immediately filed a claim for it. Despite a preponderance of evidence proving ownership, it took the German government more than a year to return the work.

In this case, there were multiple heirs who could not agree on what to do with the art. As a result, the family put it to auction with Sotheby's. This is a common occurrence, since in many cases there is no way to equitably share the recovered work between heirs. As Peter Toren, the great-grandnephew of the original owner of the painting, wrote, "Because my father was not the only heir, we had to sell *Two Riders*."

In other cases, the heirs are united in wishing to keep the art but it turns out to be too expensive to preserve and insure, or they are forced to sell the art to pay for attorney's fees, which often run to a third or more of the value of the recovered work. I can't help but feel saddened that attorney's fees, fees to provenance researchers, and paying for care and/or restoration means there is often no choice but to auction the works. I have a personal distaste for selling recovered artwork because I am looking for works with strong personal value and connection to my great-grandfather. While the return and subsequent sale of the work might right a historical wrong for some, it wouldn't make sense for me personally.

In the case of large collections, families that keep all or most of the works face enormous responsibilities. While most museums have both a collection manager and a registrar, families typically don't. A collection manager is usually responsible for overseeing the physical care of objects in the collection, working with everyone from curators and conservators to building management and security to ensure long-term care and proper preservation. At institutions with a separate registrar, this person is tasked with documenting the collection: logging the works, maintaining contracts, tracking facility reports, recording incoming and outgoing loans, obtaining insurance coverage, and more. At smaller institutions, these two jobs generally get rolled into one.

In my family, it is a sort of generational challenge. Responsibilities for the one-hundred-plus Rynecki paintings, including physical care, tracking inventory, dealing with exhibition requests, recording history, database management, environmental control, and the like are handled on an ad-hoc and as-needed basis. In a broad sense, Moshe painted the works, Perla rescued the works we have, Grandpa George brought them out of Europe and instilled in me a sense of love for the art, Dad began documenting and archiving the paintings and sketches, and I have worked to uncover history and to share the legacy. These accomplishments are all important, but the reality is that most sizable art collections are associated with a staff trained in art history, object handling, collection preservation, and art conservation—all skills in which I feel only marginally qualified.

One solution to this increasingly complex problem is to donate paintings to a trusted museum or institution equipped with the funding resources and expertise to care for the art. This option doesn't appeal to my family for multiple reasons—most importantly, because only a tiny fraction of artworks are ever displayed. But we're not opposed to donating when it makes sense. Grandpa George donated one piece in 1982 to the Judah L. Magnes Museum in Berkeley, California, and Dad (with agreement from Mom and me) gifted a second piece in 2002 to Yad Vashem in Jerusalem, Israel.

I was twelve in 1981 when the Judah L. Magnes Museum in Berkeley, California, opened the Reutlinger Gallery. The inaugural exhibition featured a solo exhibition and retrospective of my great-grandfather's paintings. The show, on display for three months, featured thirty-five of Moshe's works. The pieces, loaned by my family for the exhibit, displayed iconic images from the collection, including *Krasiński Park* (1930), *Perla Rynecki* (1929), *Synagogue Interior* (1930), and *Refugees* (1939).

At the opening I wore a brown suit jacket and skirt ensemble Mom had picked out and a jade butterfly lapel pin loaned to me by my grandmother. In one photograph from the event, Mom and I stand in front of three Rynecki paintings, our bodies somewhat awkwardly twisted toward the photographer as if we were asked to look away from the art and at the camera. My long black hair is held back with a barrette; my arms are folded across my chest. Though I was not yet officially a teen,

I definitely exude a typical teen attitude of general distaste. In a second photograph, I stand at the exhibition entrance. On the wall behind me are my great-grandfather's *Self-Portrait* (1936) and a portrait of my great-grandmother, *Perla* (1929). I am facing the camera, hands tucked away in pockets and a small eighties girl scarf-tie sticking out from under the corners of the collar of my white blouse. I am smiling, just barely, as I try to hide my braces.

I was somewhat bored by the exhibition catalog at the show's opening, but rereading the catalog today, I find the text profound and important. I'm drawn, in particular, to a few words written by Ruth Eis, the show's curator. "Only a small segment of his oeuvre has remained in the hands of his family. Even among these precious few, mostly sketches, some traces of destruction are visible: a muddied outline of a soldier's boot here, a torn edge of a fragmented scene there, or a defacing crease in the center of a painting. Though we lament these imperfections, they are of small consequence to the overall importance of the collection."

A painting's personal value can be priceless. Of course, innumerable objects hold personal or sentimental value—your son's first-grade drawing, a sketch a girl you liked in school passed to you in class, a ticket stub from a baseball game you attended with your dad. Clearly, the vast majority have no market value whatsoever. The art market generally values art based on condition, artist, style/technique, and size. The art market is also very fashion-sensitive, so value will strongly depend on what is currently in vogue. Savvy buyers will know the market well, including how often similar works come up for sale and the last known selling price of any comparable works—if something is very similar to a number of other works, it'll probably be worth less than something that rarely comes to market. On the other hand, less unique works are easier to evaluate and sell.

What I liked about Ruth Eis's catalog commentary was that she saw past all the external factors that make a collection monetarily valuable and clearly understood the historical, cultural, and political context of the works. While in many cases the poor condition of a painting—a rip, a tear, a crease—would significantly diminish the worth of the artwork, Eis understood that calling attention to the physical marks enabled the museum to tell a larger and more important story. The exhibition was not just a show of Moshe Rynecki's paintings, but a show about the history of the Second World War, the plight of the artist during that period, and of European Jewry. Eis said as much in her introduction: "Through his choice of subject matter, Rynecki expressed his preference for political and social commentary. Although his primary intent was artistic merit, his legacy is more complex. History turned him into a witness to events of monumental consequence. . . . In light of the vastness of destruction and of all the material that was lost, it is of particular importance to examine an artistic career such as Rynecki's. The social, political and cultural history of European Jewry which shaped child, adolescent, and man comes to the surface in his works and gives credence to his artistic statement."

And then I spied at the very back of the catalog, in the appendix, a very simple sentence: "No inventory has been made of works which might have survived and are now in museum or private collections." I'd entirely missed this sentence and all it meant when I was twelve years old. Now, in my forties, it seemed to summarize everything I'd worked so hard to understand since the discovery of Grandpa George's journal in the trunk of his car. This one sentence implied a series of questions about how museums research and deal with issues of provenance. Eis's sentence acknowledged all the work not yet done regarding what might have survived, who had what pieces, and how they might have been acquired. Honestly, I couldn't decide if I wanted to laugh and rejoice at her foreshadowing of my project, or cry that I'd missed her notation and its import for more than thirty years.

The museum negotiated with Grandpa George before, during, and after the exhibition about the possibility of his gifting a painting to the museum. Grandpa George really did *not* want to part with his father's works. They were profoundly important to him, and asking him to let go of any of the pieces was a bold request. I knew from personal experience that Grandpa was fiercely protective of the paintings. He wanted to show them off, but also to jealously guard them.

I had visited Grandpa George at his home in Northern California, in Humboldt County, during one of my college summers. It turned out to be the last time I ever saw him. Dad, Grandpa George, and I sat in the living room talking and there was a lull in the conversation. While I stared out the window wishing I could walk down to the barn, Dad asked if I wanted to see the Rynecki paintings stored in what used to be the pump room—the original structure on the land.

"Come on, let's take a look," Dad said.

"Why do you want to do that?" Grandpa George asked.

"She hasn't seen them in a while," Dad said.

"I'll just take a quick peek," I said.

"Five minutes," Dad said.

The way the paintings, maybe seventy-five of them, were stacked up around the room made it difficult to see individual works. It didn't make sense for them to be stored here, but after the divorce Grandpa George had insisted they be taken out of Grandma's house, packed up, and shipped here. He no longer had a space to display them, but he wasn't willing to be apart from them.

"It's sad they're not hanging," I said.

"No room," Dad said.

I moved a few frames at the front of one of the stacks to see some of the less visible pieces.

"What do you think you're doing?" Grandpa George asked as he walked into the room.

"Just looking at the paintings," I said, gently putting the stack back into place.

"Well, don't," Grandpa George said.

"I'm sorry," I said.

"You might damage them."

"I just wanted to see them."

"If I wanted you to see them, I'd have hung them in the living room."

I looked at Dad. I knew Grandpa George wasn't trying to be mean, but his words stung.

"It was my idea to show them to her." Dad tried to rescue me.

"I asked you not to come back here."

Maybe Grandpa George was already not feeling well. Perhaps he somehow thought we were eyeing pieces we wanted when he was gone. If true, it is very sad; at the time we just wanted to see some of the art we hadn't seen in a long time. But when I think about how he felt about me looking at the paintings, it makes me wonder how he felt about the Magnes Museum asking for a painting.

In a 1981 *Marin Independent Journal* newspaper article, Grandpa told journalist Donna Horowitz that looking at his father's work was painful because it reminded him of the war years. "I see all the murdered people," he explained. And while he'd had offers from people wanting to buy the works, he would never sell them. "None of these paintings are for sale, and they won't ever be. . . . You don't sell your children." At the same time, he told her he wanted to see the collection exhibited in New York, Amsterdam, London, and Jerusalem. "I believe these paintings," Grandpa George said, "belong to the Jewish people of the world."

The truth was a bit more complicated. As much as Grandpa George wanted to shield and protect the collection from the prying eyes of those who might try to charm a piece off of him, he also very much liked being the center of attention. Being courted assiduously by the museum definitely appealed to him. But ultimately, his gift of a painting—*The Wedding (The Gift of Bread)*—seemed surprising. Grandpa George spent a postwar lifetime holding on tight to all he had left of his father—each individual painting a piece of the past. To let go of a painting must have been exceptionally difficult.

Today I think the gift created a win-win situation. It brought attention to a work that would have otherwise simply hung in a family home with limited opportunity to find an audience or share Moshe's legacy. But there is an aspect of museum collections that makes gifting them a little less positive than it might otherwise appear.

The idea of collectors amassing a large and important body of work and then making a dramatic donation to a well-known museum holds broad appeal. These sorts of stories—a prominent collector's decision to gift an important collection to a museum—are exciting for both museums and the public. Museum curators allude to announcements about forthcoming displays of works previously inaccessible to the public. Journalists love these stories because headlines about the extraordinary value of art capture attention. The reality of donating art is generally less glamorous, in large part due to the realities of museum collections.

At any given time, museums can show only a tiny percentage of the art they own. Typically between 2 and 4 percent of a collection is shown on the walls of a museum's galleries. Increasingly, museums share more of their collections on the Internet, giving art lovers greater access to what is usually in storage. And museums try to balance showing popular pieces that routinely draw in crowds with displaying lesser known pieces that give the public access to more of the collection. Objects in storage typically age much better than those displayed, since light and even humidity from nearby patrons eventually damage most artwork. Typically museums show pieces for up to six months, and then quietly put them away for years or decades. Many museums have policies that allow curators and researchers access to works tucked away, but such an option is generally not available for the public. There are not enough staff members, resources, or security personnel to accommodate such requests.

A private collector of Moshe Rynecki paintings once told me he'd donate all of his paintings to a Jewish museum if they'd guarantee the pieces would be on permanent display. When I shared this story with several different museum curators, they all shook their heads and said it was impossible. Many art collectors, like my family, know this and so we wrestle with an emotionally difficult decision—keep the painting in private hands and have access to it at all times, while trying to be as responsible as possible for its care, or donate the painting with the expectation that it will receive the proper archival care it needs but with only modest hope that it will be displayed often enough to reach a large audience.

Some collectors try to influence the fate of their art even after they've donated it. A collector may make monetary donations contingent upon the display of pieces from their collection. Or sometimes the gift isn't really a gift at all, but a long-term loan so if the museum ceases to display the art object in a way that is satisfactory to the collector, the collector can yank the donation and bring it back into the privacy of his or her own home or offer it to another museum more actively interested in the work. In extreme cases, some collectors decide to forgo gifting a museum and to build their own museum to display the work, but this is extraordinarily expensive and often doesn't work out the way that the collector intended.

The Barnes Collection is a prototypical case of how things can go wrong. In Merion, Pennsylvania, Albert Barnes assembled a legendary collection of late-nineteenth- and early-twentieth-century French masterpieces including works by Picasso, Van Gogh, Renoir, Cézanne, Seurat, and Matisse. He created a foundation to display and protect the works, and the bylaws of the foundation stipulated that after his death, no picture in the collection should "ever be loaned, sold or otherwise disposed of," unless it was hopelessly damaged, and that the paintings should always remain on display at the museum. But Barnes passed away in 1951, and in 1993, the Barnes Foundation did precisely what Barnes said they could not—they removed the works and sent them on tour around the world. And then in 2012 the foundation moved the $25 billion collection to a new location in downtown Philadelphia.

The cold, hard truth is that when you donate art (or anything, really), it's not yours anymore, and even the most strongly worded rules regarding the art object will not guarantee the art will be treated as you would have treated it yourself. I knew this theoretically, but I experienced it on a far more personal and emotional level when in 2009 my family learned that the Judah L. Magnes Museum was selling its facility on Russell Street in Berkeley and moving its collection to UC Berkeley, where it would be known as the Magnes Collection of Jewish Art and Life. Upon learning this news, Dad and I were concerned about what would happen to the Rynecki painting Grandpa George had donated more than twenty-five years earlier. We knew that the Magnes would sell some of its collection in an effort to downsize its holdings and to raise admittedly much needed funds for the renovation of its new home in downtown Berkeley. Dad and I, understandably worried about the fate of the Rynecki painting, contacted Alla Efimova, the museum's director, to ask what was in store for my great-grandfather's piece. I told Alla that if the Rynecki piece was for sale, we wanted to buy it back. She told me the painting was not for sale, but even if it was, it would have to be put up for sale in such a way as to not favor my family. I was reminded, again, that once you make a gift, it's no longer yours, and however difficult it is, you must let go.

My father and I dealt with the pros and cons of donating more directly in 2002, when we were contacted by Yehudit Shendar, deputy director and senior art curator at Yad Vashem in Israel. Established in 1953, Yad Vashem is, in its own words, "the Jewish people's living memorial to the Holocaust." Yehudit contacted us because the museum staff had seen our website and wanted to know more about my great-grandfather's life and his paintings. Yehudit wanted to view our collection in person.

We were flattered Yehudit wanted to see the collection and congratulated ourselves on the decision to build the Moshe Rynecki website. If we had not built the website, Yehudit most likely would not have learned of the paintings, and making new connections was certainly exciting. But with the palpable excitement as Yehudit's scheduled visit approached came an equally profound dread. We surmised before Yehudit's arrival that she would ask us to donate a painting to Yad Vashem. The question was whether or not we were willing to part with a second painting.

Before Yehudit arrived, I braced myself. I wanted to be on guard, so I'd be ready to say no when she asked for a painting. I was prepared to be firm. I didn't want my family giving away any more pieces, partly for purely selfish reasons and partly because I wanted my sons to grow up with access to the art. I didn't want to take something from them before they'd even gotten a chance to know their great-great-grandfather's body of work. I was ready to defend the collection from others seeking to further dismantle it. But when Yehudit arrived, I immediately warmed to her. Delightfully charming and friendly, she felt like an old family friend, who just happened to be an expert on Jewish art history and the Holocaust. She didn't just politely look at the paintings on our guided tour; she was insightful and personally reflective about her visit and the collection. We showed Yehudit numerous paintings hanging in the living room, dining room, and hallway, as well as those in the special rack Dad had purchased for flipping through the matted but unframed portraits that just wouldn't fit on the walls. And then Dad took Yehudit into a closet space where more framed pieces were stacked. One by one he began pulling paintings out. It was both a serious moment and a completely absurd endeavor because as much as Dad wanted to show Yehudit all the pieces, it was awkward and difficult to pull them out of what was essentially storage.

In that moment I realized the irony of my family's situation. Lacking wall space to display all the art, and absent the financial resources to build a museum dedicated to my great-grandfather's art, we had the exact same problem that made me critical of museums, though not to the same degree. Although the paintings might physically be in my family's possession, the question was, to what end? I love my great-grandfather's paintings, and I find both his work and the history compelling. But to do his legacy justice means finding a way to be comfortable with letting go; it means allowing the art to shift from a very private and personal space to a far more open and public sphere. It was an incredibly difficult dilemma for Grandpa George, a challenging one for Dad, and a perplexing one for me.

Yehudit and I watched Dad struggle with the paintings in the closet and I wished it would stop. Dad must have sensed the ridiculousness of his efforts and eventually announced he would check with Mom on the status of lunch.

Lunch was a light affair—San Francisco sourdough bread, a sliced tomato salad, and a vegetarian fritatta. We set aside discussion of the paintings over lunch and enjoyed an exceedingly pleasant conversation about our lives, travel, and family. And then, just as Mom set down dessert, Yehudit pulled some materials out of her bag.

"I want to tell you about the new history museum Yad Vashem is building," she told us.

The new wing on Yad Vashem's forty-five-acre campus, she explained, was designed by world-renowned architect Moshe Safdie. The building was to be a triangular concrete structure going through the mountain, the exhibition galleries all below. The gently sloping floor of the museum would give visitors the feeling of descending as they went deeper into the history and darkness of the Holocaust, and then ultimately would ascend through the northern exit, a route that would go to a dramatic cantilevered deck overlooking Jerusalem. The exhibition itself would be presented in galleries just off the designated route taking visitors through the museum. Between galleries, visitors would cross a prism floor, which ran the length of the museum, symbolic of historical memory. The displays, filled with "original artifacts, documentation, testimonies, film, literature, diaries, letters, and works of art," were all intended to provide intimate and personal views of the Holocaust. One of the galleries along the exhibition's path was a space to be called *Between Walls and Fences*. Yehudit wanted a painting for this exhibit. In fact, she wanted art throughout the museum because her goal was for visitors to experience the Holocaust through the eyes of Jewish artists who were witnesses. Testimonies, film footage, and artifacts can tell an enormous part of the history, but as an art historian, Yehudit yearned to use the power of art to convey the story to visitors in a unique and moving way.

"I am asking," she said, coming to the conclusion of her presentation, "for you to gift *Refugees* (1939) for permanent exhibit in the core exhibit of the history museum."

Dad and I looked at each other. We had agreed to a "no decisions during this visit" policy. We would listen, we would learn, and then we would talk about it as a family later.

"Well," Dad said, "that was an impressive pitch."

Yehudit smiled. We all laughed a bit nervously at Dad's attempt to break down the formal nature of the conversation.

"Really," Dad said. "I'm very moved by all you've presented. But we'll need to think about it and get back to you."

"Of course," Yehudit said. "I understand perfectly."

And then we finished our coffee, tea, and dessert, shared some pleasantries, and brought the visit to a close. We walked Yehudit to the door, waved goodbye, and sat down for a family discussion.

"What do you think?" Dad asked.

"She's good," I said.

Dad nodded.

"Whatever you two decide," Mom said. "It's really not my decision."

"It's a family decision," Dad said.

Mom shrugged her shoulders and looked at me.

"I'd like to think about it," I said, still feeling a bit reluctant at the notion of donating a painting.

"Did you hear her talk about the numbers of visitors they anticipate each year?" Dad asked.

"Close to a million a year, right?"

Dad nodded his head. "We have an obligation, I think, to donate the painting. It's an incredible opportunity for the painting to be seen by so many."

"What if we just gave it on a long-term loan?" I asked, searching for a middle ground. I wasn't entirely certain I was ready to give up *Refugees*. It was too good a painting and a final touchstone to my great-grandfather. It was one of the last known paintings he ever made.

"That won't work," Dad said. "You can't gift something with strings attached. It's too complicated for everyone. We either donate or we don't."

I stared at Dad, not sure what to say. He'd been involved in Grandpa George's negotiations to donate the Rynecki painting to the Magnes. Surely he knew more about it than I.

"But I have an idea," Dad said. "I'll write to Yehudit and offer her a different piece. Let's see what she says," he suggested.

"All right," I agreed, skeptical about how it would play out.

Dad sent an email to Yehudit a few days later. Eventually we heard back. Yehudit's response was hardly surprising. She wrote, in part, "I had a meeting with our historian in charge of the research and implementation of the material concerning the Warsaw Ghetto in our new museum. Here is our decision and choice: Due to the historical evidence that the phenomena of refugees arriving in Warsaw from the vicinity of the city and other provinces, is a major component of understanding what the ghetto was all about, we all feel the watercolor describing that phenomena titled *Refugees*, is what we would like to receive for our display."

We had another family discussion, albeit a brief one.

"We're all agreed, right?" Dad asked.

"Yes," I said, feeling both in favor and incredibly reluctant. A part of me still wanted to say no because it was sad to part with the painting.

But Yehudit had been very convincing with her commitment to the Rynecki collection and its narrative history, and I realized her visit was about more than just wanting a painting for Yad Vashem's walls—it was about the importance of the body of work.

This was eye-opening for me. My great-grandfather's paintings had always just been the paintings on the walls of my home. From Yehudit's visit, I began to envision my great-grandfather's art legacy through the eyes of a stranger, a stranger who understood their importance more than I did. It changed the way I felt about the paintings. It made me want to commit to learning all I could about my great-grandfather, to commemorate him as an artist and part of my family.

What was ultimately convincing was something Yehudit didn't say. It was something I saw when she took the tour. Simply put, it was that the paintings struck a personal chord in her. The opportunity to strike such a chord, even in a small fraction of the visitors to the museum, was an opportunity I simply couldn't resist. If even only 1 percent of them saw something in my great-grandfather's work, that opportunity to touch thousands of lives a year was not something that could be thrown away for personal sentimentality, no matter how intense.

And so with my okay to proceed, Dad replied to Yehudit with this note: "We are pleased to donate the painting *Refugees* to the permanent collection of the Museum. We consider it an honor to Moshe Rynecki both in terms of memory and art for the work to be displayed in the New Museum at Yad Vashem."

In early 2003, *Refugees* was picked up in California and delivered to Yad Vashem. In May 2003, we received notice from the museum thanking us for our donation and providing us with photographs from the display. Today the painting is part of the museum's Art Department, and occasionally the original is on display in its art museum. A "facsimile" of the painting—the museum's wording—is on permanent display in the *Between Walls and Fences* exhibition in the Holocaust History Museum. It can also be seen in their online exhibition.

ELEVEN

Serendipity

Sometimes the greatest opportunities arise in the unlikeliest of places. In 2012 I signed up with a friend for a "women's boot camp." In boot camp we rotated through a series of interval exercises intended to get us into shape. Twice a week we met in the early morning hours to run through many repetitions of simple exercises, including abdominal crunches, jumping jacks, and, ultimately, the dreaded burpee. A burpee requires you to stand with feet shoulder-width apart, squat, place your hands on the floor, and kick your legs backward so you can do a push-up. Then you reverse the motions, stand, and jump in the air. That sequence is one burpee. The teacher was an enthusiastic cheerleader who pushed us hard to reach our goals. One day she had each of us make a dream board—a collage of images cut from magazines to inspire us to reach our life-changing diet, exercise, and body shape goals. Frankly, I thought the project was stupid. I didn't want to do it, so I rebelled. I created a dream board, but it had nothing at all to do with the exercise class. Instead, mine focused on my great-grandfather's paintings, as well as my ambition to write a book and make a documentary film. I didn't really know what most of the women in the class thought about my completed assignment, but one woman, Juanita, found my story interesting, and she shared the project's website with her mother-in-law, Nancy. Nancy liked the project so much, she asked me to speak at her synagogue in Davis, California, for *Yom Ha'Shoah* (Holocaust Remembrance Day). I said yes much faster than I could ever do a burpee.

In the months before the talk, I excitedly composed a lecture about the Rynecki art, the paintings' story of survival, Holocaust-era art restitution, and my quest for the lost pieces. The date loomed on the calendar taped to my refrigerator; my anticipation of sharing the story was partly offset by my dread that I would have no audience. I wrote a PowerPoint presentation with more than forty slides, then deleted them all and started again. It was too academic, not really showing the power of Moshe's art and story. So I made a bargain with myself—I could have thirty-five slides if I showed only images, practiced the lecture, and used no vocalized pauses, such as "um" or "uh." I even practiced to my cat Meisha, silently perched on my living room sofa and almost certainly wondering about my sanity. I rehearsed difficult sections while driving to work. And when the Davis newspaper, the *Enterprise*, published a front page story about the upcoming event, I cajoled my family into listening, hoping an actual audience would help me prepare for the real deal. Steve, Tyler, and Owen patiently sat through my rehearsal, then made only a few editorial critiques. Almost before I knew it, the day of the talk arrived. I packed my laptop, notes, and jumbled nerves into the car, and drove the hour and a half to Davis, timing it so I would arrive an hour early—plenty of time to set up, see the space, and deal with any last-minute technological snafus.

While I drove from Oakland, Dad drove from his vacation spot in Lake Tahoe. The room set aside for my presentation at Congregation Bet Haverim was large. I mean it looked positively cavernous. Nancy greeted me with a hug and many questions. Where would I stand? Did

I need the podium? Could I help her connect the laptop with the projector? Would I please do a sound check with the microphone and sound system? Nancy's questions were good—they gave me time to focus on a list of tasks and not on my nerves. But then Nancy and some other people began setting up chairs—first a row of ten, then ten more behind. As a third row was put in place, my intimidation grew. It seemed like an awful lot of empty chairs. It would be exceedingly embarrassing to speak to a small group and have a large, unfilled room.

"Hey, Ace," Dad said, looking at me looking at the chairs. "How you holding up?"

"That's a lot of chairs," I said, nodding toward the increasing mass of empty seats.

"You'll have the placed packed."

"I don't know."

"Nancy?" I called out across the room. "Uhmm, don't you think that's enough?"

"Actually, we need a few more."

"But I already see fifty."

"Oh, yes," Nancy said. "We've got an RSVP list for at least that many. We're going to put out a hundred chairs."

I gulped. A crowd of one hundred was fantastic, almost too good to be true. For so long the *Chasing Portraits* project had been my hobby. While it was obsessively engaging for me, it was often only modestly interesting to my family, who at times grew fatigued at hearing the seemingly endless stream of detailed stories, events, and discoveries related to my project. Steve always listened and offered support, but Tyler and Owen were more interested in telling me about their video game exploits than hearing my own real-world trials and tribulations. Knowing that my family's own level of interest in the topic had waned, I had lost perspective on what others might think of the story. It seemed absurdly unlikely that a hundred people would come on a Sunday afternoon to hear me speak.

Thirty minutes before I was scheduled to begin, people began to arrive. Some took their seats right away, others introduced themselves to me, while a few approached Dad—one man even conversed with him in Polish. Astonishingly, seat by seat, row by row, the seats filled.

At a little after three o'clock Nancy took the stage. "Thank you so much for coming today!" she told the gathered audience. "What I love about this story is Elizabeth's passion for her great-grandfather's art. I met Elizabeth several months ago," she explained. "Her story, and the art she will share with us today, is very important."

I stood toward the front of the room, but off to the side, my hands grasped behind my back, and looked on as Nancy introduced me. Her words seemed to fade out as I looked from her, to Dad in the front row, and then to those in attendance. Nancy told the story of how we met and how excited she was by the fabulous turnout. As she wrapped up her introduction, she gestured to where I stood, and invited me to approach the podium. The audience clapped, I waved, and then walked to the podium.

My talk covered a lot of ground—my great-grandfather's body of work, information about the whereabouts of missing pieces, Holocaust-era art restitution, and my quest to see pieces held by others. It was a rush standing in front of a captive audience sharing the story. I was thrilled to see an audience enamored by the sweep of history, from the sadness and tragedy of the war, to the humor and absurdity of parts of my journey. They were right there with me, along for the ride. I was supposed to speak for forty minutes. I lost track of time; I didn't have a watch or a visible clock. I looked at Dad hoping he would give me a "wrap this thing up signal" if I'd gone on too long. But I realized that if I was looking for a signal, I'd definitely gone on too long. I zipped through the last two slides, and brought the whole thing to a close. I had spoken for close to an hour, but the audience didn't leave when I finished. Instead, they had questions, and lots of them.

How many paintings had I found? Where could they see pieces in person? Were there materials about the project they could buy? Why hadn't the *New York Times* written about me? Had I called *60 Minutes*?

When would there be an exhibit? Did I need translation help? Did I have a research staff? When would my film be released? There were questions about my ambitious agenda to write a book; raise funds to finish filming in Canada, Poland, and Israel; write an educational resource guide; and establish relationships with academics in Art Education, Religious Studies, Sociology, Jewish History, and Holocaust Education.

"That's an awful lot of goals for one person," a woman up front noted. "There are a lot of people here today," she said. "Perhaps some of them can help you work towards these goals."

I stared. Help from other people? Caught off guard by this suggestion, I murmured thanks and said something vague about how that was an interesting idea.

"I'd be happy to translate Yiddish for you," a man called out.

"I speak and read Polish," an older gentleman added.

Nancy stood up. "We need to wind up," she said. "Elizabeth will be here for a while if anyone wants to talk with her," she said.

As I packed up my notes, I realized a group was forming around the podium.

"Would you sign this?" a man asked me, handing me the flyer for the program.

"Who should I make it out to?" I asked, somewhat stupefied anyone would want my autograph.

As I finished scrawling my name, a woman approached. "I have a relative who is on a Fulbright scholarship in Warsaw," she said. "I can ask him to do research for you at the Jewish Historical Institute, if you'd like."

"Really?" I asked.

"Maybe he can get some of the information you can't get yourself," she said.

"Well, I would like details and photographs of the Rynecki paintings in their possession," I said.

"Give me your email," she said. "I'll put the two of you in contact. His name is Richard."

A few more people spoke with me about the talk, shared their own family genealogy stories, and told tales of their own quests and discoveries. Then Dad and I packed everything up and went out for an early dinner at a nearby Tex-Mex restaurant. Over enormous, spicy Southwestern salads with corn and jicama, tortilla chips, and a large bowl of guacamole, we swapped impressions of the afternoon.

"Maybe it's time for me to open source the project," I said.

"Meaning?" Dad asked.

"Put more of what I know online. Give people access to images, articles, and stories I've come across that might help uncover more clues," I said.

"It's an interesting idea," Dad said. "It reminds me of an article I read about medical research crowdsourcing. Researchers make data accessible and ask the public to sift through the vast amounts of data to help discover answers."

"People seem so excited about the story," I said. "The offers to help are incredible."

Dad nodded. "I think you're really onto something," he said.

"So you don't mind if I post more online?"

"Why would I mind?"

"I don't know," I said. "Maybe it's making the personal too public."

"Grandpa George would be proud of all you've done."

"I wish I could do more."

"Maybe by accepting help from others you *can* do more," Dad said.

"I'm definitely up for trying," I said.

A few weeks later, the woman I'd met at the talk wrote me an email to introduce me to her brother-in-law, Richard Sapon-White, the Fulbright scholar in Warsaw. I had serendipitously been connected with my first crowdsourced research assistant. I expressed my deep appreciation for his willingness to help and asked Richard to spearhead work on two tasks. One was to find and print out pages from *Nasz Przegląd Ilustrowany* (a Polish-language Zionist paper published on a daily basis in Warsaw between

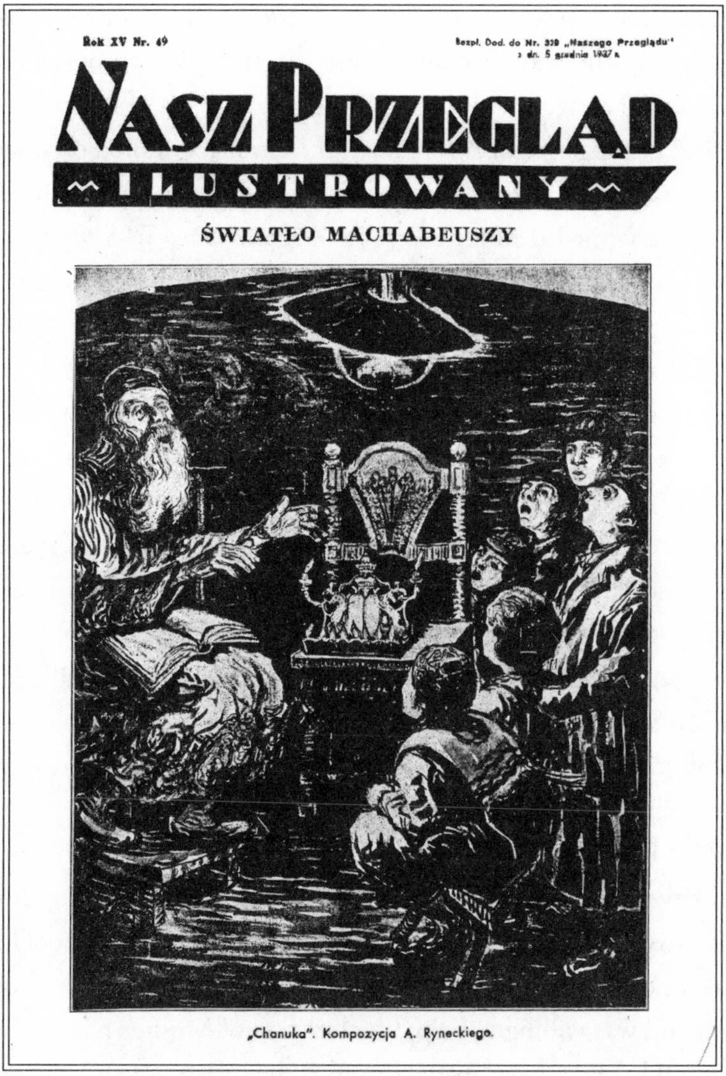

Rok XV Nr. 49

Bezpł. Dod. do Nr. 339 „Naszego Przeglądu" z dn. 5 grudnia 1937 r.

NASZ PRZEGLĄD

ILUSTROWANY

ŚWIATŁO MACHABEUSZY

„Chanuka". Kompozycja A. Ryneckiego.

Cover of Nasz Przegląd Ilustrowany
showing the Rynecki painting Chanuka *(1937, issue 49).*
Whereabouts of this painting and whether it survived World War II are unknown.

1923 and September 1939) containing images of a few Rynecki paintings I'd seen referenced in print. I also hoped he could visit the Jewish Historical Institute to uncover any information, details, and photographs of the Rynecki paintings in the collection. And then I waited.

I didn't have to wait long. Although there were some technological glitches along the way, Richard came through. Two months later, in June, an email arrived with three JPEG attachments of images Richard had found in the pages of *Nasz Przegląd Ilustrowany* stored on microfilm at the University of Warsaw Library. The first image, a piece titled *Chanuka*, was a work I'd never seen. The second one, *W Sukoth* [*During Sukkot*], was dark and difficult to see. The style seemed to be my great-grandfather's, but the title was strange. The subject didn't look like a celebration of Sukkot (a holiday to commemorate the years the Israelites wandered the desert after their exodus from slavery in Egypt); it looked much more like Simchas Torah (the celebration of the conclusion of the annual cycle of public Torah readings; after the recitation of the *attah hareita*, a collection of biblical verses in praise of God and the Torah, the Torah scrolls are removed from the ark and carried in procession in the synagogue). The third painting, *Modlitwy Dnia Pojednania* [*Yom Kippur Prayers*], appeared familiar. After a quick search I realized I had seen it at Stanford University's Green Library, in a book by Jerzy Malinowski about Polish-Jewish artists. I still didn't know the whereabouts of the original.

I wrote Richard and thanked him profusely. It was incredible that someone I'd never met, who didn't have any connection to my project except that his sister-in-law had attended my lecture, had taken time out of his own schedule to do research for me. Because he was in the right place, because he cared and was willing to help, I had images of Moshe's paintings I otherwise wouldn't have been able to see. As if that wasn't enough, in late June Richard visited the Jewish Historical Institute to see what he could uncover about the Rynecki paintings in their collection.

What Richard discovered at the Jewish Historical Institute might be called a card catalog system, a decidedly low-tech inventory of all the artwork held by the institute. On the front of six-inch-by-six-inch cards were boxes the museum staff filled out with the name of the artist, the painting medium, the size, an inventory number, and a description of the work. On the back of the cards were spaces for details about the art object's condition, conservation procedures for it, previous exhibition information, the date the piece was acquired by the museum, and the name of the person filling out the card. There were fifty-two Rynecki cards. Richard built an Excel spreadsheet of information culled from the cards. There were no images on the spreadsheet, but every piece had a title and an inventory number. It was a start, and it included details about the works I'd craved for years. Immediately I set about trying to match images in my files, from both online sources and books of art, with the descriptions in Richard's spreadsheet.

Richard's spreadsheet made a world of difference in my ability to understand the Rynecki collection at the Jewish Historical Institute. It also brought home, in a very concrete way, the tremendous potential, impact, and value of networking. My quest to find my great-grandfather's work had always seemed daunting at best, more quixotic than realistic, for me alone. But groups of people have more of everything that matters: knowledge, skills, connections, ideas, and time. If I wanted to find more Rynecki paintings in my lifetime and, even more to the point, during my father's lifetime, I would need help. But I had never dared hope that anyone would want to help until after my presentation led to Richard's contribution.

I had been sharing the story online on my blog and on social media, so I had seen the power of networking in a number of ways. But the talk at Congregation Bet Haverim in Davis made me realize that while valuable connections can be made online, there is no substitute for a personal connection. If speaking to a crowd in Davis led to the solution of my research question in Warsaw, more talks might open doors to further discoveries. I realized that I needed to give my talk in more places and to more people.

So, soon after the presentation in Davis in April, I looked for a new opportunity. Steve and I had planned a family trip to Boston in June, and I took the travel date as a challenge to find an East Coast venue for my lecture. The answer came from a group I discovered online: Boston 3G—the grandchildren of Holocaust survivors.

The year 1993 marked the first time I heard the phrase "children of survivors," also sometimes called 2G. I still felt a little odd that others' histories played a role in my personal identity, and that there were others like me trying to come to terms with their own legacies. It seems obvious in retrospect, but the discovery that the second generation's children identified themselves as the "grandchildren of survivors," or 3G, astounded me. The discovery briefly left me with pangs of jealousy that the next generation already knew their grandparents' stories, and embraced their legacy in a way I had yet to fully grasp. It also made me realize that my age put me in a strange place—I was right between the second generation born in the baby boom years of late 1940s and early 1950s and the third generation millenials born in the 1980s. My birthdate in 1969 meant I was more than a decade away from the middle of each group. Conversely, because both Dad and my grandparents were Holocaust survivors, I was simultaneously a very young 2G and a very old 3G.

After emails and phone calls to Boston explaining who I was and why I was inviting myself to speak to their group, Liz said the Boston 3G group would be delighted to host me. My talk, she explained, would take place in the common room of an apartment building on Tremont Street, right off the Boston Commons in the heart of the city. They announced the talk in several places, including the *Jewish Advocate*, the oldest continually circulated English-language Jewish newspaper in the United States (since 1902). The *Jewish Advocate* published an article by Alexandra Lapkin called "A Brush with the Holocaust." Friends, family, and a variety of people who read the story in the paper came to hear about my search. The audience at the Boston talk was smaller than at the Davis talk, but the discussion afterward was engaged and enthusiastic. Of particular interest to the audience was mention of a collector in Toronto, Canada, whom, I explained, I planned to meet in October, just four months away.

"You have to give your talk while you're there," a college student at the back of the room told me.

"Do you know someone who might host me?" I asked.

"Not really," she said, "but you really should talk in Toronto. The Jewish population in Toronto is active, there's the Jewish film festival, and several universities have Jewish studies programs."

"I can certainly ask around," I said.

While I was contemplating whom to ask about hosting my lecture in Toronto, our family vacation transitioned from Boston to New York City. Our trip was a balance between places the boys wanted to go (the Apple Store on Fifth Avenue and the Lego Store at Rockefeller Center) and places Steve and I insisted the boys see (the 9/11 memorial, the Met, MoMA, where my sons enjoyed an exhibit of video games, and Central Park). We didn't always want to do the same things, but we agreed the crowds at Times Square were too much and that the view from the Top of the Rock was quite spectacular.

A few days into our trip I received an unexpected email from the Canadian collector I was scheduled to visit in October. His email said he was sending me photos of Rynecki paintings held by his Israeli cousin. These pieces, like the ones he had in Canada, he explained, were all from "the same collection recovered by my father in Poland in 1945." Attached were seven JPEG images of paintings.

I'm not sure I squealed, but I made an awfully similar sound. Perhaps it was a cross between a delighted shriek and a gasp of surprise. Steve was asleep before the email arrived, but not after my joyous exclamation.

The hotel Wi-Fi meant the JPEG images downloaded quickly to my iPhone, but the small screen and the poor resolution of the images made it hard to discern details. Two images stood out: a blacksmith and a cobbler. In some of the paintings I could see my great-grandfather's signature. In almost all of the photographs I could make out the shadow of the photographer reflected in the glass of the framed image.

The shadow somehow seemed to be about more than the presence of the photographer—a person I didn't know. It felt symbolic of the history of the paintings: always present but somehow slightly out of my reach. I desperately wanted better images. Even more, I wanted to go to Israel to see the paintings in person. But first, I needed to focus on the interview with the collector in Toronto and find a place to give my talk.

TWELVE

Toronto, Canada

Back in spring 2008, I received a voice mail message from a man with a Polish accent and a Canadian telephone number. His name was Moshe Wertheim, he'd read Grandpa George's memoir, *Surviving Hitler in Poland: One Jew's Story*, which we'd published a few years earlier, and he wanted to talk with me about a passage in the book. Intrigued, I picked up the phone and dialed his number.

"Hello?" he answered.

"Hi," I said. "This is Elizabeth Rynecki. I'm returning your call."

He said nothing. It was as if he had recently left a lot of voice mail messages and couldn't quite remember who I was or why he'd called. So I continued. "You said you read my grandfather's memoir and you had something to tell me."

"Oh, yes! Thank you for calling me back," he said. "I'm sorry I didn't recognize your name. How do you say it?" he asked.

"Rye-neck-ee," I said.

"But you know it's Rih-net-ski, right?" he said.

"Yes, that's the Polish pronunciation," I said. "My family Americanized it in the fifties."

"You know it probably comes from the Polish word *rynek*, which refers to a marketplace," he said.

"Yes, you're right," I replied, and tried to be polite. This wasn't the first time I'd heard this explanation of my last name. I wondered where this all was going.

"That's not what I called to talk to you about," he said and cleared his throat. "I want to talk to you about your grandfather's memoir, the one listed on your website."

"Surviving Hitler in Poland?" I asked. It was the memoir Dad had found in the trunk of Grandpa George's car in 1992. We'd done some slight editing for spelling and the like and self-published it in 2005.

"Yes," he said. "I bought it from Amazon. It's interesting."

"I'm glad you enjoyed it."

"There's a passage in the book that caught my attention. It's about one of your great-grandfather's paintings. The description of the pogrom. I think I may have it."

"You have what?"

"Your Grandpa George describes a painting in the book—a Russian pogrom. I think it's hanging in my living room."

I looked around wildly, then lunged for a copy of the book I saw on the side of my desk, and frantically flipped through its pages trying to find the description. There it was, on the bottom of page 61.

"This one?" I asked, interrupting Mr. Wertheim, who was still talking about the painting hanging in his living room: "'When the Polish came to power he painted a painting, oil on canvas, which became a controversial one in Warsaw. He created a Russian pogrom, an attack of the Cossacks on a synagogue in which raping of women was shown, dead men wrapped in the holy scrolls, a very strong political painting against the White Russians. Of course the story of Russian pogroms was well-known, but had never been shown in a painting of such dramatic dimensions.' "

"Right. That's the one," he said. "I think I have it."

"But how?" I asked somewhat incredulously.

"After the war," he said, "my parents bought it."

"Bought it?"

"My parents, Anatol and Anna, were Polish Jews," he said. "During the Second World War they went into Russia and became partisan fighters—part of the resistance." I knew a bit about partisan fighters, but not a lot. Partisans were guerrilla fighters, Poles or Russians or Yugoslavs, among others, who fought behind German lines. Among them were a number of Jews who had escaped ghettos and camps and lived mostly in the woods. These independent fighters plotted sabotage missions (like cutting train tracks, ambushing convoys of trucks, or attacking poorly guarded communications or command-and-control facilities). In some cases, they actually grew their own food, but mostly they lived by taking supplies from the Germans or from the local populace. Sometimes partisan and resistance groups worked together, sharing military intelligence to coordinate sabotage operations.

"My parents were in a camp created by Shalom Zorin," he continued. "After the war they returned to Poland. At one point during their journey, near Lodz, they passed a farmhouse. The farmer asked them, 'Are you Jewish?' My parents told the farmer that, yes, they were Jewish. The farmer said, 'I always knew the Jews would return. I have this bundle of paintings showing Jewish life. Do you want to buy them?' My parents bought the paintings, maybe about fifty pieces."

"You have fifty Rynecki paintings?" I gasped.

"Oh, no," he said. "There are just four here in my home."

"What happened to the others?" I asked, feeling incredibly crushed.

"My parents gave them away."

"They gave them away? But why? Who has them?"

"They were gifts," he said. "My parents gave them to friends and family because they wanted to share them. They did this quite a bit with all the art they collected. People would come for dinner and they'd send them home with a painting," he said.

I'd never heard of such a thing. People gifted bottles of wine and books, chocolates and bouquets of flowers, not paintings. Especially not my great-grandfather's paintings.

"Do you at least have photographs of all the pieces?" I asked.

"Not of all the pieces," he said. "But I can make you photographs of the four I have. And I can ask my brother in Poland and aunt in Israel to photograph the ones they've got."

"This is incredible," I said, scribbling his story onto a pad of paper. "Just astonishing, really."

"I thought you'd want to know."

"I do, I do," I said. "I'm so glad you called. It's just all a bit overwhelming."

"Sure, I understand," he said.

"Can you tell me how you found me? Why you called?"

"I recently decided to reframe a few of the Rynecki pieces," he said. "Really, just on a whim, I decided to Google the Rynecki name to see if I could learn more about the artist. My parents really never knew anything about him except that he was clearly a Jewish painter. That's how I found your website."

"Incredible."

And then we exchanged email addresses, Mr. Wertheim assured me he would send me photographs of the paintings, and I hung up the phone.

2008 passed with no photographs from Canada.

"Maybe he's just forgotten," Dad said that winter.

"Maybe," I said. "Or maybe he's nervous about letting me see them. He might be afraid I want to claim them."

Several years passed, and several rounds of correspondence later, I wasn't sure I would ever get to see the paintings. In 2012, four years later, it occurred to me that if I wrote a follow-up email to Mr. Wertheim and mentioned my documentary, he might be willing to be part of the film.

I drafted and redrafted my email message, finally settling on "I wish to see the paintings you and your brother have. Can we arrange to talk? Perhaps even meet? It would mean so much to my father for us to see the paintings you have. I am trying to gain a better understanding of the oeuvre of my great-grandfather's work and the paintings you have are part of that link. You hold an important link to my family's past."

Mr. Wertheim responded the next day thanking me for the reminder, and said he would send pictures the following week. I waited a month and heard nothing. I wrote again, this time telling him about my recent discovery of two Rynecki paintings held by the National Museum in Warsaw and a newspaper clipping held by their Iconographic and Photographic Department, showing a Rynecki painting titled *Na Wywczasach* [a prewar spelling of *Na wczasach*, meaning "on holiday" or "on vacation"] in which a man (presumably my great-grandfather) is painting, a small crowd watching him. I explained that I'd never seen the painting before and was unsure if it had survived the Second World War. I asked if Mr. Wertheim knew it. Perhaps, I mused, it was part of the collection his parents had bought from the farmer in Lodz.

Mr. Wertheim replied. He didn't mention the newspaper clipping, but that was beside the point, because attached to his email were photographs of the four Rynecki paintings in his home. My heart raced. I couldn't decide between the immediate gratification of opening the JPEG attachments by myself and my desire to share that excitement with someone who had seen all of the ups and downs of my quest. It was too early to call Dad, and though I tried to wait, I failed pretty quickly. It was just too exciting, so I double clicked on the JPEGs to download them. In a moment, like magic, there they were—four Rynecki images on my desktop.

Na wczasach (Vacation) *by Moshe Rynecki,*
featured in a 1931 Warsaw Courier *illustrated Sunday supplement.*
Whereabouts of this painting and whether it survived World War II are unknown.

I jubilantly clicked back and forth between the four. I knew, instantly, that these were the work of my great-grandfather. I enlarged the images on my screen, trying to see more details, but enlarging them just made them too pixilated. As I toggled between the four, trying to learn and absorb their scenes, I heard my older son pouring cereal in the kitchen.

"Tyler," I called out, "you have to come see this!"

He mumbled something about needing to put the milk away, but because I couldn't wait I marched into the kitchen to convey the importance of the moment and the need for him to come at once.

"It's absolutely amazing," I insisted, grabbing his hand and pulling him toward my office. "You have to see these photos. They are ones I have *never* seen before!"

"Where'd you get them?"

"A man in Canada emailed them to me."

"I like the black-and-white one best," he said, slipping into my desk chair and using the mouse to click back and forth between the four images.

"Me too, although I'm really just so happy to have photos of all of them."

Tyler stood up and hugged me.

"Congratulations, Mom. It's really great," he said, and then went back to the kitchen.

I sat down to stare at the photos a bit longer. I understood Tyler really was happy for me, but I felt dismayed at my inability to express the amazing confluence of events that had brought the images into my life. I don't think he was able to comprehend the magnitude of the moment, or at least he wasn't able to appreciate it the same way. For me, it was surreal. I didn't want to take my eyes off the screen, as if perhaps the images would mysteriously disappear, almost as miraculously as they had appeared. I thought about the passage of time, not just the four years it took Mr. Wertheim to send me the photographs, but the more than seventy years since my great-grandfather had divided and hidden his collection. I gazed at each of the paintings, wishing I could hear my great-grandfather's voice in the shadows of his brushstrokes.

Mr. Wertheim's email arrived in May. In August the documentary film received its first donation. It wasn't a lot compared to the cost of the whole project, but it was generous enough that if I was frugal, I could fly to Toronto and hire a crew to film my visit. I wrote Mr. Wertheim and expressed my desire to film a segment with him for the documentary. Together we agreed October looked like a good time, so I began to look around for a cameraman.

My original plan had been to take Johnny and Leo, the same people who filmed the interview with Dad several years earlier, with me to Canada. This would have meant paying for three flights to Canada, three hotel rooms, plus meals, per diems, and day rates. I just couldn't afford it. The much less expensive solution was to find a film crew in Toronto. Finding someone in my budget, who was willing to work just the one day I required, and who had experience filming documentary interviews, was extremely stressful, especially from thousands of miles away. After a fairly lengthy search, I found someone and we tentatively set a date for late October.

In mid-September, Mom and I got together for lunch to discuss my pending trip to Toronto, and to catch up on a trip she and Dad had recently taken to Lake Tahoe. We met at a cute Japanese restaurant in Larkspur, a small town north of San Francisco. We sat at a window table, and while we waited for lunch and sipped tea, I jabbered on about the upcoming trip, my excitement at seeing the paintings in person, and my nervousness about interviewing Mr. Wertheim. Mom expressed excitement, but also concern that I had become overly preoccupied with the Moshe Rynecki project. She didn't want it to overtake my life. I nodded and shrugged. At that point, our food arrived, and we ate in silence for a while, until she said, "I need to tell you something."

I looked up. I was sure she was going to tell me she needed hearing aids. I'd been worried for some time about what I perceived as her growing loss of hearing. She hadn't admitted it, and it wasn't exactly that I had to raise my voice in order for her to hear me, but if I didn't look right at her and speak clearly, she often needed me to repeat myself. For her part, she claimed I'd started mumbling more frequently. I prepared myself for her to share this news, and for me to feign surprise and to offer support.

"I went to see a cardiologist," she said.

I stared, perplexed and increasingly worried.

"I've been feeling short-winded, and Dad made me go to the doctor," she explained.

"And?"

"Well, it seems that I'm supposed to have surgery."

"But you don't want to?"

"I don't really have a choice."

"You always have a choice," I said.

"I need a heart-valve replacement. The surgeon says it's a pretty common surgery."

"Common for the surgeon, but not for you."

"I'm going to schedule it for early October."

"You tell me when, and I'll be there."

She nodded and switched the topic to Tyler and his new fifth-grade teachers. He had been a bit uncertain about a new school principal and a rotating class schedule for all subjects rather than a single teacher. I assured her the teachers were fantastic and Tyler was thriving. As for Owen, she wondered about his transition from summer back into school and what he thought of third grade. Owen was perfectly capable of doing well in school but didn't particularly like it. Unlike many children who dislike school, surprisingly, his least favorite time was recess. He wanted recess to be unstructured time and had difficulty with the many rules about exactly how you had to play certain games. Fortunately, the new school year had started off on the right foot for him, and while I had a preemptive parent-teacher conference scheduled, I assured Mom that things were going well.

After lunch I emailed Mr. Wertheim and the film crew. I explained that something personal had come up and I wasn't sure about being able to come to Canada in mid-October.

On the day of the surgery, October 4, Mom and Dad were already at the hospital by six a.m. I called Mom's cellphone to check in. "We are earlier than we need to be," she said. "Dad and I are at the hospital just waiting for a free bed. I won't be admitted until ten o'clock."

I got in my car in Oakland and drove fifty miles south to the hospital in Santa Clara. Arriving a bit after eight-thirty, I found parking and went inside. Mom was already checked into the Cardiovascular Surgery Department on the third floor. I went upstairs, gave the nurse my name, and entered the patient area. Despite the delay, the nurses were busily getting Mom ready for surgery. She had changed into a hospital gown, was wearing a blue hairnet, and sat propped up in the hospital bed with several blankets piled on her legs to keep her warm. Dad was in a chair next to the bed. I grabbed another chair and sat down.

It was strange to see Mom in the hospital, and carrying on a normal conversation was difficult. We talked about Tyler and Owen, what costumes they might wear for Halloween, and Dad's upcoming birthday: all things to help pass the time while she waited to be prepped and wheeled off to surgery. Then the nurse came to give her a shot—"It's a sort of truth serum," she laughed. "Not really, but people really just speak their mind after the shot kicks in," she said. At first Mom seemed really out of it. Then she seemed to doze in and out of consciousness, sometimes mumbling, other times looking asleep. Dad and I watched her and watched each other. Then Mom said quite clearly, "The only way I'm going out of here is in a body bag." Dad and I looked at each other. Mom must have known she had said something out loud that she had been thinking privately, because she became more alert and asked us, "Did I say anything strange?"

"No," I said, hoping Dad wouldn't reveal what she'd said. I wanted Mom to remain positive. I was afraid if we told her what she had said it would somehow make things bad. Dad stood up and walked over to her bedside.

"Look at your arm," he said, pointing at the black-and-blue mark where she'd been given the shot. "I have a Band-Aid. I'll patch you up," he said.

"Is it bad?" Mom asked.

"This should be the worst of your troubles," he said, putting the Band-Aid into place.

And then word came that Mom was ready to be wheeled down the hallway. I hugged her and told her I'd see her tomorrow. Dad and I walked down the hallway and turned right toward the waiting room while Mom was wheeled through double doors toward surgery.

I spent a few hours with Dad. We walked around the hospital grounds. We had a cup of tea. It was getting late and I really needed to get home. The boys would be home from school soon, and I needed to make dinner.

"Are you sure it's okay if I leave?" I asked.

"Of course," Dad said. "There's really nothing for you to do here."

And so Dad and I hugged goodbye and I drove home.

We ate dinner early, about six. Around seven, when I was doing dishes, the phone rang.

"Everything is okay," Dad said. "I saw her. She's out of surgery. She's a little groggy, but the nurses say she's strong and doing well. She might actually move out of the ICU a little early."

"Great!" I said. "I'll come down in the morning," I promised.

At 10 p.m. my cellphone rang again. I almost didn't hear it. I go to sleep early—ridiculously early—and I usually kept the ringer off. By the time I woke up and realized the phone was ringing in the kitchen, I had to run to catch it in time. Caller ID showed it was Dad.

"It's not good," Dad said.

"What's not good?"

"It's Mom," he said, choking up. "She died."

I was silent.

"I'll put on the doctor," Dad said.

I heard the phone change hands. The surgeon came on the line.

"I'm really so very sorry," he said. "We aren't sure what happened. Surgery went exceedingly well. She was strong when she came out. About an hour ago the nurses reported her heart slowing down. We did CPR. We even opened up the stitches and tried to see if we could see what was wrong. We tried everything," he said.

"I'm going to throw up," I said, sitting down on the floor and crying.

"I'm so very sorry," the surgeon said again.

Dad came back on the phone. "Can you come down tomorrow?"

"Do you want me to come right now?"

"No."

"I love you."

Mom's death was horrible. It put my life into a tailspin. I stopped writing. I crawled into bed and cried a lot. The Moshe Rynecki story wasn't Mom's story, but she had always been there for me—to explain why Dad couldn't watch films about the Holocaust, or why he didn't like leftovers (they reminded him of the war), or why my grandparents sometimes yelled at each other in Polish. She was my go-to person for answering questions about the Rynecki family history when I just couldn't ask Dad. She even went on a research field trip with me to the Stanford library, where we discovered books with Rynecki paintings we'd never seen before. Her loss was a complete and total shock. For a surgery said to have a 98 percent success rate, Mom had landed on the very bad side of the odds.

Beyond my own troubles, I was at a loss for how to help Dad. He told me her death "was the worst thing that has ever happened to me." This was difficult for me to process. Really? Worse than the war? Worse than the losses experienced by his family in the Holocaust? It was, for me, a completely stunning statement. And yet in a lot of ways it made sense. The war had ended when he was eight years old. He had lived most of a lifetime since then, and had been married to Mom for the better part of it. He told me sometimes it seemed like the war happened to somebody else. For him, Mom's death was so much closer and more real. He had gotten over the war because he'd been young. He went to school in Italy and then the United States, and ultimately worked hard to integrate himself into American life. At seventy-five, losing Mom was entirely different. We buried Mom a few days later, on Simchas Torah. My trip was supposed to be less than a week away, but there was no way I could recover, or even function normally, much less adequately support my father, if I went to Toronto. Needless to say, I canceled my trip.

It was an emotionally exhausting time for both my father and me. To help escape our loss, we rented a beach house on the California coast for Thanksgiving. Facing Thanksgiving at home without Mom was just too hard. The whole winter was especially gloomy, and it was really difficult for me to start looking forward again, when all I wanted to do was look back and question why it happened. Eventually, though, I came around. In about six months or so, I started thinking about the project again, and a few months later, I started to feel that Mom's death was no longer an ever-present lodestone that I couldn't escape. In fact, I began to feel that going to Toronto was a bit like a light at the end of the tunnel. It was something to look forward to and something to distract me. Because of the feedback I'd gotten from the talk in Boston the summer before, I decided to find an organization in Toronto to host my talk.

In some senses, pitching my talk was easy; there was a large Jewish community in Toronto. In addition, because four Rynecki paintings were in the city, I had a connection to the community. Also, given the growing interest in issues of Holocaust-era art restitution, I thought my story might be appealing. In short, it didn't seem like a tough sell, since I was merely asking for the opportunity to speak.

As it turned out, I was surprised at how many organizations were not at all interested in my talk. Well, maybe you wouldn't be surprised given all the strikes against me: I was not an attorney specializing in Holocaust art recovery, I was not an academic, and there was no movie to share, or book to sell. The unknown Rynecki story, it turned out, was a very difficult sell. The organizations I contacted were unfailingly polite about saying it just didn't fit their needs. Eventually, I found one person, Dr. Adam Cohen at the University of Toronto, who said yes. I had only one yes against many no's, but that was all I needed.

And so on Monday, October 14, 2013, Canadian Thanksgiving, I flew from San Francisco to Toronto. In my carry-on bag I had my interview outfit, two hard drives for backing up the digital film "footage," my list of interview questions, and my laptop.

My hotel was on Bloor Street, on the edge of the University of Toronto campus, in a cute neighborhood filled with fabulously cheap and varied ethnic restaurants. The night I arrived, I ate at a mouthwatering Thai place. My hotel room wasn't much, but the price was affordable—while the University of Toronto's Center for Jewish Studies could not pay me for my talk or travel expenses, they were able to get me a discounted room rate. I kept pinching myself the night before the interview; I couldn't believe I was just a cab ride away from seeing in person four of my great-grandfather's paintings, at least one very different from any I had seen before.

Tuesday morning I woke up early to read over my interview questions and prepare. I was so excited I was a little over the top in worrying about being on time. The cab ride took far less time than anticipated, and I arrived on Mr. Wertheim's doorstep forty-five minutes early, well before the film crew was supposed to arrive. Although I was embarrassed to ring the doorbell so early, I couldn't make myself wait. Fortunately, Mr. Wertheim was welcoming and warm. He offered me a cup of tea and we sat at his breakfast table and chatted. He had just returned with his wife from Italy and told me about their adventures. I admired the beautiful view of the fall leaves in his backyard; we talked about my flight and where I was staying, and then naturally moved to talking about my great-grandfather and his art. About twenty minutes later he said, "Well, come, I'm sure you'd like to see the paintings."

I thought he'd never ask.

He led me into the family room to see the black-and-white painting of, as he called it, *Men Studying*. It looked so much like a wood-block print, but then I peered closely and saw pencil marks where my great-grandfather had sketched the work before inking it. Mostly black, in sharp contrast to the white background, were seven men gathered around a simple wooden table. In front of each of them was an open book. A man somewhat to the left of center, seated in the middle of four other men, was the focal point of the piece. This man's right hand rested on a book, while his left hand was in the air, gesturing, as he spoke. Across from him, two men covered their eyes.

I didn't want to move. I just wanted to stare, uninterrupted, indefinitely. I reached out to touch the frame, hoping that feeling it in my fingertips might assure me that the moment was, indeed, real. A mixture of immense sadness and profound gratitude washed over me. This house, these walls, they were home; not my home, but home to my great-grandfather's paintings. They were concrete and indisputable proof of

The Water Carriers *(1930)*.

Street Performers *(undated)*.

Unless otherwise noted, all paintings held by and all photographs courtesy of the Rynecki family.

Left:
Reading the Megillah
(1919).

Below:
Shemoneh Esreh
(undated).

The Reader *(date illegible).*

The Chess Players *(undated).*

Curious Children *(1928).*

Girl in a Sailor Outfit *(1935).*

Self-Portrait *(1931).*
Held by the Jewish Historical Institute.

Forced Labor *(1939)*.

Old Jew *(undated)*.

The Hoop *(1934)*.

The Seamstresses *(1931)*.

Krasiński Park *(1930)*.

Party with Violinist *(undated)*.

Luna Park *(undated)*.

At the Market *(1937)*.
Held by the Jewish Historical Institute.

Left:
The Wedding (The First Dance) *(1919).*

Below:
Russian Pogrom *(undated).*
Held by Moshe Wertheim.

Refugees *(1939).*
Painting gifted from the Rynecki family to Yad Vashem, Israel.

Prayer *(circa 1927).*

Men Studying *(date illegible).*
Held by Moshe Wertheim.

Jews Reading Books (House of Learning) *(undated).*
Held by the Jewish Historical Institute.

Jews with Candles *(undated).*
Held by the Jewish Historical Institute.

Eve of the Day of Atonement *(1929).*
Held by the Jewish Historical Institute.

Synagogue Interior *(1930).*

Jews of the Book *(1932).*
Held by Maciej Rauch Grodecki.

Catherine (Cathy) Greenblatt, Sławomir (Sławek) Grünberg, and me at the Jewish Motifs International Film Festival, May 2015.

A wood carving by Moshe Rynecki (undated). Carving held by Shula Eliaz, gift to her family from Perla Rynecki. Photograph © Chuck Fishman.

My father, Alex Rynecki, and I pose beside Moshe's paintings Self-Portrait *(1936) and* Perla Rynecki *(1929). Photograph © 2014 Shoey Sindel Photography.*

yet another bundle surviving. I smiled. It felt glorious and victorious just to be here. Grandpa George and my great-grandfather would have been pleased to know I'd found these paintings.

I turned toward Mr. Wertheim, who guided me out of the living room and into a more formal sitting room at the front of the house. Above the couch, I saw it right away, the Russian pogrom piece—*Attack of the Cossacks*. It was the piece described in Grandpa George's memoir. It is such an amazing painting; it defied simple description. There was so much going on in the painting, so much to see, I was literally stunned to look at it.

Eventually, thinking about the painting in terms of action in the foreground (where the scene was darker) and in the background (where the people were more illuminated) and working my way across the painting from left to right, I was able to piece together the individual components comprising the whole. At the front a man lay dead. Across his chest rested a Torah in a yellow mantle (or cloak), decorated with a Star of David. To his right a man on his knees begged for his life as he looked up at a soldier. The soldier steadied himself as he prepared to stab his bayonet into the kneeling man. Behind the soldier were two more soldiers in green uniforms. They were by the front door and seemed engrossed in a book one of them held. At the far left was a woman. She had long hair and wore a white flowing dress or gown. Behind and beneath her were outlines of bodies—one dead on the floor below her, another crouched with head in hand, a third and fourth appearing in form but not detail, and a fifth, a man with a beard, reaching toward the woman. One of the soldiers, an older man with a mustache, had his arms wrapped around the woman. Her right elbow jutted against his chin while her hand rested on her forehead. The position of her elbow forced the soldier's head back a bit. Her left arm reached up, presumably flailing as she struggled with the soldier. Behind him stood another soldier in a prominent green jacket.

Along the upper edge of the painting were several chandeliers, but most of the light came from two windows. At the back of the room a Star of David was painted on the wall. A man clad all in white stood in front of a large gathering of people at the back—both soldiers and villagers. He was leaning backward, pulling on the arms of someone kneeling on the floor, desperately trying to resist.

"See here?" Mr. Wertheim asked, pointing to cracks and wrinkles in the painting. "It seems like someone once crumpled up the entire piece into a small ball of paper."

I moved my head in closer, closer than a security guard at a museum would ever allow me to get to a painting. I stared at the hairline wrinkles and cracks in the paint. These weren't gaping holes like the ones in the pieces we had, but there were still clearly small wrinkle lines. Mr. Wertheim explained that an art restorer had recently worked on the piece to smooth it out. I wondered how wrinkled it had looked before it was worked on.

Mr. Wertheim showed me a third piece—a man working with a wooden book press, but I wasn't so interested in that piece. It was clearly my great-grandfather's work, but the subject didn't grab me as much as the first two. We returned to the kitchen to finish our tea, and I asked Mr. Wertheim about the fourth painting. He looked at me sort of quizzically and asked if I meant the painting his brother had in Poland. I pulled out a photograph of the piece I wanted to see—a blind man and a young girl walking together. This jogged his memory a bit and he stood up. "Oh yes, where is that piece?" First he headed to the spare bedroom (it wasn't there), then the dining room (it wasn't there). After a momentary pause to think, he said, "Wait a minute, I'll be right back," and he disappeared to the upper floor of the house. He returned a few minutes later with the painting in his hands.

"It was in my wife's study. I don't go in there very often, so I forgot that's where it hung," he said. He laid it down on the table, and together we looked at the old bearded man walking with a cane, a young girl beside him, her hand holding on to his upper arm.

"It's so faded," I said.

Mr. Wertheim nodded.

"Do you think the face of the man might once have been clearer?"

"Hard to remember," he said. "I'm not sure."

The morning seemed to slip away, and finally it occurred to me that all the things Mr. Wertheim and I were discussing really ought to be captured on film. Certainly it was important to create a sense of comfort for an interviewee, to ensure that the interaction was genuine. But it was just as important to maintain the spontaneity of the initial stages of interaction, so the film captured the moment rather than looking rehearsed and wooden. I looked at the time on my cellphone and saw that my camera crew was running late. I made a phone call, but got no answer. Chris Logan, the cameraman, had visited Mr. Wertheim's home the previous week to scout out the site, so I was sure he must be on his way. I walked to the front door, looked out the window, and was relieved to see Chris and David Balodis, who would handle the audio, creating a growing pile of lights, tripods, cables, and cameras on Mr. Wertheim's doorstep.

I excused myself so I could help bring equipment into the house; it quickly took over the entryway. Chris and I conferred about where to set up and decided the best place was in the family room, where there was plenty of natural light. We positioned Mr. Wertheim in a cushioned living room chair with his back to the window and me opposite on an ottoman with the camera right behind me; the shot of Mr. Wertheim would show him talking almost directly to the camera. We even set up a second camera so there would also be film of me interviewing him.

It took Chris and David almost an hour to set up. Mr. Wertheim passed the time by setting up his own camera to film the filming of the interview, while I read through my notes again. Then it was time for the interview. David stepped in front of Mr. Wertheim with a clapboard and said, "Camera 1, take 1," and I laughed. It was so official, it almost seemed unreal, more like Hollywood than real life.

I interviewed Mr. Wertheim for close to two hours, about his recollection of his parents' story telling how they acquired the Rynecki paintings, his childhood memories of the art, if he could tell me where each of the pieces hung in his parents' home, and what his parents titled each of the pieces. I even had him read the description of the painting in Grandpa George's memoir because it was what had prompted him to call. Of course, there were also questions I didn't ask. It was not so much that I chickened out, but that I wanted to be careful about what I asked and how I asked it. My goal was to share Moshe's work, and that required a softer touch than being an investigative journalist. Of course seeing the paintings and capturing their story on film was critical, but I also wanted to build a foundation with Mr. Wertheim so we could collaborate again in the future.

One of the questions I asked Mr. Wertheim was about his children's relationship to the Moshe Rynecki paintings held by their family. I explained that while I had not always felt protective about the paintings, they were important to me, that I understood them in relationship to my family's story of survival, and that I hoped someday my children would relate to and respect the paintings in a similar way. Then I asked him about his children, if as grandchildren of survivors they felt the tug of history, and if they knew the story of how the Wertheims had acquired Moshe's paintings. He said his children knew a bit of the story, but that they were at a point in their lives where other things were more pressing. Chris, the cameraman, tapped me on the shoulder; he needed to stop filming and change the CF card in the camera.

Mr. Wertheim's son, who I guessed was in his twenties, had been sitting in the kitchen listening. While the camera was off, he spoke to me. "I can tell you what I think about the paintings and what I'll do when my dad is old and sick. I'll put him in the old person's home and we'll donate the paintings to a museum." I was dumbfounded. His comment seemed so callous—so insensitive to the idea of his father growing old and so utterly unconcerned with art that his family and I both clearly valued. Momentarily stunned by his lack of empathy, I recovered enough to ask if he was willing to be interviewed on camera. His father gave him the equivalent of a "look"—a warning, it seemed to me—and the son quickly backpedaled. He told me he was joking, he was teasing his dad. He said he would go call his sister, an attorney, and get a coherent sibling response to the question. A few minutes later he returned and sat down where his father had previously sat. I gave him time to be comfortable in front of the camera before I asked what he one day would do if he was to inherit the paintings. "The paintings," the son said, "are very important to my family. We treasure them and will always have a place for them in our lives. I hope to someday proudly hang them in my own home."

At first I was angry. That was not what he had said off camera, and what he had said in that earlier moment had been enough to really upset me on a number of levels. If this was how the next generation thought of the art—to flippantly give it away without understanding its place in history—then maybe my choice to be an observer was a mistake. Maybe the Wertheims, I thought, fuming, didn't deserve to have Rynecki art in their home.

To be clear, upon reflection, I knew that wasn't fair. Mr. Wertheim had been incredibly gracious, and his son would inevitably shift his opinions as he gained more life experience. Many young people were glib about important issues because they hadn't fully considered the consequences of their actions or the impact of their words. That was not a new and noteworthy phenomenon, no matter how upsetting it was to me in the moment. Mr. Wertheim's son may not even determine what happens to his father or the paintings—family dynamics are quite complicated. But with all that said, at the time I was steaming mad, and it was all I could do to remain stoic and tactful.

At the time I felt even angrier than I should have because I'd had, in the back of my mind, a fantasy of Toronto that reality could never live up to. In my dream world, I would visit the Wertheim family and they would be so inspired by my story that they would take a painting off the wall and hand it to me. "It belongs to your family," they would tell me. I would cry and accept it with open arms. "Thank you," I'd whisper.

I knew my fantasy was unrealistic, but that hadn't kept me from hoping it might come true anyway. However, even though it was clear Moshe Wertheim was not going to give me a painting, I still felt incredibly grateful to him. If Mr. Wertheim had not reached out to me, I'd never have even known the paintings existed. Without his kindness, allowing me not only to visit, but to film an interview, I wouldn't have seen them in person, wouldn't have known the story behind their recovery, and wouldn't have been able to share them with others. So despite a couple of discordant notes, partly of my own creation, the visit to Mr. Wertheim was a great success. An even bigger success than I thought, because serendipity was about to come into play once again, during my visit to the University of Toronto.

THIRTEEN

University of Toronto

My talk at the University of Toronto was in the late afternoon, two days after my interview with Mr. Wertheim. I admit that prior to the trip, I had spent so much time preparing for the interview that I hadn't thought much about the talk, though I had put together an updated PowerPoint presentation. So the morning of the talk I woke up early, feeling nervous and a bit unprepared. I calmed myself by making small edits and practicing the transitions between slides. At around 10 a.m. I took a break to chat with Professor Cohen, the man who had arranged my talk.

He arrived at my hotel by bike. I immediately liked him. He was a friendly kibitzer—we talked about his morning commute, my time in Toronto, and university life. At the coffee shop—a faculty hangout—we sat at a table in the window and sipped hot tea, which he insisted was his treat. He joked that although the department couldn't give me an honorarium, he could certainly afford to buy me a cup of tea. We both chuckled. We chatted about his research (primarily medieval art), how he'd ended up in Toronto, my great-grandfather's art, Jewish art history, and Holocaust studies. And then Adam shifted gears.

"I want you to know, we've never had anyone ask us out of the blue if they could come be part of our speaker series."

"I'm really grateful you're giving me a chance," I said.

"I'm looking forward to hearing your story," he said.

We parted ways, and I enjoyed the day in Toronto. I took the underground metro downtown to St. Lawrence Market—a food-shopping market hall—and had a leisurely walk back toward the University of Toronto campus. Along the way, I enjoyed viewing famed Chinese artist Ai Weiwei's 3,144 *Forever Bicycles* near City Hall. Then it was back to the hotel to rest and look at my slides before giving the talk.

I always like arriving early to talks—being in the room where I'll speak somehow calms my nerves. Eventually the audience arrived; the crowd seemed friendly and polite. I saw Mr. Wertheim and his wife and said hello. At the appointed time, Professor Cohen introduced me and then I got started. The presentation went well, although there were some technical glitches with the sound system. Eventually I finished up and asked if anyone had questions.

There were a few questions: How long had I been searching? How many pieces had I found? Where was I from? Was I an artist too? Then a woman in the front row asked me multiple questions related to my decision to be a historian and not a claimant. Her questions made me uncomfortable because Mr. Wertheim was sitting in the audience. I glanced at Mr. Wertheim and his wife and wondered if they registered the significance of these questions. They didn't seem to have any reaction at all. I answered that I was trying to build bridges. That I wanted to see the Rynecki art and that if I was a claimant those who had his pieces would be less likely to step forward. I moved on to questions from another gentleman, who wanted to know if I ever considered donating my family's collection to a museum. I told him we'd made donations, but despite our desire to share, it was hard to part with such a personal legacy.

Professor Cohen stood up and said we had time for one more question before we needed to bring everything to a close. I called on a man seated at the back of the room.

"Are you aware," he asked, "that the University of Toronto's Thomas Fisher Rare Book Library has the papers of Otto Schneid, and in its archives are photographs of several of your great-grandfather's paintings as well as original handwritten letters he wrote?"

"Excuse me?" I asked. It was hard to put all that together, and it seemed to come completely out of left field.

"The Schneid archive," he said again. "It has information about your great-grandfather."

"I have no idea what you're talking about," I said. I didn't know what to say, but I couldn't wait to find out more.

Professor Cohen stood up. "We really need to wrap this up," he said to the audience. I had enough presence of mind to lean over to the microphone and speak to the man in the back: "Please don't go anywhere."

"That's Professor Barry Dov Walfish. He won't go anywhere," Professor Cohen said.

As the audience dispersed, I focused on the man at the back, who slowly (too slowly, it seemed) worked his way toward me, and introduced himself.

"I'm Barry," he said. "I'm the Judaica specialist for the University of Toronto libraries. I looked in the Otto Schneid archive index before coming over to your talk. It has all sorts of material about your great-grandfather."

"Who's Otto Schneid?" I asked.

"It's a long story," he said. "If you have time, the Thomas Fisher Rare Book Library, where the materials are kept, happens to be open late tonight. I can take you over if you want."

As hard as it may be to believe, I was in a dilemma of sorts. Of course I had to go to the library, no doubt about it, but I also had accepted an invitation from Mr. Wertheim and his wife to take me out for dinner. So I was torn between my prior commitment (my parents taught me to never break a commitment) and the one chance to see this library collection before my early morning flight back to California. I quickly spoke with Mr. Wertheim and explained I had to go to the library. I asked if he minded postponing dinner for an hour. He understood and told me to call him when I was ready. As I packed up my laptop and speaking notes, the woman who had asked me the pointed questions about Holocaust-era art restitution approached me and handed me her card.

"I'm Fern Smiley," she said. "I'm an art researcher and consultant for Holocaust-era cultural property. Do you mind if I come with you to the library? I sometimes write for the *Canadian Jewish News*."

"Sure," I said. A journalist was a great addition to the mix, but now I desperately wished I had a film crew.

The three of us headed toward the exit. It was raining. I was wearing a cotton Lands' End wraparound dress and chunky-heeled black leather boots, and as we stepped out onto the street a bit after 6 p.m., I realized it was freezing cold. Unfortunately, I had no jacket, no hat, and no umbrella, and no time to retrieve anything from the hotel. I slung the strap of my soft-sided briefcase bag across my chest, letting the bag rest on my backside while my purse was strapped in the other direction and clanked against my thigh. The three of us made quite a sight, as we futilely dodged the rain, continued introductions, and ran toward the library. Eventually we arrived. Out of breath but full of curiosity, I circled the conversation back to the beginning.

"So, Otto Schneid?" I asked. "Who is he?"

"Right," Barry said. "Otto Schneid was born in Czechoslovakia, to Polish parents. He was an artist, writer, and professor of art history. In the 1930s he worked on a dictionary of twentieth-century Jewish artists. It was set to be published in Vienna in 1938, but the Nazis confiscated the plates. In 1939, he was able to escape Vienna, fleeing with his materials and manuscripts to Warsaw. He then made his way to Palestine, where he settled down. Eventually he married, taught at the Israel Institute of Technology, and continued to write and make art. He immigrated to the United States in the early 1960s and ultimately ended up in Canada, where he died in 1974. After he passed away, his wife donated his research materials to the library. The collection includes letters he exchanged with more than a hundred Jewish artists, exhibition catalogs, and photographs of their art."

We entered the library at street level, where we were told to leave our bags at the front desk. Then we took a small, rickety elevator down to the reading room. Still dripping from the walk in the rain, I filled out paperwork that allowed me to access the library archives. Barry disappeared into a back hallway, returning a few minutes later carrying two white archival boxes. I probably wouldn't have remembered standing there except that somehow I had the presence of mind to hand Fern my small digital camera and she snapped photos of me gazing longingly at the boxes while I wondered what was inside. It took all my self-restraint to not just grab the boxes and paw through them. It was like being handed a special birthday gift, but only to look at, rather than unwrap. Was Barry right? Were the contents of the boxes actually about my great-grandfather? Or had he made a mistake and I might soon discover absolutely nothing? I tried to temper my feelings and calm my thoughts, which were bouncing around like a pinball. I managed to relax by focusing on my breathing.

After a few moments that seemed like an eternity, Barry, Fern, and I moved into the reading room. I wiped my hands on my dress to dry them off. Barry set the boxes on the table, and I sat down while he leaned over to open them and started to set things in front of me. I sat and stared at everything Barry placed before me on the table. I couldn't believe what I was seeing. First, there were black-and-white photographs of many of my great-grandfather's paintings, some of which I'd never seen before. There were handwritten letters in Polish with his distinctive

Untitled (Chess Players).
Whereabouts of this painting and whether it survived World War II are unknown.

Szewczyk (Shoemaker).
Whereabouts of this painting and whether it survived World War II are unknown.

signature at the bottom of each page. Even the envelopes that had originally contained the letters were included, with the return address of Moshe and Perla's art supply store at 24 Krucza Street in Warsaw. There was also a handwritten note in Yiddish. Barry translated the first line, "I was born an artist," so we thought it likely was a brief biographical summary Moshe had written for Schneid. In the files there was also a German newspaper article about a "winter salon" exhibit; the article

In Beth-Hamidrasch *(a hall or school where Jews study).*
Whereabouts of this painting and whether it survived World War II are unknown.

The Kabbalist.
Whereabouts of this painting and whether it survived World War II are unknown.

featured photographs of several of my great-grandfather's paintings as well as the work of another artist in the show.

Of all the photographs of paintings I'd never seen before, one in particular caught my eye. It looked so familiar, reminiscent but somehow not the same as something I had seen. I stared hard, trying to remember what the connection was, and then it hit me like a ton of bricks. I had seen this painting before, but the bottom left corner had been torn away.

Prayer *(1927).*

This was what the whole painting had looked like before the war. It showed both my great-grandfather's signature and the word *"Warszawa"* ["Warsaw"].

My head spun trying to process this trove of indescribably precious treasure. It not only was treasure in itself, but it represented the hope of all the undiscovered treasure everywhere—it was a symbol of just how much had miraculously survived. First, I needed copies of everything. I also needed to know more about Schneid and his heirs, in case there was more to the story or more material not included in the archive. Finally, I couldn't believe I had less than an hour to reconnect with Mr. Wertheim. As calmly but rapidly as possible, I snapped photographs with both my digital camera and my iPhone. The librarian explained that if I had a flash drive I could use their book2net kiosk overhead scanner to digitize items. I moved as quickly as I could while following library decorum at least in spirit, race-walking back to the elevator. The trip up the rickety elevator seemed to take a hundred times as long as the trip down. Outside, I temporarily retrieved my bag to get to the flash drive, gave my bag back to the librarian, then took an interminable ride back down the elevator. Then I scanned everything—the black-and-white photos, the letters, newspaper articles, even the envelopes. I wanted all of it. Fern took notes and then said she had to go, but promised a story for the *Canadian Jewish News.*

As I finished up, I thanked Barry effusively. "Now you're part of the story," I said. I took his business card and promised to stay in touch. One more elevator ride up allowed me to retrieve my bag so I could race back out into the pouring rain. As I ran down the street, I fumbled with my phone, trying to call Mr. Wertheim to tell him I was on my way, but I discovered that a touch screen really doesn't work at all when it's wet and your hands are cold and clammy. I arrived back at the hotel, wiped off my phone, and dialed Mr. Wertheim. He said he'd come pick me up in ten minutes—it was just enough time to run upstairs, drop my bags, and grab a jacket.

Mr. Wertheim and his wife took me to a French restaurant for dinner. We chatted about what I'd seen at the library, my quest to find more information about my great-grandfather, and how I might find information in other archives. At the talk it had been suggested that perhaps an exhibit of Moshe's paintings could be brought to Toronto to coincide with Holocaust Education Week—a large event in the city. Mr. Wertheim said he thought that was interesting, but then told me a bit about the Kraków Jewish Cultural Festival that he'd seen several years before; he thought it was a bigger, more important event. That led us into discussion about the return of Jews to Poland and the growing interest in Polish-Jewish history. It was a discussion as much about POLIN Museum of the History of Polish Jews as about where I might find interested audiences and fund-raising sources for my documentary film. As the conversation wound up and we finished dinner, we talked about lighter issues—my children's interests, my husband's work, and the Wertheims' planned trip to Asia. And then the meal was over and Mr. Wertheim and his wife drove me back to my hotel.

"Thank you so much for dinner, and allowing me to visit your home and the Rynecki paintings," I said.

"Our pleasure," Mr. Wertheim said.

"It was incredible."

"Come back anytime you like."

"I'd like that."

I stepped out of the car and into the rain. Toronto, I thought. Who would have ever predicted all that I had found in Toronto? It seemed one of the most unlikely spots imaginable for such a cache. I rushed up to my hotel room to call Dad and tell him all about it.

FOURTEEN

Schneid Archive

"Are you sitting down?" I asked.

"No, but I can be," Dad said.

"You're not going to believe this."

"Okay, now I'm sitting. Did the talk go well?"

"It was great. But what happened afterward was amazing. There's an archive at the University of Toronto with photographs and newspaper clippings of twenty-two Rynecki paintings, thirteen of which I've never seen before."

"I'm not sure I follow."

"I know. I barely get it myself."

For the next thirty minutes I told Dad about Barry Walfish, Otto Schneid, and the Thomas Fisher Rare Book Library. I told him that I'd held an actual handwritten letter my great-grandfather wrote in 1931. Not a copy of the letter. The actual letter.

"It's a good thing you gave your talk in Toronto," Dad said when I finally finished.

"That's an understatement."

"Did you take photos?"

"I got scans, but I am going to pay the library to make higher-quality photos of everything."

"I look forward to seeing them when you get back," he said. We talked a bit more about my trip and made some small talk before saying goodbye.

Among the Otto Schneid papers at the rare book library were two handwritten Moshe Rynecki letters. Schneid had these letters (as well as a typewritten one in German) as a result of his research. In order to write his book he contacted various artists, including my great-grandfather, to request further information on their work. Unfortunately, Schneid's book was never published. First, he intended to publish it in German, but the Nazis halted its printing. He rewrote the book in Hebrew while living in Israel, but for a variety of reasons, it never saw the light of day. Thankfully, Schneid held on to my great-grandfather's letters. The incredible amount of material Schneid managed to save, while fleeing not only from the Nazis, but across Europe, to Palestine, and thence to North America, really spoke to how meaningful the topic was to him. Perhaps it was corny, but to me it felt as if Schneid had saved it all because he knew someday someone like me would come looking for it. Even then, there was yet another stroke of fortune required for me to see the material. I didn't know this at the time, but I found out from the testimony of Otto's widow, Miriam Schneid-Ofseyer, to the USC Shoah Foundation, that she had tried to sell the archive to a private collector.

Taken altogether, it was a tremendously serendipitous chain of events: if Schneid hadn't saved the archive for almost forty years over multiple moves across three continents, if his wife had sold it, or thrown it away, if I hadn't been fortunate enough to give a talk at the University of Toronto, or if Barry Walfish had not seen the announcement or hadn't bothered to look up Moshe's work in the Schneid archive, I wouldn't have had this fantastic opportunity to peer into the past, to get another view of my great-grandfather's life and art.

In any event, Moshe's letters to Otto, penned in beautiful cursive, were visually stunning. Because they were in Polish, all I could do was stare at the smooth loops and dramatic, artistic flair of my great-grandfather's writing. Even before translation, the letters begged to communicate through their artistic expression.

As soon as I returned home from Toronto, I had the letters translated. The first one was pretty straightforward. It thanked the "Honorable Doctor" for his letter of 1 December 1931 and said Moshe looked forward to meeting Schneid on his next visit to Warsaw. "Again I express my hope that at your next visit to Warsaw I will have the honor to welcome you to my home, with the aim of more closely acquainting you with my work." Schneid had apparently reached out to my great-grandfather about seeing his paintings in person, and my great-grandfather looked forward to meeting him and showing him his work.

The second letter, dated just a few days later, was easily translated but much sadder. "I suppose that only a sudden necessity to leave Warsaw explains your absence from my home on the 17th, when you promised to view my works and give me your opinion of them. I am extremely sorry that I did not have the honor to offer you hospitality at my place, but I hope that during your next visit to Warsaw you will be kind enough to visit me. At the same time I am sending 12 photographs of my works, as I promised. I hope that my work will interest you, at least a little."

Had Schneid stood up my great-grandfather? Or maybe something had come up? I wasn't sure how to interpret the tone of the letter. Of course, maybe the letter in English was missing some nuance that existed in the original Polish—translation is notoriously finicky and difficult. But I read the last sentence again and again: "I hope that my work will interest you, at least a little." My great-grandfather seemed so crushed that Schneid had not stopped by. And even worse, he seemed filled with self-doubt that Schneid might not really want to see his work at all.

I wrote Barry and asked to see the portion of the Schneid manuscript that contained information about my great-grandfather. Barry replied, a bit apologetically, that he had reviewed both the German manuscript as well as the Hebrew one and that neither contained anything about my great-grandfather. Even though Schneid held on to my great-grandfather's correspondence, photographs, and newspaper clippings, my great-grandfather had failed to make the editorial cut. Perhaps my great-grandfather had been right to be concerned in the tone of his letter.

At first, I felt bad Moshe was left out, but I soon realized that was silly. The more I thought about it, the more I appreciated how difficult this project must have been for Otto. In a way, if there was a snub of my great-grandfather's work, it was a pale parallel to the snub of Otto's own life work. He carried his material with him for decades, and he had written manuscripts in multiple languages, but none was ever published. The first time, the printing plates had already been constructed; he was literally as close as one could be to being published, but the Nazis destroyed them. To try to recover years later, after the war, to rewrite the material in another language, and be rejected, must have been crushing. I am curious whether he ever considered writing a third manuscript in English, or if it was just too demoralizing to consider. In any event, like Moshe, his career was stolen by the Nazis, although of course he was fortunate enough to escape with his life.

Though I'm sure it was disappointing, being left out of Otto's manuscript had no lasting impact on Moshe's life or work. While it would have been interesting to see what Schneid might have written, the fact that he'd held on to the materials for so many years and that they were now accessible in an archive in Toronto was so impressive that it overshadowed the sadness I felt for Moshe.

In addition to the letters, there was a document written in Yiddish.

It took me a bit to find a Yiddish translator, but not as long as I'd expected. Interest in Yiddish was growing. There were language study programs at many colleges and universities. There were Yiddish music festivals, and Yiddish language immersion retreats in the United States, Israel, and Lithuania.

Surprisingly quickly, I was able to read what my great-grandfather wrote about himself in December 1930:

> *Otto Schneid!*
>
> *I am an artist, a painter, born in the year 1885 in the small Polish town of Siedlce. My name is Moshe Rynecki. I now live in Warsaw at 24 Krucza St. Apt. 9. I studied with Professor Gajewski in Siedlce, and later at the Warsaw Art Academy with Professor Stabrowski and with the painter, Trzebiński, and Professor Herstein. He now lives in Berlin. My specialty is only painting Jewish folk scenes. I have been exhibiting paintings the last few years at the Jewish Art Exhibition in Warsaw at 51 Kralevske St, Society of Encouragement of Friends of Fine Arts in Warsaw, and at the Christian exhibition as well. The Polish press, as well as the Jewish Press, have written a lot about me already. And what they wrote was favorable. I am enclosing a German newspaper and several reviews of my paintings. With much hope that I will be honored by your response.*

The thing I loved about this handwritten autobiographical statement was that in it I heard my great-grandfather's voice. The letter explained his artistic life and career in his own words. For so long I had only had deductions and guesses about his life and how he saw himself. For the first time, I had something of how Moshe saw himself or wanted to present himself, a more nuanced view than I had gotten from studying his paintings and occasional self-portraits. I was greatly moved by his simple characterization of his work as "Jewish folk scenes." Perhaps it was overly simplified, to save time and space, but it came from the heart, and that was powerful to me.

I was surprised to see him say he was born in 1885. Grandpa George always said his father was born in 1881. Although this four-year difference hardly mattered more than seventy years after his death, I was curious about the discrepancy. There were a few plausible explanations, none of which I really liked. Perhaps Grandpa George remembered it incorrectly or purposefully changed it. Or maybe my great-grandfather purposefully misstated his birth year because he wanted Schneid to think he was younger. I searched for a birth certificate by contacting Polish archives, but I was unsuccessful in locating one.

And these new works—well, not exactly new, but new to me—were both reminiscent of everything I already knew about my great-grandfather's work, yet fantastic because they were paintings I'd never seen before. I instantly recognized the people and the scenes in them because they reminded me of other pieces I knew. Of the twenty-two photographs in the Schneid archive, I knew my family had five of the paintings. One painting, a market scene, I knew about because my family had a photograph of it, but not the painting itself. I was pretty sure the Jewish Historical Institute in Warsaw had three more, although there was one I had doubts about. As for the other thirteen—these were pieces that I could only hope had survived the war, and the whereabouts of which I knew nothing about.

The first piece, whose title I didn't know, depicted a building, perhaps a home, in the background. Out front stood musicians, and at the center of the painting a man held a loaf of bread and danced toward a woman and her family. The woman was wearing a white dress, and was presumably a bride on her wedding day. It looked, I realized, very much like another painting, *The Wedding (The Gift of Bread)*, which Grandpa George had donated to the Judah L. Magnes Museum. There was no doubt it was the same wedding. Clearly my great-grandfather had painted the scene at least twice, and had created slightly different

The Wedding (The Gift of Bread) *(1919).*
Whereabouts of this painting and whether it survived World War II are unknown.

versions. I knew artists made sketches and experimented with layout and colors, and that intrigued me, but I suddenly had an unfulfillable yearning to know which piece my great-grandfather preferred and if there were even more versions. I felt grateful for the survival of the black-and-white photograph, but also cheated, because each photo was a reminder of what my family had lost in the war.

The second piece was intriguing because of the writing on it. It looked like Hebrew, but I knew from Barry that the language was Yiddish, which is written using Hebrew letters. The translation, I eventually learned, made it clear this piece was a deathbed painting for Moshe's father. It said, "Avraham Zvi, son of Shimshon, died on Wednesday, on the week of reading the Torah portion, *Acharei Mot-Kedoshim*. Fifth month of the year, 5682 (1922). Siedlce. By his son Moshe Rynecki."

I'd never seen such a deeply personal painting. For me, this painting was not only about the death of his father, but about my great-grandfather's grief. Moshe struggled as a young man to find his own identity, and to pursue his passion for art—a career his father opposed.

On the death of Avraham Zvi ben (son of) Shimshon, 5682 *(1922).*
Siedlce. By his son Moshe Rynecki.
Whereabouts of this painting and whether it survived World War II are unknown.

And yet the loss of a parent, as I knew only too well from the loss of my mother a year earlier, was deeply personal. The painting, it seemed, was a way to mourn the loss, to pay tribute to his father, to stay true to his passion for art, and to say goodbye.

I felt an abiding guilt that I didn't know the whereabouts of this painting. I desperately hoped the painting had survived the war, but it seemed inexorably wrong that this piece might be in the home of a stranger. There was little chance they would understand the personal significance of the piece.

And then I remembered another painting, a companion piece to this work. It was one my great-grandfather made two years later, when his mother died. That painting, I knew, was held by the Jewish Historical Institute in Warsaw. Someday, I thought, these two deathbed pieces should hang together again, as I was certain they once had in Moshe and Perla's apartment on Krucza Street.

So much of the *Chasing Portraits* project was about my pursuit of unknown works. My search for the lost and missing pieces was based on Grandpa George's memoir, and specifically a single line which mentioned Moshe's prolific production of more than eight hundred works. But it was one thing to see that in writing, and another to see numerous photographs of pieces from before the war. The Schneid find confirmed my underlying belief—that if I kept looking, kept making the project known, and refused to give up, eventually more paintings, more records, and more details would surface. It also made me realize something I had been dreading for more than a decade. If I was truly serious about my project, I could no longer avoid going to Poland.

FIFTEEN

Poland

I once read a memoir about a Holocaust survivor who left Poland after the war in a horse-drawn wagon. As she crossed out of Poland, she leaned out the back and spit: a vituperative farewell to her homeland. I don't think my father or grandparents spit on Polish soil when they left, but I grew up knowing they still harbored hostile feelings toward the Poles. Grandpa George wrote in his memoir that he could forgive the Germans, but never the Poles. I'm certain the same was true for my grandmother. I'm not sure about Dad; he was very young during the war, but I did know he had never had any interest in returning to Poland.

My family's feelings were not uncommon for survivors. In the interwar period many Jews considered their Polish neighbors as friends, so when some of these same Poles exposed them to the Germans or refused to help them, survivors became embittered. Clearly, the war was exceptionally difficult for almost everyone. Poland itself suffered terribly. Further, Poland was the only occupied territory that mandated the death penalty for those who helped the Jews *as well as their families*. So it was very dangerous to even be thought to be helping Jews. And yes, even though it was terribly risky, a number of Jews were saved through the efforts of many kind Poles. But my grandparents witnessed a number of Poles who charged Jews steep prices to keep them hidden, a number who would sell them out to the Nazis, and some who would do both. This led to a great disdain for Poland as a whole.

Not surprisingly, Polish sensitivity on this topic is extraordinarily high, and many work to combat the negative wartime stories of Poles by sharing stories of those who did help Jews. Jan Karski tried to warn the world about the nature of the Holocaust. Irena Sendler rescued children from the Warsaw Ghetto, and Jan and Antonina Zabinski hid Jews in the empty cages of the Warsaw Zoo. Again, a number of Poles offered Jews shelter, food, false papers, and more, and those who did these things should be remembered and honored for their heroic efforts. But Grandpa George's personal wartime experience was that no one helped him out unless they got paid. It was probably fair to say that while I didn't personally understand the inconsolable grief my father and grandparents carried with them about all they lost in the Holocaust, I grew up with a sense of anger and, to be honest, a prejudice against Poland. It was a country I knew only through black-and-white photographs and film footage of Jewish ghetto roundups, deportations, and skeletal bodies. Poland conjured up a generation of tragedy and trauma. Frankly, I was afraid to go. Out of fear not so much for my safety, but for my emotional and mental well-being. I was afraid I wouldn't be able to handle the history. I didn't want to think of myself as a "thanotourist," or "grief tourist," visiting places where great suffering and violent death were directly associated with their historical importance. I only wanted to visit if there could be something positive, some hope, and not just grief for the loss, the suffering, the dead.

The Rynecki paintings at the Jewish Historical Institute were a definite draw, as the largest known set of my great-grandfather's paintings not held by my family. I was also looking forward to learning firsthand about ongoing efforts in Polish-Jewish reconciliation. And while I didn't want the trip to be all about the past, ignoring it wouldn't make it go away. As much as I didn't want to address it, there would be value in seeing what remained of my family's history: visiting the remaining walls of the Warsaw Ghetto, retracing parts of Grandpa George's wartime experiences, going to 24 Krucza, site of the Rynecki art store and family apartment. Although I didn't really want to go, I needed to go. And then, if I was really being honest with myself, there was another reason to visit. I was committed to making a documentary film, and I couldn't very well tell the story of my quest for this lost art legacy without actually going to Poland.

"You'll be the first one in the family to go back," Dad said when I told him about the contemplated trip. This wasn't quite true, but almost. Grandma Stella had returned to Poland from Italy to sell things—she once told me nylons—on the black market. I didn't know much about the trip, but I did know that it was unpleasant and she never wanted to do it again.

I knew if I were to go, I couldn't do it alone. There was absolutely no way Dad would go with me. So in November, just a month after I returned from Toronto, I wrote to Catherine (Cathy) Greenblatt, a friend I had met when our sons were in the same preschool class. Cathy had always been interested in *Chasing Portraits* (before it even had that name) and in its early days had helped me brainstorm about the project over Thai lunches near Lake Merritt in downtown Oakland. Cathy knew the story well and would be an excellent consultant, sounding board, and reality check in Poland. She had a strong and varied academic background, with a Ph.D. in History of Consciousness from UC Santa Cruz, followed by work in program development and planning involving a diverse array of literary, arts, and cultural studies. Our shared academic interest in visual arts and Jewish history gave her a deep understanding of my project.

"I am s-l-o-w-l-y starting to think about the possibility of going to Poland in the fall," I emailed Cathy, my hyphens between the letters placed to let her know that even though I was writing the email, I was still reticent.

"Let's talk! I am thrilled by the idea and would like to figure out how to make it work," she replied.

We talked by phone (by that point Cathy had relocated from Oakland to Portland, Oregon), swapped numerous emails, and pondered a trip for the fall of 2014. The final tipping point was an advertisement I saw in *San Francisco* magazine for the grand opening of POLIN Museum of the History of Polish Jews. If we could, we'd use the *Chasing Portraits* film project to attend the opening as part of the press. But before booking tickets to Poland, I wanted to secure permission from the Jewish Historical Institute for access to my great-grandfather's fifty-two paintings.

I had exchanged emails with Teresa Śmiechowska, head of the Art Department at the Jewish Historical Institute, once before, in the summer of 2013, when Richard Sapon-White, the Fulbright scholar, had put together the spreadsheet of Rynecki holdings for me. The exchange had been friendly and Teresa offered to send me photographs of my great-grandfather's paintings. My spirits had been greatly buoyed by the interchange. I told Teresa, "You are the first person at ŻIH [*Żydowski Instytut Historyczny*, the Polish name for the Jewish Historical Institute] who has been so forthcoming and friendly to me." It took several months, but eventually I received an email from Jakub Bendkowski, a member of Teresa's team, with photographs of seventeen of my great-grandfather's paintings. The arrival of the images in my inbox sent me reeling. I used four adjectives to describe my delight in an email reply to Jakub: stunned, THRILLED—yes, I wrote it in all caps—ecstatic, and astounded. It was a momentous occasion, and I savored it before asking for photographs of the other thirty-five Rynecki paintings in the institute's possession.

Planning my trip almost a year later, I had not heard back. I was nervous because I now had a much bigger request. But if you don't ask, you don't get, so I emailed Teresa and Jakub telling them I was coming to Warsaw in October, and that I wanted to see all of the paintings. I wasn't sure how they would react, but Teresa's reply was polite. She said an October visit was not a problem and that I was welcome to visit the institute on the proposed dates. But I had to admit I was not fully reassured. Although Teresa's response sounded pleasant, and Richard assured me she was lovely, I wasn't sure how to interpret her email. It was all rather vague. Instead of proposing a time, and assuring me that the fifty-two pieces would be available for viewing, she had written, "There is nothing to prevent your visit." This left me feeling uncomfortable with what my plan would be if they just forgot about it. From a cost and opportunity standpoint, it had to go right the first time. From an emotional standpoint, everything hung on this moment going well. It's hard now to capture just how anxious I was about my trip. I had anxiety about going to Poland in the first place; if I couldn't capture the hope represented by the largest group of surviving paintings outside my family, I would be devastated. Filming the outside of the institute if they didn't have the paintings available wasn't going to be nearly enough, but I tried hard to remain calm even though I felt frantic. What I wanted was confirmation of details, and I wanted them etched in stone. I obviously wasn't going to get that in an email, so in June I called.

Teresa wasn't in the office. Jakub answered the phone.

"This is Elizabeth Rynecki," I said. "I'm calling about my great-grandfather's work held by the institute."

Jakub was quiet.

"His name was Moshe Rynecki," I said.

Jakub was still quiet.

"Moshe RinEHtski," I repeated, suddenly remembering to use the Polish pronunciation.

"Right, right, of course," Jakub said.

"I'm calling," I said and cleared my throat because I had choked up and felt on the verge of tears, "because I want to confirm that you know my plans to come in October. I want to see all fifty-two paintings," I added, my voice now audibly shaking.

"Yes, yes, we know you are coming," Jakub said.

"I just want to be sure you'll have the paintings out," I said, feeling a lump in my throat and choking back my tears. "This is my one chance to see them."

"Of course," Jakub said. "It's on the calendar."

I thanked him, hung up, and burst into tears. Sobbing, I had a new reason to worry. If I cried this hard in relief, at the mere prospect of viewing the paintings, what kind of emotional wreck would I be once I saw them?

Between June and early October, Cathy and I worked to pull together an itinerary, interview questions, sites we needed to film, and a checklist of moments we needed to capture. By the time we were done, it was a detailed, inch-thick document outlining all we were setting out to accomplish.

I hired a cinematographer, Sławomir Grünberg, the Emmy award–winning documentary filmmaker, for my trip to Poland, and in mid-September he sent me an email. He'd just been to the Jewish Historical Institute. It was, he warned, "a mess and practically closed to visitors." It was to be closed for quite some time—the institute was undergoing a major remodel. He said he'd managed to "smuggle myself inside" and visit with Janek Jagielski, a good friend of his and a historian at the institute. But Sławomir told me not to worry. "We will have to do it the Polish way," he assured me. He signed his email, Sławek.

Worse than bad news, this was essentially my worst nightmare. I was again imagining flying six thousand miles to film myself peering into a window. I crossed my fingers and hoped for it all to work out. If Sławek was willing to do it Polish style, I was too. Whatever that meant.

So it was with a mix of trepidation and excitement that Cathy and I boarded a plane for Poland in mid-October. After a ten-hour flight to

Me on a flight to Poland.

Zurich, a two-hour flight to Warsaw, and a nine-hour time difference, I landed on Polish soil. A long flight, but a journey far easier than the one my father and grandparents had made when they left Poland sixty-nine years earlier.

Despite weeks of planning, I felt nervous for my first interviews at POLIN. My initial visit was eleven days before the museum's inaugural celebration, so both Barbara Kirshenblatt-Gimblett, the program director of the core exhibition, and Renata Piątkowska, the coordinator for the Core Exhibition Planning Team for POLIN, were incredibly busy. I was grateful to them for making time for me, and anxious about the interviews.

My interview with Renata was first. I knew from my research that she had written quite a bit about my great-grandfather and his work held by the Jewish Historical Institute. But I also knew that my family's refusal to loan an original painting from our collection to POLIN had upset her. I started the interview delicately, trying to give the translator I'd brought along a moment to process my words and ask the question in Polish. But Renata didn't need a translator. Her English was fine and the translator never had a chance to ask the question.

As Renata and I tried to get to know each other, I realized that her passion for my great-grandfather's work outweighed any negative feelings she might have toward me. If Renata had any lingering frustration about my family's decision to not loan a painting, it didn't show. In fact, Renata spoke with great passion about my great-grandfather's work for well over an hour. She not only knew his pieces, but understood his contribution in a larger perspective. She was, I realized, the first person I'd met personally who could expertly hold forth about my great-grandfather's artistic style, subject matter, and place in Polish-Jewish history. The Rynecki collection at the Jewish Historical Institute, she told me, "is unique." The core of her message was that my great-grandfather's paintings help us "to think about Jewish life differently."

That my great-grandfather's worked inspired Renata to think about prewar Jewish life differently amazed me. If nothing else had happened on my trip, this interview would still have made it worthwhile and rewarding. That we could come from such dissimilar backgrounds but mutually agree on the insights of Moshe's work filled me with joy. It was inspiring to hear an expert make a strong, passionate argument for the historical importance of my great-grandfather's work.

My other interview at POLIN was with Barbara Kirshenblatt-Gimblett. Barbara wore many hats—as an academic who chaired the department of performance studies at Tisch School of Arts at New York University, as an affiliated Professor of Hebrew and Judaic Studies in the Graduate School of Arts and Science at New York University, and as the head of POLIN's exhibition team. She was intense. A petite and vivacious septuagenarian, BKG (a nickname used by her friends) was a powerful force. Raised in Canada by parents who'd left Poland in the interwar period, she had spent much of her professional career in New York City. Barbara radiated a perspective that was hard for me to parse—a passion for Polish-Jewish art, culture, and history and a deep-seated desire to tell the unfettered story of a thousand years of Polish-Jewish history, a story much deeper and broader than the story of the handful of years of the Nazi occupation and the Holocaust.

I was skeptical about Barbara's viewpoint the first time I spoke with her on the phone. Barbara had contacted me to revisit the discussion of my family lending the Rynecki painting to POLIN, but although the answer remained no, a friendship was born. While I'm sure she was disappointed by the decision, her incessantly upbeat attitude showed through, as she eagerly asked me questions about my quest and the next steps.

"You must come to Poland," Barbara insisted. She wanted me to witness firsthand the interest in Jewish history, the number of institutions celebrating Jewish culture, and for me to see that Poland was evolving away from the static past I'd envisioned. Poland, she assured me, wasn't stuck in the past, but was moving into the twenty-first century at an incredible clip. When, several months later, I finally decided to visit, I emailed Barbara to see if she would sit for an interview. She immediately agreed and said she would be delighted.

I knew my interview with BKG at POLIN had to be short. With the museum opening in days, she had only a snippet of time.

"Where," I asked, "does my great-grandfather's work sit within the milieu of Polish-Jewish art history?"

"What was special about his work," Barbara said, "was that while it was clear he came from a religious family and that he found his Jewish upbringing a great source of inspiration, his paintings showed a traditional world refracted through a modern sensibility."

Given that my great-grandfather was born in the late nineteenth century, "modern" wasn't a word I'd ever used to describe his work. But Barbara was right. Moshe's entire adult life he had one foot in the small town and insular Jewish community he'd left behind and the other in cosmopolitan Warsaw. He lived a contemporary life, and gave his children a home outside the traditional boundaries of the Warsaw Jewish community, but he could never really step away from his traditional Jewish roots. He had an irresistible urge to paint the world he and his family were inexorably leaving behind.

Following my interview with Barbara, I really wished I could see where Moshe worked and painted. Sadly, it wasn't physically possible, because so many of those places simply no longer existed. I could retrace his steps, but the places themselves had been destroyed in the war and rebuilt in new and different ways. As a result, my journey was as much an exercise in imagination and spirit as it was about history. Despite this difficulty, Cathy, Sławek, and I set out to visit many of the places mentioned in Grandpa George's memoir. One of our first stops was on Mazowiecka Street, the scene of one of Grandpa George's close calls in the early days of the Second World War.

"Grandpa George was sitting in his office," I said as we spotted the street name, "reading a newspaper. Three men came in to talk to the receptionist. He sensed something was wrong. He stood up and walked toward the door. As he exited, he heard one of the men ask, 'Where is Jan Trzaska?' He raced out of the building, skipping steps to get to the bottom faster. And then he ran along this street towards Jerozolimskie Avenue."

Grandpa George raced down this street, running for his life. He had compromising papers under a blotter right on top of his desk. If the Gestapo searched, they'd find them and a photograph. He had to run, but in order to get his papers out he returned later, climbing through a window so he wouldn't break the seal they'd put on the door. He lost his stock of merchandise when it was confiscated, as well as his office. But he lived and didn't leave a trail behind.

Just like Grandpa George, we continued down Mazowiecka Street toward Jerozolimskie Avenue and took a streetcar headed south. Unlike Grandpa George, we didn't have the Gestapo chasing us, so we calmly rode the streetcar and enjoyed the day. We got off near Tamka Street, the street where my great-aunt, Bronisława, had had her dental practice.

Bronisława's dental practice was at 29 Tamka, but when we arrived there was little doubt that the building that had housed that address was gone. The site was ringed with fencing, and a new building was under construction.

"Ask the woman across the street if she can help you find the address," Sławek said.

"*Dzień dobry* [jen doughBRAY]—good morning," I said to an older woman I found standing on the corner. "Can you help me find 29 Tamka?" I asked in English, pointing to the map. The woman, bless her heart, wasted no time telling me all about 29 Tamka, the cross street, and much more. At least I think that's what she told me. She spoke Polish, and I understood none of it. I nodded my head and pretended I understood perfectly.

"*Dziękuję* [jenKOOya]—thank you," I told her, and then crossed the street toward 29 Tamka, and past Sławek filming it all.

"Why don't you ask that young couple for directions?" Sławek asked, pointing to a man and a woman in their twenties. "They probably speak English."

I headed up the hill and swallowed my fear to ask, again, for directions.

"Why do you want to go there?" the man asked me in English. I tried to answer, but I started to cry.

"My grandfather's sister had her dental practice in the building," I said.

The couple pointed to the building at the corner.

"It's closed for construction, but you might be able to get into it on this side street," he said, pointing up a side alley. I nodded and thanked him. The couple walked down the hill as Sławek walked up to me.

"Why are you crying?" he asked.

"It's so stupid," I stammered. "I don't even know why I'm here. There's nothing to see. There were Rynecki paintings at this address more than seventy years ago. Why am I here now? There's nothing here. I'm chasing the idea of a painting. I'm too late."

Sławek turned the camera off and I wiped away tears. I really was too late, and I was bubbling over with emotion and not quite sure how to cope with it.

We silently walked up the hill a few blocks toward the Chopin Museum. We didn't have time to visit the exhibition halls, but we popped into the gift shop looking for souvenirs. I wandered aimlessly, idly fiddling with pads of paper, key chains, and assorted trinkets. A souvenir was a token of remembrance, an object to be taken home as a memento of a visit. But I didn't want to take home a new memory—I wanted to rescue old ones, ones that weren't even mine.

We left the Chopin Museum gift shop and walked toward Nowy Swiat (a rather swanky street). Sławek hailed a cab to whisk us away to 25 Szucha (the former Warsaw Gestapo offices). This was where Grandpa George went to obtain papers to travel to Gdynia, to go and check on his fish-import business. While he was there, standing in line, a local pharmacist recognized him and whispered in his ear that he'd best leave immediately or face arrest. Today this was the site of the Mausoleum of Struggle and Martyrdom. A place, I later learned, that was one of the best preserved sites of the Nazi massacre of Poles in Warsaw. I didn't stay long; thankfully, neither did Grandpa George.

Then we walked for a few minutes toward Ujazdowski Avenue, the place where seventy-five years earlier Hitler had reviewed a victory parade of his troops in October 1939. I involuntarily shivered as we passed. From there, it was only fifteen minutes to the site of my great-grandparents' apartment—the building at 24 Krucza.

There was a multistory, glass-clad building at the address, with a bank on the ground floor. This was clearly not my great-grandparents' building. The only thing their building and this building shared was a street address. I'd known for years that the building was gone. Grandpa George wrote in his memoir about it being bombed, and friends had sent me photographs of the modern building that stood in its place. Sławek filmed me at the side of the building staring at its address plate.

"Put your head to the window," he said. "Peer in."

I cupped my hands around my eyes to block the sunlight and to see inside the building more easily.

"What do you see?" he prompted, the camera waiting for my reply.

"Nothing," I said, and stepped away. "There's a reflective coating on the window. I can't see anything."

I literally couldn't see in. But even if I could have, what exactly was it I thought I would see? Moshe wasn't behind the glass. The paintings weren't hanging inside for me to see. What precisely did I think I would find in Poland? Suddenly the trip seemed futile. There was nothing for me at the building. Here again, the past had vanished without a trace. I turned my back to the building. I wanted to leave, but I couldn't. I had scheduled a meeting nearby with Alex Wertheim.

Alex, the brother of Moshe Wertheim, the man I'd interviewed at his home in Toronto, had agreed to squeeze me into his schedule for a quick afternoon tea at a nearby café. I had wanted to go to his home to see a Rynecki painting his brother said he had. He assured me he didn't have a painting, but said he'd still be delighted to meet. And, true to his word, Alex came to 24 Krucza and escorted us to Green Caffé Nero, just two blocks away. It was in the early afternoon, around two o'clock, so the sun was still out, but it was a cool October day, and while we chose to sit outside to have privacy to film the interview, it was chilly. I was wearing a wool coat, scarf, and fingerless purple mittens but was still awfully cold. While Sławek set up his camera, Alex went inside the café to get us both hot tea.

"I already know from your brother how your parents ended up with the Rynecki paintings," I said, "but it would be good to hear you tell it too."

"So the story, as I understood it from my father, is that when war in September 1939 broke, the paintings of your grand-grandfather were coming back to Poland, and the train was bombed, and the Polish villagers, from what I understood, robbed the train, and they had boxes, crates with the paintings," Alex said.

I looked quizzically at Alex. "I've never heard this," I gasped.

"A hundred percent, that's what I remember from my father, and they hid them in the barn. 1945, my father was working in Lodz, in the Jewish community, he was one of the leaders, and one of the villagers came to his office on a horse with a buggy. My father went downstairs, and all the paintings were rolled, and he bought it, all the paintings that were in the crate."

"How many?" I asked.

"I do not know. If I'm not mistaken, around fifty. And then my father said, 'I don't need fifty.' And he shared with his cousin, whose daughter is living now in Israel, and they shared the paintings, between my father and his cousin."

"This isn't what your brother told me," I said, shocked by the variations in their stories.

"What did he say?" Alex asked.

"There are similarities," I said. "But there's no train and there's no box falling off of it." And so I told Alex the story his brother had told me, about his parents walking back to Poland after fighting as partisans in Russia and meeting a farmer who asked if they wanted to buy a bundle of paintings.

Alex shook his head.

"That's not the story you know," I said.

"For sure not. And I heard this story from my father many, many times," he said.

"Are you the older brother?" I asked.

"No, I'm the younger," he said. "That's why my memory is better."

My mind raced. How could this be? Had Moshe Wertheim misremembered the story? Or maybe he thought it would be easier if he simplified it? Or was Alex making up a different version? There were similarities for sure, but the differences were critical. In Moshe's version, the paintings were already at the farmer's home, the implication being that they'd been placed there, perhaps, I'd assumed, by my great-grandfather. But in Alex's version the paintings came back from somewhere, an exhibition he thought, in the early days of the Second World

War, and the train was bombed, and in an opportunistic moment the villagers took the boxes hoping to recover something worthwhile—something valuable they might be able to sell, barter, or even eat. But I didn't know about a 1939 exhibition that would have required the transportation of fifty of my great-grandfather's paintings. If they were on a train, where had the train started and where was it heading? Lodz is west of Warsaw. If the paintings were bound for Warsaw, that means they were coming from the west. But from where? Germany? Czechoslovakia? Austria? Or further? Maybe Belgium, France, or even Spain? My great-grandfather exhibited at the International Exposition in Brussels, but that was four years earlier, in 1935. The pieces of Alex's story didn't add up. I knew most of my grandfather's bundles had each contained fifty to sixty paintings; maybe this was one of his bundles. It seemed like too large a number for an exhibition, unless my great-grandfather was featured, in which case it seems likely I would have heard of the show. And why would an exhibition not have had the works framed? It seemed unlikely they would have been transported so sloppily.

"I am perplexed," I told Alex, trying to remain levelheaded so I might wrap my mind around all the pieces of the story, many of which just didn't make any sense at all.

Alex looked at me, not really knowing what to say. He had told me the story he knew. The story was one he had inherited from his father, and it was more than sixty years old. In any memory, some details were bound to be wrong, some aspects fragmentary or simply misremembered. In this case, the story was secondhand as well. And the big picture was perfectly clear: after the Second World War the Wertheim parents acquired a bundle of fifty Rynecki paintings and then gifted away many of the pieces to others. While I desperately wanted to straighten out the confusing elements of the Wertheim family story, I wanted, even more, to know the location of the other paintings. And if there was one thing both the Wertheim brothers did agree on, it was that their cousin in

Israel had some Rynecki pieces and that neither of them knew where I could find the others that had once been part of their parents' original purchase from the farmer in Lodz. Although Alex was gracious, and tried very hard to be helpful, the conversation capped a depressing day.

The next day, Sunday, we headed out to Koło Bazar, a sort of antique market with a slightly kitschy feel, a place where you could buy just about anything—from furniture and books to chinaware, flatware, and art. It was known to have vendors selling Jewish art. However unlikely it was, I thought there was some chance to find a Rynecki painting at one of the vendors' stalls. That I might actually find a painting seemed pretty crazy, but nothing is impossible. If not, perhaps I would just enjoy the shopping, the people-watching, and the slower pace of the day. Sławek mic'd me and I began asking people for help. I handed them my postcard—five by seven inches, with a photograph of *The Water Carriers* (1930) on one side, and information about the *Chasing Portraits* project on the other. I approached vendors and asked, "Do you speak English?" Sometimes they did, but mostly they didn't. Sławek helped translate.

"I'm searching for my great-grandfather's art," I told several different vendors. "He was a Polish-Jewish Warsaw-based artist in the interwar period. Have you seen his work?" Most just shook their heads. They didn't know my great-grandfather's work. They didn't have anything of his to sell. An older gentleman was more opinionated on the topic.

"It's impossible," he said. "Nothing here is real. It's all fake. You won't find anything."

"Impossible?" I asked.

"Impossible," he said. "Why don't you speak Polish?" he both asked and demanded of me.

"I'm American."

"But Rynecki," he said, "it's Polish."

"Yes," I said. "But I was born and raised in California. I'm not Polish." He seemed confused. And I felt a bit confused too. I thanked him for his time and walked deeper into the market, searching for a Rynecki painting amid the bins, containers, and nooks and crannies of the bazaar.

I didn't see any of my great-grandfather's paintings in the market. I saw some historical items and some Judaica—a sketch of a Jewish wedding, photographs from the interwar period, and history books about the Holocaust. There was a physical market and an audience interested in these items. If a Rynecki painting ended up in a place like this, what sort of chance would I ever have of learning about it? The odds that Rynecki paintings had been sold at places like this were very good; certainly if sales had happened at auction houses, it was more than likely that they would also have happened at flea markets or the like. But the chance that I would be at the right market in Poland on the right day to see one was vanishingly small. Fortunately, not all of the Rynecki paintings in Poland would be as hard to find. I knew exactly where fifty-two were located.

Monday morning I made my way to the Jewish Historical Institute at 3/5 Tłomackie Street in Warsaw, a building that before the war had served as the main library for the Institute for Judaic Studies. While the Great Synagogue that had once stood next door to the library had been destroyed in the Second World War, the library building had survived, although not unscathed. When the precursor organization to the Jewish Historical Institute had been established in Lublin in 1944, it created a historical commission to document Nazi crimes and to collect Judaica, such as books and art. Among the pieces the commission collected were my great-grandfather's paintings. I intended to see all of these pieces, but I was still worried because Sławek had told me before I left the U.S. that the museum was officially closed. And when we arrived at Tłomackie Street, the sign on the building was not promising:

We kindly inform you that from 1 September to
30 October 2014 the Institute will be closed for visitors.

(MUSEUM, LIBRARY, ARCHIVES AND BOOKSTORE ARE CLOSED)
GENEALOGY IS OPEN!

It was the twentieth of October. Ignoring the sign, and hoping for the best, I pushed on the door. I was quite surprised when it opened, and I sighed with relief as I went inside.

SIXTEEN

The Jewish Historical Institute

Inside the lobby there were signs of construction, including tools, dust, and paint cans, but it was otherwise deserted. Ahead of me was a stairwell, to the right a vacant reception desk, and to the left a large map of Poland. I recognized the names of the bigger towns—Warsaw, Lublin, Kraków. I tried to find Siedlce, as if pointing to it on the map might help me better understand the place where my great-grandfather had spent his youth. It was nothing more than a dot among other towns and villages whose names I didn't recognize.

"I'll see if I can find someone," Sławek said.

"Can you find the town where your great-grandfather was born?" Cathy asked.

"It's east of Warsaw and near Siedlce," I said, pointing in the general direction.

"Do you remember the name?" Cathy asked.

"Sure, but I can't possibly pronounce it."

"Something with an M?"

"Medz, Mier, Mmmm . . . ," I said, staring at the map.

Cathy pointed to Międzyrzecze.

"Right!"

Sławek joined us. "Międzyrzecze," he said, the ecze combination rolling off his tongue with great ease.

"You make it sound so easy," I said.

"You should film this," Cathy said.

"Really?" I asked.

"Yup," Cathy said. "It's a good visual."

"Sławek?" I asked. "Let's do it."

And so Sławek turned on the camera and I stared at the map, pointed to the names of towns where Moshe had lived, pointed to his path of travel. I sounded out the Polish words in my head so I might form them correctly when I spoke their names. My ancestors may have been Polish, but I struggled to shape the sounds needed to bring the words to life.

I turned away from the map and back toward the reception desk. A woman had returned while we were looking at the map.

"We're here to see Teresa," I said as we approached.

She looked up, seeming unsure about my presence. The museum was, after all, closed.

Sławek said something to her in Polish that seemed to help. Just as Sławek finished, we heard the clatter of shoes on the stone floor. I turned, seeing a woman headed toward us.

"Teresa!" Sławek exclaimed, rushing forward to hug her with one arm while holding his camera in the other hand. They exchanged kisses on both cheeks.

"This looks promising," Cathy said.

Indeed, it was. Sławek, we would soon learn, was a beloved fixture in the Polish-Jewish community in Warsaw. Because he had produced many films on Jewish topics, everyone knew and adored him. His avuncular disposition and delightfully warm smile inspired jovial greetings from friends and acquaintances. As was already becoming apparent,

Sławek's charm and charisma would open many doors for the *Chasing Portraits* project.

"Come, come," Teresa insisted. "Bring your bags," she said, gesturing toward a door adjacent to the reception desk. "This is our temporary office. You can put your things in here."

Cathy and I followed her into what looked like a staff research library. Bookshelves wrapped around the room from floor to ceiling with titles of Polish and English books and journals on topics of Polish-Jewish art history and culture. I recognized some of the titles from my own research. Three people sat at a large conference room table in the middle of the room, where they quietly worked on laptop computers. At the right side of the room was a largely empty table. The room wasn't small, but with all the furniture and the growing number of people, it was a tight fit.

"I'll go find Jakub," Teresa said, "and we'll bring up the paintings."

"I'd like to come with you," I said. "To film it."

Teresa looked at Sławek. They spoke in Polish.

Cathy and I looked at each other. We had discussed the importance of filming absolutely everything at the Jewish Historical Institute. I hoped we weren't getting off on the wrong foot. We listened to their conversation, and hoped things would play out in our favor.

Sławek turned to me and smiled, his whole face lighting up, giving me much-needed reassurance. We followed Teresa to the far end of the lobby, where Jakub joined us as we went down a set of stairs. We were headed to see my great-grandfather's paintings. It was a path I'd been on for so many years, and now I was actually here. And to know that in just a matter of moments I would see the room where the Rynecki paintings were stored left me speechless. I hastened my pace.

"Slow down," Sławek said. "I want to film you on the stairs." I slowed down, feigning calm, though I felt more like racing than walking sedately.

At the bottom of the stairs was a locked door. Jakub fished a key out of his pocket. As he fitted the key into the lock, I put my hand against the wall to steady myself; I was already getting a bit wobbly from anticipation. Jakub jiggled the key, unlocked the dead bolt, and swung the door inward. I stepped forward, peering into the climate-controlled storage room, which was filled with different cases, metal structures, and bins to hold the institute's collection. Jakub stepped down the few steps into the room and picked up a framed piece.

"Is that my great-grandfather's?" I asked.

He turned the piece toward me. It was the blind beggar, a piece I'd seen in an article years before. It was very exciting to find evidence of a work, to see a photo of or an article on a piece; but it was indescribably joyous to actually see the piece in person, and revel in its continued existence—to enjoy the moment of *knowing* that it too somehow survived.

Teresa and Jakub watched me study the painting.

"I can hardly believe I'm standing here," I said. "I've been waiting for this moment for so many years." I felt emotionally unhinged; I couldn't decide if I wanted to cry or shout with joy.

Jakub and Teresa nodded politely.

I felt incapable of articulately expressing myself, but I didn't really care. It was my moment and no one could ever take it away from me. And then I felt sad because I knew the person who would have understood this moment best was Grandpa George. Searching for the paintings, finding the stories, and trying to reclaim Moshe's legacy—these were all things Grandpa George had inspired me to do. I wished he was there, to share the moment with me, to delight in my getting to see works he once knew so intimately.

"I'll carry it upstairs," Jakub said, breaking me out of my reverie as he stepped past.

I followed him back to the room where we'd left our things. When we arrived, Jakub set the painting down and excused himself to retrieve more paintings. I got my Canon DSLR camera out of my camera bag and tried to photograph the piece. It was awkward, since the piece was behind glass in its frame. In a few minutes, Jakub returned with a stack of Rynecki pieces, and fortunately these were in mats, each piece separated by a protective piece of acid-free paper. Jakub set it all on a table in the corner, then picked up the first piece and placed it on a clear space in front of me.

It felt strange to have so many sets of eyes on me. Cathy took photographs with her iPhone. Sławek filmed everything I said and did. Teresa and Jakub studied me studying my great-grandfather's art. The unveiling of each piece felt pivotal. It was the core reason for my trip to Poland. After all the planning of having a film crew document my journey, I had a strange desire to be in a quiet space, alone with the art. This was a delightful and bittersweet day when I would make my personal acquaintance with my great-grandfather's paintings and then bid them farewell when they were put back into the storage room. It felt hard to share it with all these well-meaning observers. Nothing is ever quite the way you imagine it, but this was exactly what I had hoped for, which is about as good as it can ever be. The people in the paintings leaped into my life, each rushing to tell me their story. The social documentary quality of my great-grandfather's paintings of Jewish life seemed particularly revealing here in Warsaw, in the very building that had once housed the Institute for Judaic Studies. It was the closest I had ever felt to the vanished past depicted in Moshe's work.

Jakub set down a piece of a market scene, a small crowd gathered around a vendor selling fruits and vegetables.

"You can see the carrots," Teresa said, gesturing toward the painting.

I nodded and leaned in to see more details.

"I've seen a photograph of this piece before," I said, "but it was a small reprint in a book. It said it was from Kazimierz Dolny."

"Yes, yes, of course," Teresa said.

"How do you know that?" I asked. "It could be so many places. Why Kazimierz Dolny?"

"This was an artistic community popular with artists in the 1920s and 1930s. Many artists went there for plein-air sessions," Teresa said.

"And you think my great-grandfather went there too?"

"I think so, yes," Teresa said.

"The town hasn't changed much since from before the war," Jakub said. "Of course the population has changed, but the buildings themselves, the layout and structure of the town, they are all quite unique."

"So there's something about this piece that just really says Kazimierz Dolny?" I asked.

Teresa, Jakub, and Sławek nodded.

"Perhaps when I visit next week I will understand," I said.

Jakub continued placing my great-grandfather's pieces in front of me one at a time. Some I'd seen before on Lookgalleria's website and in books about Polish-Jewish art history: chess players, an accordion player, women sewing, a violin player, a metalsmith.

I established a routine. Jakub would place a painting on the table. I'd peer more closely, look at details, observe creases, search for my great-grandfather's signature and date, and then I'd take a photograph. I would hold the camera up high over the piece, where I couldn't actually see through the viewfinder, and snap the shutter. Then I would look at the LCD screen and assess the shot: Was I too crooked? Did I miss a corner? Was it blurry? I tried to take multiple shots of each painting, hoping something would turn out so that by the time I left I would have complete photographic documentation of all the Rynecki pieces in the collection. After I'd taken a photograph of the front of each piece, Jakub would turn the painting over. We were looking for exhibition stamps, or any other clues about the past of the piece. On a number of paintings, we found a stamp indicating the inclusion of the piece at the 1935 International Exposition in Brussels. At a point when everything felt sort of routine, Jakub set down a piece and pulled away the protective sheet to reveal a painting I didn't know.

"I've never seen this one before," I gasped, bending closer to the

Szachisci (Chess Players) *(undated). Held by the Jewish Historical Institute.*

painting, my eyes growing big at the sight of a new work. Well, new to me. Art doesn't speak, not in ways we wish it would talk to us. It whispers its secrets, gently revealing meaning and its mysteries over time. I stood up on my tiptoes and snapped a photograph, then crouched down low to peer at the work from an intimate angle. My physical movements—up and down—perfectly echoed my internal emotional roller coaster of complete delight interrupted with pockets of dread that my visit would inevitably end all too soon.

The style and composition of the piece was familiar, though the work itself was not. The black-and-white ink drawing showed four men, each with a tallith draped over his shoulders, prayer book in hand. Three were hunched over reading while the fourth was engrossed in prayer. Though very similar to a piece I had seen in a newspaper clipping at the Schneid archive at the University of Toronto, its execution was bolder, livelier. There was something lighter, more playful, about this version. Although still a respectful depiction of a religious moment inside the synagogue, it contained delightful line work that gave each of the men likable personalities. I stared, wondering about the evolution of my

Modlacy sie Zydzi (Jews Praying) *(undated).*
Held by the Jewish Historical Institute.

great-grandfather's work. There were clues that the men in these two paintings were the same people, but I had no idea which piece had been done first. Neither work was dated. Had my great-grandfather done the more reverential piece first and then decided to try it again with a more lighthearted approach? Or maybe, since the piece I'd seen at the Schneid archive was from a newspaper clipping, he'd done the more playful one first, but then gone with the more somber one for an exhibit. It was impossible to know. I loved how these two pieces allowed me a peek into Moshe's artistic process.

While we looked at the painting, the director of the museum, Paweł Śpiewak, stopped by to check in on our progress.

"I've never seen this piece before," I told him.

He stepped closer to the table, looked down, and then stepped away. He seemed nonplussed by my pronouncement. I'm not quite sure what he thought I meant, or perhaps he had misheard what I said, because he responded, "We are here to take good care of the art. This is its home."

The Jewish Historical Institute has always felt secure in its mission. During the Second World War, Emanuel Ringelblum and his family were forced into the Warsaw Ghetto. Ringelblum started what he called

Modlitwa w synagodze (Praying in the synagogue) *(undated)*.
Whereabouts of this painting and whether it survived World War II are unknown.

"Oyneg Shabbos," Yiddish for "Sabbath Delight," an underground effort to collect diaries, underground newspapers, documents about life in the ghetto, and art. On the eve of the Warsaw Ghetto Uprising, when the end was near for nearly everyone there, items were hidden in milk cans and metal boxes, and buried in the cellars of buildings inside the ghetto. It was a time capsule, if you will. Ringelblum died in the Holocaust, but after the war some of the archive was recovered. Among the items recovered was some artwork by Gela Seksztajn, who drew and painted portraits and landscapes. She left a will with her drawings. She wrote, "While standing on the verge of Life and Death, more certain that I shall die than live, I wish to say goodbye to my friends and my work. I donate my work to the Jewish Museum to be founded in the future to restore prewar Jewish culture up to 1939, and to learn the terrible tragedy of the Jewish community in Poland during the war." Seksztajn's plea for a museum is a core part of the Jewish Historical Institute's mission—to be the repository and advocate for not only Seksztajn's work, but for other Polish-Jewish prewar artists, like my great-grandfather.

"I appreciate you allowing my visit," I said.

"It makes the most sense for the art to be here," he said. "It is the place where people come to look for Polish-Jewish art. We are glad to have your great-grandfather's works here."

I hadn't brought up the issue of provenance and legal rights to my great-grandfather's paintings held by the Jewish Historical Institute, but I felt Paweł was trying to address the topic by asserting the importance of the museum's mission and purpose. It seemed unlikely that I would have had the same level of access to the paintings if I had asked to see my great-grandfather's art as a claimant, so this was perhaps the best that could be hoped for. While I often yearned for more of Moshe's works, these had a good home, a safe home, in a place with like works and an important purpose. As sad as it was for me to prepare to leave them, I think that Moshe would have been happy for some of his works to be in such a museum.

Paweł left the room and Jakub placed one of the last paintings on the table. I stepped away from the table and looked at Teresa.

"I have something to tell you that's a little hard to talk about," I said.

Teresa looked at me, waiting for me to say more.

"A lot of people, when they come looking for paintings, they're coming to reclaim them," I said. "I'm here not as a claimant," I said, pausing to compose myself, "but as a historian. I want to better understand my great-grandfather's body of work, his legacy."

"Of course," Teresa said.

But I wondered if she really did understand, if she knew how difficult it was for me to look at the paintings and not crave them for my own collection.

"For so long my relationship with the institute has not been particularly good," I said. "I'd like for that to change."

"I am learning things from you," Teresa said. "And this will help me in my own work as a curator."

I smiled. If my visit inspired more attention to my great-grandfather's works—a solo exhibition, a journal article, attention for more lost works—

this was all good. My persistence and perseverance created opportunities for new projects. This excited me.

Sooner than I would have liked, our day at the Jewish Historical Institute was over. It had been an emotional day for me, and Teresa and Jakub had been exceedingly helpful. We would be back again tomorrow to see eight pieces that weren't in storage. I was happy to find out that these were in the art conservation studio being prepared for display in the *Ocalałe/Salvaged* exhibition, which was opening in a few days.

SEVENTEEN

A Tour of POLIN

In the morning, Cathy, Sławek, and I returned to the Jewish Historical Institute to see the Rynecki paintings in the conservation studio. I knew from looking at the work yesterday that the institute took great care of my great-grandfather's paintings. Because many of the Rynecki pieces had been damaged during the war, the high level of care gave me substantial peace of mind. And many pieces in the institute's possession had clearly suffered the same sorts of damage—creases, rips, slashes, and water damage—as the works in my family's possession. I looked forward to observing their efforts to conserve the pieces and extend the life of Moshe's works.

The studio itself was small. I felt awkward invading the space, but the woman working there seemed delighted to have us and more than happy to talk. Because there were so many terms and processes for which she didn't know the English words, Teresa offered to translate and explain the museum's conservation methods. I heard the explanations, and although I didn't understand all the details, the woman's pride in her work was clear. I was extremely happy to see the meticulous and painstaking techniques used to preserve and safeguard each piece.

The Rynecki pieces stacked on the conservator's table included pieces under consideration for inclusion in the not yet opened *Ocalałe/Salvaged* exhibition. The work on top was my great-grandfather's self-portrait. This was the piece I'd first seen years ago on the Polish stock photography website. I moved over to the self-portrait and looked down on it, carefully studying Moshe's face. Perhaps surprisingly, there were no known photographs of my great-grandfather; self-portraits were all I knew of his likeness. I reached out toward his hand, the fingers of his right hand wrapped gently around his chin and the side of his face. His eyes looked kind, understanding. He seemed almost able to see me. Unlike so many of his paintings or portraits, this one showed him in a modern shirt, a button-down. It was a view of him as an artist, an outsider in some ways to the culture he documented. If I could have had just one piece, this was the one I wanted more than any of the others. I loved it, and ultimately this was the painting to which I struggled to say goodbye.

As the conservator prepared to show me the next painting, I impulsively asked Teresa, "Can I hold him?"

The conservator looked at me and then Teresa.

"I'll put on gloves and be very careful," I promised.

"Yes, yes, that's fine," Teresa said, reaching for protective gloves for me to wear.

And then Teresa handed me my great-grandfather's self-portrait, and I turned toward Sławek with an enormous grin on my face. I hardly cared what else was in the stack; if I could just stand all day holding my great-grandfather, I'd be blissfully happy.

The previous night Cathy and I had carefully reviewed the spreadsheet Richard, the Fulbright scholar, had originally put together for me, with all of the photographs I'd later added. We looked at all the paintings

I'd photographed and then made notations by paintings we hadn't yet seen. As we finished photographing, I realized there were some pieces I had thought were held by the museum but weren't. I had a hunch two of them might be held by Maciej, the private collector in New York. I had first spotted the images on the websites of Desa Unicum and Rempex, Polish auction houses, which had listed the pieces for sale, though they had failed to find a buyer. I seriously hoped when I returned to the States I'd be able to track down Maciej and schedule a visit. However, on the spreadsheet there was one photograph of a painting I'd seen in a book, the whereabouts of which were unknown.

"Jakub, where is this painting?" I asked, pointing at the photo in my spreadsheet, of a Rynecki painting I'd first seen in Jerzy Malinowski's book at Stanford. The piece was titled *Modlitwa w Sukot* [*Prayer during Sukkot*].

Jakub looked perplexed. He went to the shelf, pulled down Malinowski's book, and flipped to the index.

"Look," he said, pointing to item number 355. "The first five items in the book are identified as being at the Jewish Historical Institute, but the item you're asking about says that it was printed in *Nasz Przegląd Ilustrowany* in 1937."

I was familiar with the publication. I'd seen different issues and reproductions of my great-grandfather's works in its pages, but I had just assumed the piece was here.

"Well, that's a new mystery," I said. "I wonder if it survived the war."

Jakub looked expectantly at me. "You'll have to let me know if you find it," he said.

"Absolutely."

After two days at the Jewish Historical Institute, we packed up our things and headed back over to POLIN. This time I wasn't going to interview anyone. We were going back to meet briefly with Renata, and to take a tour. She had said during our interview that she'd forgotten to bring along something I would find interesting. Renata met me in the lobby, where she approached with a bundle of papers.

Modlitwa w Sukoth (Sukkot Prayer),
featured in the journal Nasz Przegląd Ilustrowany *(1937, issue 39).*

"I found this while doing some research," she said, handing me a page printed in Polish with a bit of cursive. I recognized my great-grandmother's name "P. Rynecka." The P was either for *Pani* ["madam/lady"] or for Perla. Rynecka rather than Rynecki because in Polish gender is indicated in one's surname and "a" is the vowel at the end of women's surnames.

"What does it say?" I asked.

"It's very interesting," Renata said. "This is an application Moshe Rynecki made in 1934/1935 to the Institute of Propaganda, an organization that promoted artists, to have two paintings included and sold in a salon [an exhibition]. On the application you can see the price he asked for each of the works: 74 zlotys and 150 zlotys."

"And the handwriting?" I asked.

"This is most interesting," Renata said. "The paintings didn't sell, and Moshe has written a note asking that the paintings please be given to his wife, Perla."

"And the other document you've brought?" I asked.

"It's from the magazine *The Synagogue and the Hazzans' World*," Renata said. "It's a publication for cantors. On the cover is this Rynecki painting of a Passover seder. See the Haggadah and the stack of matzo?" she asked.

"It looks like the youngest at the table is asking the four questions," I said.

"Have you seen this piece?" Renata asked.

I shook my head.

"Perhaps someday you'll find it," Renata said optimistically. "Wouldn't that be fantastic?"

I thanked Renata and put the papers into my bag. Our tour group was waiting for us, so I handed my bag to the woman at coat check, and joined Cathy, Sławek, and the others. Our guide explained that the museum had much to offer, and that this two-hour tour couldn't do it justice. Her goal was to highlight the importance of each room and point out some of the unique objects on display.

"You're welcome to look around," the guide said, "but there's a lot to see, so please keep up."

Forty-five thousand square feet is quite large, but given the museum's ambitious goal to share one thousand years of Polish-Jewish history, a substantial amount of history is packed into each exhibit. While I could read the exhibition tags—they were in Polish and English—there were so many new names, places, and dates to track and remember. I found the lineage of Polish kings alone to be a bit overwhelming.

As we explored each of the galleries, I looked for my great-grandfather's painting. Well, the photograph of the painting my family had made available to the museum. But I couldn't find it and when I asked our tour guide, she didn't know its whereabouts. We wandered through the rest of the exhibition, getting lost even in the relatively small portion of the museum dedicated to the Warsaw Ghetto and the Holocaust. As we tried to retrace our steps and find our group, I heard Renata's voice down one of the hallways.

"I can't find my great-grandfather's painting," I said when we came face-to-face with her.

"It's not up yet," she said rather apologetically. "It's supposed to go up tomorrow. But I can show you the exhibit case," she said.

When we finally stood in front of the exhibit case that would eventually hold the photograph of the Rynecki painting, I saw that there were two exhibit tags about my great-grandfather's work. The first tag had the name of the piece, *Wedding*, with the subtitle, *The First Dance*, and the words "Collection of the Rynecki Family, United States. Reproduction." The other was a description of my great-grandfather's painting, accompanied by the words of Grigorii Isaakovich Bogrov (1825–1885), a Russian Jewish writer known for having rebelled against tradition and his family. The quote said, "I sighed with relief when the last official dance with the bride started. . . . All her male relatives, one after another, led the bride many times through the room, during which she may not touch her partner's hand directly—she holds one end of a handkerchief and he the other." And then it said of my great-grandfather, "Moshe Rynecki was born into a Hasidic family. He painted in loving detail the Jewish world he knew so intimately."

EIGHTEEN

Majdanek

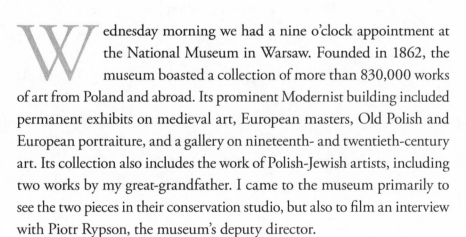

Wednesday morning we had a nine o'clock appointment at the National Museum in Warsaw. Founded in 1862, the museum boasted a collection of more than 830,000 works of art from Poland and abroad. Its prominent Modernist building included permanent exhibits on medieval art, European masters, Old Polish and European portraiture, and a gallery on nineteenth- and twentieth-century art. Its collection also includes the work of Polish-Jewish artists, including two works by my great-grandfather. I came to the museum primarily to see the two pieces in their conservation studio, but also to film an interview with Piotr Rypson, the museum's deputy director.

The museum's conservation studio, quite a bit larger than the one at the Jewish Historical Institute, was lined with a number of storage cabinets and work spaces. The staff was clearly prepared for my visit, as they had already laid out my great-grandfather's paintings on a side table for easy viewing. The woman who brought me to the studio pointed to the two pieces covered with a piece of acid-free paper.

"Would you like to do the honors?" my guide asked.

"Absolutely!" I said, and gently placed my hand on the overlay sheet and lifted it up to reveal *W Parku* [*In a Park*] (1935), a painting showing four men seated on a park bench, one man reading a newspaper, the others holding canes. The painting was somewhat similar to *Krasiński Park* (1930), a work held by my family. I gently lifted the piece and moved it to an empty space on the table so I could look at the other painting, *Talmudysci* [*The Talmudists*] (undated).

I looked at the two pieces for a while, my hands clasped behind my back, but I just couldn't rally much enthusiasm. It wasn't that these paintings were bad, but I was certainly spoiled by the recent bounty of seeing the many works at the Jewish Historical Institute, including Moshe's self-portrait. In hindsight, perhaps I should have visited the National Museum first. I felt guilty. My goal was to find, see, and share my great-grandfather's paintings, not to play favorites.

"Do you know how these pieces ended up here?" I asked.

"I've put out the logbook for you," she said, pointing to the open pages of a book on the counter.

When a museum takes works of art into its collection, it records each and every item. The log contains a description of the painting (e.g., "four men sitting on a park bench, three holding canes, behind them are trees," etc.), information about the condition of the work, and the name of the person who either sold or donated the work. The open page of the logbook contained two entries in regards to the Rynecki paintings, one for each piece.

I put my finger on my great-grandfather's name. Interestingly, the name written in the book was not Moshe, but Maurycy—his Polish name—Rynecki. The entry was, of course, in Polish, so I couldn't read the rest of it. The page was wide and there were multiple columns, at least eleven. There was one for the inventory intake number, one for the description, another for the artist's name, and then there was one that provided information about how the museum had acquired the piece.

On each line for my great-grandfather's paintings that last column said that in 1963 a Mr. J. Żebrowski sold both pieces for a combined price of 2,000 zlotys.

"Who is Mr. Żebrowski?" I asked.

"I'm sorry, I don't know," she said.

"How can I find out?"

"We don't have any other information, and Żebrowski is a pretty common last name."

"Do you know why he sold the painting to the National Museum?"

She shook her head.

"Another mystery."

When we finished looking at the paintings we returned to Piotr Rypson's office. Piotr, though scheduled to leave town in a few hours, kindly made time for me and happily answered my many questions over the next hour.

"It seems odd," I said, "that in 1963 Mr. Żebrowski approached the National Museum in Warsaw with an offer to sell the two Rynecki paintings. I wonder why he didn't try to sell them to the Jewish Historical Institute. Do you know if the National Museum was making an active effort at that point in time to acquire the works of Polish-Jewish artists?"

"It's hard to know," Piotr said. "It does seem a bit unusual and beyond the museum's general acquisition focus. But museum boards and curators change and shift, and so perhaps the museum wanted to expand its holdings to include Polish-Jewish artists from the interwar period."

"Have either of the Rynecki pieces held here ever been included in an exhibition at the museum?" I asked.

"I believe the answer is no," Piotr said.

"Has the museum ever loaned either piece for exhibit?"

"Again, I believe the answer is no," Piotr said.

"Would the museum ever be willing to loan the pieces for exhibition?"

"I don't see why not. The work you are doing is important and we would certainly support you in your efforts."

"Do you know how I might track down more information about Mr. Żebrowski? I wish I knew who he was, how he obtained my great-grandfather's work, why he sold these two pieces, and if maybe he has more."

"Anything is possible," Piotr said, "and I hope you can find him and learn more answers to your questions. But Żebrowski is a common name and with a fifty-year-old trail and little to go on, you might have a hard time finding him."

I nodded. The odds were certainly stacked against me, I understood that. But every piece of information, every clue, might lead to a discovery later.

Later in the day we caught a train out of Warsaw's central train station to Lublin. Tomorrow we would visit Majdanek—the Nazi concentration camp. I felt I must visit Majdanek, but there were few things in my life I had dreaded more than visiting the camp. As I took a window seat on the train, I couldn't help but think about cattle cars loaded up with Jews beyond counting, crushed and almost unable to breathe with the crowding. I stared out the window and thought about those who boarded trains and perished in the Holocaust. As if I were watching a horror movie, but one that was all too real, I always wanted to shout, "Leave! Run! Get out while you can!" to my relatives and so many others in the past. But of course the past is fixed, so I felt hopeless, as if each of the dead was another weight pushing down on me. Eventually, I looked up at Cathy and Sławek, absorbed in reading email on their phones. Somehow, the very normalcy of their actions helped to slowly pull me away from the ghosts of the past and back to the present.

Cathy and Sławek had turned out to be the perfect team. Sławek, a Polish native with U.S. citizenship (he became a citizen when he was caught in the United States on a business trip in 1981 after Polish leaders declared martial law), was affable and easygoing. He didn't exactly hide behind his camera, but it gave him the perfect cover to quietly observe the world. I loved that everything with him was understated. In fact it wasn't until several days into filming that he told me he'd come into his Jewishness later in life. And Cathy, like me, was a Reform Jew, a cultural Jew. Both of us, slightly nerdy ex-academics, were just as likely to discuss a *New Yorker* article as we were to share stories about our kids. I was fond of the small team I'd assembled.

"Cathy?" I asked.

She looked up.

"Look," I said, and pointed out the train window. "It's raining."

"Really?" she asked. "We've had perfect weather up to this point."

I nodded.

"You okay?"

"I guess." I leaned my head against the glass and looked out the train window as the city gave way to suburbs and then fields. The view alongside was just a vague blur of green as we sped through the countryside.

We arrived in Lublin around 7 p.m. and were met by both a steady cold rain and Lublin native Dariusz Baran, an old friend of Sławek's. A tall, balding man with broad shoulders and a short, gray beard, Dariusz greeted us with hugs and inquiries about our well-being. His English was excellent and he was happy to chat, but Cathy and I could tell he really wanted to catch up with Sławek, whom he hadn't seen in many years. The most comfortable and quickest way for them to chat was in Polish, so we told them to go ahead, we understood.

Dariusz drove us to our hotel, the Rezydencja Waksman Hotel on Grodzka Street. Grodzka Gate, known as "the Jewish Gate," once was the passage between the Christian and Jewish parts of the city. We left our bags at the hotel and walked along Grodzka Street, a moderately steep, cobblestone road with old stone buildings and narrow alleys, toward a place Dariusz had recommended for dinner.

"It's a Jewish restaurant," Dariusz told me.

"A Jewish restaurant?" I asked.

"It's called Mandragora," Dariusz said.

Cathy and I looked at each other and shrugged. What we'd experienced of Jewish life in Poland so far was chasing ghosts in Warsaw. I have to admit I wasn't clear on the concept of a Jewish restaurant. The only Jewish restaurant I could conjure up in my mind was a classic New York City deli.

"Some Polish people really miss the Jews," Dariusz said, as we started to cross the rynek, the town square. "Some young Poles feel guilt for the deeds of their ancestors; others feel a nostalgia for the neighbors they never knew. Some study Hebrew, attend religious services, and help maintain Jewish cemeteries. Others enjoy eating traditional Jewish foods. And here it is," he said, pointing toward Mandragora, a cute little restaurant with a menorah in the window.

Once we entered the restaurant, we were quickly seated by the hostess and handed thick menus detailing the restaurant's offerings, which included Jewish herring with almonds and raisins, fried chicken liver, chicken soup with kreplachs (Jewish dumplings, the menu assured us), latkes, Jewish duck ("Half duck stuffed with apples, glazed with honey, served on carrot tzimmes. A dish prepared for all family celebrations," the menu said), and gefilte fish.

"I can't decide if it's cool or totally creepy," I said to Cathy.

"Have you seen the mural?" she asked.

I looked at the drawings Cathy gestured to across the dining room—a wall scene showing five or six men, with beards, hats, and long coats. The men were all dancing—their hands in the air, their right feet forward, and their bodies animated to indicate they were in motion.

"I don't think I've ever felt more Jewish in my life than these last few days," Cathy said.

"Really?"

"Maybe it's just that everything makes me feel hyperaware of being Jewish."

I nodded. I knew exactly what Cathy meant. At home my Jewishness, even my more secular form of Jewishness, was a part of me, but not something I was always keenly aware of.

"Is it appropriate to eat at a Jewish restaurant the night before we go to Majdanek?" I asked. "It feels wrong."

"What are you ordering?" Cathy asked.

"Latkes."

As we waited for dinner, Cathy and I continued to take in the restaurant's kitsch, and Dariusz and Sławek chatted amiably in Polish.

Soon enough the waitress approached the table carrying a number of dishes. One of them seemed suspiciously overburdened with food. Sławek, Dariusz, and Cathy looked up as the waitress put down in front of me a plate filled with many large pancake-sized latkes.

"This is my order alone?" I asked. Sławek and Dariusz laughed.

"I hope you're hungry," Sławek said. "Hold up the plate. I'll take a picture."

"But then she'll post it on Facebook!" Cathy said, both laughing at me and egging me on. I was, despite Cathy's best efforts to resist, slowly chipping away at her negative outlook on Facebook and Twitter. A mostly private person, Cathy was beginning to see that it was sometimes fun to share behind-the-scenes moments of the *Chasing Portraits* journey on social media. Although her short brown hair and angular glasses projected the image of a bookish, studious, and contemplative woman, she also had a strong whimsical streak.

I held up the plate of latkes and Cathy leaned in too, both of us laughing while Sławek took a picture with his iPhone. But then I turned serious.

"My extended family murdered, everything taken, lost, destroyed, my dad and grandparents barely made it through the Holocaust in one piece, and now I'm eating latkes in Poland."

"It is strange, isn't it?" Cathy said.

"I'd say." I tried to stay in the present, but as I had on the train, I started to feel the pressure of the past all around me.

As much as I had not wanted to come to Poland at all, I *really* didn't want to go to a Nazi concentration camp. I had had a bad experience with the Holocaust Museum in D.C., and that was with just displays of objects taken from camps. This prospect seemed more than scary; it was nauseating.

But for Jews visiting Poland, visiting a death camp had become obligatory. It was both a physical and emotional journey, providing a connection to their identity and to one another through the shared horror of the past. For some the camps were primarily evidence of the crimes, a memorial to those who perished, and an opportunity to remember. I felt obliged to visit Majdanek, but I was reluctant to do so because I feared its emotional power.

Majdanek is not as well-known to most people as Auschwitz and others, although it was the first camp to be liberated—by Soviet troops on July 23, 1944. Originally established as a forced-labor camp, it became an extermination camp in the spring of 1942 when three camps built specifically to murder Jews (Belzec, Sobibor, and Treblinka) could not handle the large Jewish populations in southern Poland. The well-preserved gas chambers and ovens in the crematorium told part of the story.

It was written in some places that my great-grandfather was murdered at Treblinka. This was a guess based on a historical chronology of events and the fact that a preponderance of Jews were deported to Treblinka before the Warsaw Ghetto Uprising in April 1943. According to the United States Holocaust Memorial Museum's website, of those who survived the uprising, "the Germans deported about 7,000 more Jews to Treblinka, and about 42,000 to concentration camps and forced-labor camps in the Lublin District. . . . Of this group, approximately 18,000 Jews were sent to the Majdanek camp."

I knew the odds my great-grandfather had survived the Warsaw Ghetto Uprising and had been deported with the group of Jews sent to Majdanek would be slim in the absence of other evidence. But I knew from Perla and Grandpa George's stories, and the timing of Perla's escape from the ghetto, that Moshe's survival until the uprising was pretty clear. And of those who survived the uprising, a substantial portion went to Majdanek. I also had another very important piece of evidence. Grandpa George's memoir said Perla received a postcard from Moshe telling her he was well and hoped to paint at Majdanek.

I wrote to the Majdanek Museum before coming to Poland, both to request permission to film for the documentary and to ask if they knew anything about my great-grandfather. Permission to film was granted, but in regards to my great-grandfather, they knew nothing. Of course, records from the war were spotty at best, so that told me very little. It would have been nice to have independent confirmation, but as with so many things from the war, certainty was hard to come by. The best evidence I had suggested that Moshe died at Majdanek, so to Majdanek I went.

On Thursday, October 24, I woke to steady rain and a blustery wind. It was almost absurdly appropriate; I don't think I could have imagined visiting a death camp on a beautiful sunny day. Cathy, Sławek, and I ate a quiet breakfast in the hotel. The stress of the trip had gotten to me; I felt sick—my throat hurt and my voice was hoarse. Cathy and Sławek both expressed concern and insisted I drink some hot tea. When we packed up for the day, I put on as many layers as I could—a wool hat, mittens, and my mother's yellow rain jacket with the hood pulled up over my hat.

"Are you going to be warm enough?" Cathy asked, eyeing my attire.

"I hope so."

"We should get an umbrella," Sławek said.

"Maybe the hotel can loan us one," Cathy said.

"I'll ask," I said, spying a few umbrellas in a stand by the front door.

Sławek opened the front door of the hotel and looked worried. With sheets of rain coming down and the wind whipping against the building, he was understandably concerned about his camera getting wet. I convinced the receptionist to loan me a small umbrella and tried to hold it over Sławek as we darted out the entryway and hailed a cab. We asked the driver to first stop at a drugstore, where Sławek consulted the pharmacist in Polish and then insisted I buy an abundance of cough drops and tissues.

The visitor center at Majdanek was a modern building with large glass windows overlooking the length of the camp. From inside the building I saw barbed wire fences, guard towers, fields of green, a few buildings, and two large monuments—an enormous, abstract stone sculpture at the camp's entrance and a large mausoleum holding the ashes of the victims at the opposite end. I introduced myself to the man behind the desk. He told us which areas were off-limits to filming and asked us to be respectful of the site.

The Monument of Struggle and Martyrdom at the entrance to Majdanek is gargantuan: a wide, squat structure with two small pillars as a base, apparently struggling to resist the massive weight above. Its dark form was intended to evoke the gates of hell, but it struck me as equally about the crushing weight of memory. The sculpture was dedicated in September 1969, exactly thirty years after Germany's invasion of Poland and less than two weeks after I was born. An abstract form on a hillside, its base was a gateway for visitors into the open fields and barracks below. I felt an almost irresistible desire to turn back, but I managed to keep my feet plodding forward.

Cathy tried to hold the umbrella over Sławek as we walked along one of the trails to a barracks off in the distance. But the wind picked up, and in a matter of moments the umbrella turned inside out. I stuck my hands deep into my raincoat pockets. Soon my fingertips lost feeling and my leather boots were soaked. My cold, wet feet, numb fingertips and toes, and the driving rain on my face only heightened the dread and helplessness I felt inside. I couldn't imagine being in this environment, even during the "work camp" era of Majdanek, with inadequate clothing and food, to say nothing of backbreaking work and abusive guards. It was hard to imagine surviving a single day here, much less months or years.

The weather made my pilgrimage to Majdanek even more isolating and solitary, though I was with Sławek and Cathy. I walked, head bent forward against the wind and rain. I stopped between two guard towers to peer through the barbed wire fence and the downpour, toward buildings in the distance, outside the camp. I put my hand on the barbed portion of the fence, its sharp points threatening my fingertips. There was nothing particularly haunting or horrific about the scene in and of itself; the context I brought with me made it so. After a time, I let go of the barbed wire and turned toward Sławek. He said something which I couldn't hear because the rain was so loud. Realizing I couldn't understand, he gestured that he wanted to head toward the barracks, and I followed.

Once inside the small, plain wooden building, I appreciated the respite from the rain and wind. The building we stepped into had bunks—stacked wooden platforms, really. I knew from photographs I'd seen of prisoners held in other camps that the wood platforms were all prisoners had had to sleep on, and they shared these spaces with far too many others. There were no mattresses, no pillows, no down comforters or even threadbare blankets to keep them warm. There was no privacy, and little comfort save the presence of shared hardship. I pondered the stark living conditions and bleak prospects of the prisoners and then headed back out into the elements.

It was hard to tell where I was going. Between the rain, wind, and my increasingly frozen feet, I focused on following Sławek. We went into another nondescript wooden building. It was dark inside, and it took me a while to figure out where I was. When I finally realized what

I was looking at, I wanted to flee. Inside were rows of metal wire cages from floor to ceiling, filled with shoes. It was endless, the individuality of each shoe utterly lost in the monstrosity of what each represented. I tried to deny the nameless and faceless monument the shoes presented. I tried to find unique characteristics in shoes—to acknowledge and memorialize people rather than the mere numbers who were murdered. But it was impossible.

There was an easy exit at the United States Holocaust Memorial Museum to escape when I felt overwhelmed. There was no easy way out at Majdanek. I came to know the horror of the Holocaust in a new and more personal way here. The buildings and preserved artifacts were an actual link to incomprehensible numbers of people, families and children, who had suffered and died here, in a nondescript bunch of buildings behind a barbed wire fence. I felt like I was reaching my breaking point, which was a problem, because though I could feel the death around me, this was the easy part. I hadn't yet seen the crematorium.

Cathy, Sławek, and I went back outside. We looked toward the crematorium, which was near the other end of the camp. They weren't ready for a walk in the rain either. We saw a sign for a museum—a heated space with a photographic exhibition about the camp. I felt a wave of guilt that I couldn't handle the weather or my feelings. Clearly, the prisoners had never gotten a break. We went inside anyway.

It was warm in the museum, and I discovered that there was a bathroom with a hand dryer. I turned it on again and again, trying to defrost my fingers and my boots. I felt like I was cheating. Of course, getting sicker in some pale imitation of solidarity was also misguided, so I tried to take care of myself. In the museum's historical exhibition and education center there were photographs, documents, stories, and information about the camp, guards, and prisoners. While the entire outside museum of Majdanek relied on knowledge the visitors brought with them, the inside space tried to commemorate victims, by showing preserved relics and documents associated with the camp. Camp officials had already told me they had no information about my great-grandfather. I looked anyway, hoping against hope for the unlikeliest of clues—sketches, signatures, anything that suggested my great-grandfather had been here—but I saw nothing.

After looking through the exhibits, we went to the shower rooms. For the first time in the camp, we were not alone; there were multiple groups of students from Israel there, many carrying the Israeli flag. A large number of them were seated on the floor, and group leaders spoke to them in Hebrew. I walked around them and moved farther into the building. I looked at the shower fixtures installed in the low ceiling and thought of how the Nazis had dispersed Zyklon B, which they used to murder so many. I wanted *out.* I wanted to leave right then. But there were no exit doors. To leave this space I had to, once again, walk through the middle of these large groups of students. I felt like I was trespassing in their space, though of course that was absurd. I was desperate for fresh air, torrential downpour and all.

"Can we leave now?" I asked Cathy.

"We need to go to the far end, to see the crematorium and mausoleum memorial."

"Can't we skip it?"

Cathy just looked at me. I knew she was right, though I wasn't happy about it. I pulled the drawstrings of my hood tighter and tried to wiggle my toes. I couldn't feel them at all.

"Let's get this over with," I said, and began the long trek down to the far end of the Majdanek complex.

The crematorium itself could be seen from far away—the brick chimney towered over the smaller wooden buildings it served. Inside, the crematorium was a row of four or five red brick ovens. The doors to the ovens on some were open and others were closed. There was a crowd here, and the teeming humanity felt oppressive. I looked at the front of the ovens and then walked around to the backside. I felt extremely nauseous. I had seen enough. I was more than ready to leave.

"We should film you here," Sławek said.

"Is it really necessary?" I asked.

Sławek nodded.

"Cathy?" I asked.

Cathy nodded too.

I hated their answer, but I trusted Cathy and Sławek. I was too close to the moment, and it was emotionally too difficult for me to judge anything given my state of mind. We got the shot relatively quickly, and I was intensely relieved to be back out in the cold and rain a few minutes later.

Nothing quite prepares you for visiting a Nazi extermination camp, and there aren't any crib notes for how to reenter day-to-day life. A quick cab ride later, and we were physically back to the heart of Lublin's old Jewish quarter, where we dried off and warmed up. My mind could not keep up; the transition was intensely jarring. I struggled to compose myself inside, before meeting Piotr Nazaruk for lunch.

Piotr was a Facebook friend I had met through a group dedicated to helping those interested in Jewish heritage in the towns of Łuków, Międzyrzec Podlaski, Siedlce, Radzyń Podlaski, Biała Podlaska, Łosice, and Łomazy. I had originally joined the group to search for information about Moshe's parents, who I thought might be buried in Siedlce. Piotr offered to help me, and although he couldn't find any information about their graves (they died of natural causes in 1922 and 1924), he tracked down information from Polish archives and even discovered some photographs of Moshe's paintings that I hadn't seen, in Polish and Yiddish newspapers. We had only been online friends for about seven months, but he'd been so helpful, I felt like I'd known him for years.

Piotr joined us for a lunch of *zupa grzybowa*, my increasingly favorite Polish mushroom soup, and pizza. As curious as Piotr was about the Polish-Jewish past, I was equally curious about why Piotr, a contemporary, non-Jewish Pole, was so engrossed in Jewish history. He explained that he had grown up in a town where there once were many Jews, but now there were none. Somehow, though the war happened before he was born, he keenly felt their absence. He felt a deep sorrow for the transgressions that had occurred in his town and an obligation to remember and memorialize those who had perished. His town's history was intimately tied to Polish-Jewish history and he wanted to rescue it. If not him, then who would? So he started searching archives for information about the Jews who had once lived in his town in eastern Poland. He even taught himself the Hebrew alphabet so he could read and translate Yiddish newspaper articles.

After lunch we all went to visit Brama Grodzka Gate Theater, an organization housed in the actual Grodzka Gate. With a small but dedicated team, the cultural institution brought stories of Lublin's Jews to the people of present-day Poland. Their physical presence, their archival research, and their performance art—a form of interactive storytelling—were all dedicated to engaging Lublin residents about the city's Jewish past. Both a metaphorical and physical bridge to the past, Grodzka Gate Theater worked to reclaim Lublin's lost history.

There was something profoundly heartfelt about Grodzka Gate Theater's indomitable spirit and passion to make Lublin's Jewish past culturally relevant. It made the ghosts and dark shadows at Majdanek feel a little less oppressive. I was inspired to see others also searching for a way to make the past relevant. It gave me hope for my own project, and enhanced my feeling that Moshe's art was meaningful to contemporary Polish and Jewish communities. That optimism buoyed my spirits as I left Lublin and headed for Kazimierz Dolny.

NINETEEN

Kazimierz Dolny

My favorite line about the historical importance of Kazimierz Dolny comes from *The River Remembers* by S. L. Shneiderman. He wrote, "The Vistula is to Poland what the Mississippi is to America and the Volga is to Russia." In one sentence Shneiderman helped me understand the town's reliance upon the Vistula as a hub for commerce, industry, and transportation. But Kazimierz Dolny is also stunningly beautiful. Nestled on the banks of the river, its gently rolling hills are dotted with whitewashed facades and red-tile roofs. Its visitors delight in its historic architecture and cobblestone streets, strolling along the dusty river path, touring the ruins of medieval Kazimierz Castle, or exploring the nearby gorges.

In the early twentieth century, the Warsaw School of Fine Arts sent groups of students to the historic town of Kazimierz Dolny for plein-air workshops. The quaint town appealed to the professors and students used to city life, and it gave them an opportunity not only to admire the Polish countryside, but to paint it, and live, at least for a time, surrounded by its charms. One of the artists believed to have painted in Kazimierz Dolny in the interwar period was Moshe. I'd come to step back in time and see a place where my great-grandfather once found inspiration.

By the time Dariusz, the same man we'd eaten dinner with in Lublin the night before, delivered us to the town square, it was dark and we couldn't see much. We grabbed our luggage and checked in at Dom Architekta, a hotel on the north side of the *rynek*, or market. The lobby was deserted, and when we finally found the receptionist, she told us we were the hotel's only guests. Not surprisingly, a rainy Thursday night in Kazimierz Dolny in the middle of October didn't hold as much appeal as a sunny midsummer stay.

I had promised Dariusz dinner at our hotel, a place Sławek recommended, as a thank-you for driving us all the way from Lublin. As we sat down around the restaurant table, he handed Cathy, Sławek, and me packages of something wrapped in clear plastic wrap.

"It's from Piekarnia Sarzyński bakery," Dariusz said. "It's a bread-dough rooster."

"It's too beautiful to eat!" I said.

"Others make them," Dariusz said. "But this is the best in town."

"I'm saving mine for breakfast."

Friday was market day in Kazimierz Dolny, and farmers arrived early to set out their goods. Off the backs of trucks came colorful assortments of flowers, vegetables, and fresh fruit. The market wasn't very big. There were just three rows of vendors arranged around the historic wooden well at the center. Given that it was October and early in the day, I had the market almost entirely to myself for quite a while. I walked up and down each row, looked at the trucks, the produce, the spreads on the tables, and tried to imagine a scene from a summer day with a painter's easel set up nearby. I wandered over to a smaller souvenir market around the corner—a market with clothes, hats, and bric-a-brac. I bought a hat. And then I spied something I'd read about online, but never managed to see in Warsaw—a Jewish figurine. About four inches tall and made of some sort of polymer clay, the figure wore a top hat, had a big beard, visible *payos* (the Hebrew word for sidelocks), a long black jacket, and under his coat, a tallith. In his left hand he held a coin—a grosz, the Polish equivalent of a penny.

I'd never seen my people, my ancestors, Jews, represented as figurines, though I had heard about it. I'd heard that the most common set of instructions were to place the figurine near the front door of your home and at the end of the week to shake him upside down so that all the money he'd attracted would fall out, thereby bringing the household luck in the financial department. Some have said Jewish figurines are offensive, that they stir up racism, and the ones holding coins ("the lucky Jews") contribute to a negative stereotype of the money-grubbing Jew. At the other end of the spectrum are those who believe the figurines are meant to pay homage to the Jewish people—the figurines help recall the past, when 3.3 million Jews accounted for approximately 9 percent of the Polish population. Neither end of the spectrum seemed particularly persuasive to me, but impulsively I bought the figure anyway. I don't generally like collectibles, but I do have a strong sense of irony. Even now, though I purchased it as a darkly humorous conversation piece, I have mixed feelings about it.

In any event, with the figure wrapped safely in my purse, Cathy, Sławek, and I headed off for the Vistula Museum at Kazimierz Dolny. I had scheduled a meeting with the director, Agnieszka Zadura, and former director, Waldemar Odorowski. Sadly, I'd missed the 2008 museum exhibition, *In Kazimierz the Vistula River spoke to them in Yiddish . . . Jewish painters in the art colony of Kazimierz*, which featured six of my great-grandfather's paintings (from the collection held by the Jewish Historical Institute in Warsaw). I hoped Waldemar, who had researched, coordinated, and written a portion of the catalog for the exhibit, might have evidence that my great-grandfather painted at Kazimierz Dolny.

Waldemar didn't speak English, and it's very difficult to have conversations requiring a translator. You lose the rhythm of the dialogue and you're constantly waiting for your turn without knowing what's being said to you. It's confusing. But Agnieszka patiently translated for both of us, and Waldemar kindly tried to explain the significance of the cultural phenomenon that was the Kazimierz Dolny my great-grandfather once knew. The idea of an art colony in Poland in the interwar period was, Waldemar explained, incredible in and of itself. What made Kazimierz Dolny a special place was that it really was just about the only place in Poland where Polish and Jewish artists worked together. For centuries the Poles and the Jews had shared a homeland, but with separate and parallel lives. That Jewish artists could be known simply as Polish artists was practically unthinkable. And yet that's exactly what happened at Kazimierz Dolny. The Jewish artists who came to the town for summer painting sessions temporarily left behind the growing anti-Semitism in the cities and shtetls. In the countryside they escaped prejudice and were able to focus entirely on their art, without regard for their nationality, religion, or culture.

I nodded my head. I understood. Well, at least I thought I understood the draw and appeal of Kazimierz Dolny.

"But even if my great-grandfather came to paint in Kazimierz Dolny," I asked, "what makes you think that he painted the market here? Why might it not be a market in another town?"

Waldemar opened the exhibition catalog to a page showing three of my great-grandfather's paintings. He gestured to the buildings in the paintings, trying to emphasize their unique architecture. Then he pointed to the center of one of the pieces and Agnieszka translated. "Doesn't that look like the wooden well?" she asked.

I peered to where she pointed. I wasn't sure. But it was true there was an incredible amount of architectural detail in this painting. I could think of no other Rynecki paintings with this level of structural detail. But were they Kazimierz Dolny's buildings?

"Many of the town's buildings are legally protected historical monuments. The town considers them cultural assets," Agnieszka said. Once some of the unique features were pointed out, I could see how, correcting for time and changes in transport, the market outside my breakfast window looked very similar to the market in my great-grandfather's painting.

After the interview I went for a walk on a trail along the eastern bank of the Vistula River. From the path I could see how the town's mountain ranges and verdant valleys helped create an idyllic life for the summer artists-in-residence. It was a bucolic place, and the spirit of Kazimierz Dolny, it seemed, had a rather mystical quality: a landscape that apparently had the power to unite Polish painters and Jewish painters in their common love of art.

Initially I hadn't wanted to come to Kazimierz Dolny. It seemed an indulgent side trip with no solid connection to my great-grandfather. But now I was glad I had come. I was beginning to understand why my great-grandfather would have felt compelled to paint here. There was solace in this place, and I easily imagined how artists must have been seduced by its charms.

TWENTY

Playing Ball

Chasing Portraits is the physical search for my great-grandfather's lost and missing artwork, but you can't just show up in a city and start ringing doorbells hoping to discover a lost painting. My homework and research before coming to Poland involved tracking down leads and following up on potential sources so I could make the most of my trip. That included years of searching the Internet, Polish museum catalogs, auction indexes, and art databases. But a lot of what I found consisted of hints or clues about a painting, or images of a painting that might have survived. Some of the information conflicted, so it was hard to know how the pieces of the puzzle fit together. In the time leading to my trip to Poland, I pored over every clue, to be as well-informed as possible about what I might see, and about what other works might have survived, and where I might go to gather more clues as to their whereabouts. Several months before coming to Poland, I had found myself confronted by a particularly baffling mystery.

Gra w Piłkę (Playing Ball) *(undated). Held by the Jewish Historical Institute.*

On my computer monitor were, side by side, two paintings. On the left was a scan of an ink drawing from a book by Artur Tanikowski about Jewish painters in Poland. The credit said that the title of the piece was *Gra w Piłkę (Playing Ball)* (undated), and that it was held by the Jewish Historical Institute in Warsaw. The image at the right was the same scene, but this drawing, also titled *Gra w Piłkę*, sold in 2009 on Allegro .pl, an online auction website in Poland. I tried to figure out if it was the same painting, if maybe the Jewish Historical Institute sold the drawing from its collection, or if it was somehow a slightly different piece. Perhaps it was a drawing of the same scene, but a slightly different take.

My eyes shifted back and forth between the two pictures, trying to spot differences, and soon I was able to pick out some. For starters, the composition, the way the image was positioned on the piece of paper itself, was different. On the work held by the Jewish Historical Institute, the image filled the paper. In the work sold on Allegro, it did not. And then there was the fact that the artistic quality of the piece held by the Jewish Historical Institute seemed stronger than the workmanship in

Gra w Piłkę (Playing Ball) *(undated). Painting held by the Rynecki family.*

the Allegro piece. At first I considered that maybe it was a problem with how each image had been photographed. The truth was that the images were small, low-resolution, and grainy, and thus hard to compare. I shifted my gaze to the signatures. In the Tanikowski book I instantly recognized the familiar way my great-grandfather signed "Rynecki." But when I looked at the signature in the Allegro piece, I was less certain. It looked funny, just a little off. Letters seemed to be missing. The "n-e-c" seemed a blurry mess of letters, as if the signatory wasn't quite sure what letter belonged, and the rhythm of the loops was somehow uneven and just plain wrong.

This, I decided, meant one of two things. Either my great-grandfather was in a rush and gave one work a particularly sloppy signature, or the second piece wasn't his. Maybe someone made a copy of the ink drawing held by the Jewish Historical Institute and tried to pass it off as an original to an unsuspecting buyer. This possibility stunned me because it seemed strange that anyone would want to copy my great-grandfather's work. So instead I thought about all the times I signed my name, and how the quality of my cursive in general, and my signature in particular, was inconsistent. If you compared my signature on countless items—credit card receipts, endorsed checks, and notes to my kids' teachers—they wouldn't all match. My great-grandfather's signature seemed fairly consistent across most of his known works, but even then I'd only seen about a quarter of all the works he was known to have produced. There was a lot I just didn't know.

I needed more information from the seller. I backtracked through the Allegro website to figure out if it was possible to contact the seller and buyer. Maybe if I knew how the seller had obtained the piece, and why he or she had sold it on Allegro, the mystery of the drawing would become clearer. Amazingly both Paweł, the seller, and Edward, the buyer, replied to my email. Paweł told me he had bought the piece from another collector a few years ago, but revealed nothing about the person who had sold it to him. And then he wrote something that made the hair on my arms stand up on end. "On the art market there are some occasions when his pieces appear, but your [great-] grandfather is very keen to be copied and falsified so you need to be extremely familiar with his work to distinguish the real objects from copies." How, I wondered, did he know this? Was his expertise from personal experience? Was he, in fact, the one copying my great-grandfather's work and trying to pass it off as original work?

I was both flattered that someone thought there was enough value in my great-grandfather's art to make it worth copying and simultaneously intensely angry that anyone would produce fakes, making my goal of finding the lost and missing works from the original body of work that much more complex. Even worse, I thought, perhaps there were also works imitating my great-grandfather's style by other artists. Listings of several other supposed Rynecki paintings on Allegro made me wonder if this had already happened. The prospect of an even more difficult process of searching for works and sorting through potentially endless fakes made me dizzy.

Edward, the man who had bought *Playing Ball* from Paweł on

Allegro, generously said I could come meet him and view the painting. So when I went to Warsaw, I had an exceptional opportunity to try to sort out the conundrum in person.

It was an hour drive to the leafy suburb where Edward lived. On the drive over, I had a sense of anticipation, but I was more curious than excited. Autumn was in the air: the leaves had mostly changed color and many had fallen onto the quiet and peaceful street. The homes, many of them built before the Second World War, were elegant but simple. There was a gate in front of Edward's home, and a large, white, fluffy dog—a Samoyed—barked at me. I considered putting my hand through the fence to pet him, but Sławek told me I had best not since I didn't know anything about his character.

Edward soon appeared and I greeted him with the one word of Polish I knew. Soon we were inside, seated at the family's dining room table. His wife served us slices of homemade apple cake. I couldn't understand Edward, who spoke to me in Polish, but I immediately liked him. I was not sure how old he was, perhaps in his sixties. His hair was gray and he wore it long, just slightly past his ears. His beard was short and trim. I loved his thick, black-rimmed glasses—he looked academic and intellectual.

I was not at all hungry, but I ate every last crumb of apple cake. It was delicious and went quite nicely with my cup of hot tea. It also gave me a chance to look around and take in my surroundings.

Three sides of the room were swallowed up with floor-to-ceiling bookshelves, filled to overflowing with books. There were so many stuffed into the space that some shelves had a second layer of books piled horizontally in front. Half of one wall was taken up by an art gallery with more than a dozen portraits. My great-grandfather's painting was not here, but there were others and they all seemed to be by or about Jewish artists—a man in a tall black hat and a long gray beard, a portrait of a woman with a long neck gazing outward toward something we couldn't see, and several sketches of lone figures.

After a few minutes, Edward brought out the Rynecki piece he had bought on Allegro and set it on the table. We began a round-robin conversation. I asked him questions, the translator rephrased my questions into Polish, Edward answered, the translator explained in English. Around and around we went. I asked him to tell me about the piece, why he bought it. His answers were straightforward and from the heart. He loved the piece, he was familiar with my great-grandfather's art, and he could afford it. I asked him how he knew my great-grandfather's body of work, and Edward pulled down a book from one of the highest shelves. It was a book I knew; it was Jerzy Malinowski's work on Polish-Jewish artists from the nineteenth and twentieth centuries. He flipped open to the page that contained six of my great-grandfather's paintings. He pointed to the pieces and told me how he loved the work, how it spoke to him, and how when he found the piece on Allegro he wanted to own it. I smiled and nodded. I asked him if he had other works by my great-grandfather. He shook his head no and explained he hadn't seen others to buy.

I asked Edward, who was not himself Jewish, why he collected the work of Polish-Jewish artists. He shared two stories. The first was that the home we were in had once offered refuge and shelter to Jews. The home had not been owned by Edward's family during the war, but he knew that several Jews had hidden in the attic. He didn't know who they were or what happened to them. And then he shared a family story. He said that before the war his father was in love with a beautiful woman, a Jewish woman, but the war separated them. The girl and her family fled, and his father never knew what happened to her. I didn't know what happened to her either, but the most likely story was a tragedy. I looked at Edward, nodded, and then began to cry. I tried not to cry, because the stories Edward shared with me weren't my stories, my family's history. But they were part of the history of my people, all too many of whom had perished senselessly. For them, and their lost hopes and dreams and potential, I wept.

Edward wanted to know my story too. He wanted to know what I could tell him about my great-grandfather, about how my family rescued a bundle of paintings, about my quest. I explained about Perla and the package in Praga. I told him about the paintings at the Jewish Historical Institute. Edward pointed to his Rynecki Allegro purchase on the table in front of him.

"What is he saying?" I asked the translator.

"He wants to know if you think it's real," he said.

I took a deep breath. Weeks before my trip to Poland I had turned over this exact moment in my head again and again. I wanted to be very careful with my words.

"I'm not sure. It looks a lot like a piece held by the Jewish Historical Institute," I said, searching on my laptop for the right JPEG image of the painting held by the institute so we could look at the two images side by side.

Edward patiently waited while I searched through my hard drive. When I opened the right file, we took the piece on the table out of the plastic so we could see it a bit better. We both stared intensely at the computer monitor and the work in front of us. Neither of us said anything.

"It's so hard to know," I finally said. "The signature on the piece you have is very different than the signature he typically put on his paintings, but I also know I sign things inconsistently."

Edward wanted to know if I could show him photographs of other Rynecki paintings held by the Jewish Historical Institute.

"Absolutely," I said, opening up the right file and then slowly browsing through the images I had photographed earlier in the trip.

We paused on many of the photos, admiring my great-grandfather's style. Edward seemed to enjoy the impromptu exhibit. He had never been to the Jewish Historical Institute.

We talked for quite a while, and eventually, it was time to wrap things up. I thanked Edward for letting me visit. I told him how special it was to meet him.

Cathy, Edward's wife, and his daughter stood. They had been seated in a far corner of the room for the entire interview. None of them had spoken or moved since the interview started. Cathy excused herself to go use the bathroom. I stood to stretch and take a closer look at the art on the wall. Sławek turned the camera off and started to pack up. I felt a tap on my shoulder. I turned and Edward was holding the Allegro piece out to me. I turned to the translator.

"What is he saying?" I asked.

"He wants you to have it," he said.

"He's giving it to me? Really?"

"Yes," the translator said.

Sławek, hearing only a bit of the conversation, looked at me. Cathy came back into the room and saw a shuffle of people. Sławek told her to move because she was in the shot. Cathy was confused. Hadn't we finished the shoot?

"Say it again to the camera," Sławek told me.

"Edward has gifted me the painting. He says it belongs to my family."

I grasped the painting in both hands and stared at it. I leaned over to hug Edward. I could not tell him with words what this meant to me, so I embraced him harder. And then we posed for photographs. One with just me, Edward, and the painting. And one with Edward, his wife, and his daughter.

Edward asked us to stay for lunch, but sadly we had to leave to get the translator back to Warsaw.

Teresa told us we could come to a special presentation of the *Salvaged* exhibit at the Jewish Historical Institute, and we did, but I felt like we were imposing on their initial showing for VIPs. The museum was still not open to the public. The group assembled in the lobby to see the exhibition was a very special contingent—they were donors and a San Francisco Bay Area group touring Warsaw with Tad Taube (a substantial backer of the POLIN museum) to experience the thriving Polish-Jewish community firsthand.

I stood on the edge of the crowd. Paweł Śpiewak gave a short speech in which he warmly welcomed those gathered in the foyer. Then Teresa promised guided tours for everyone. After she finished, I approached Shana Penn, the executive director of Tad Taube's Foundation for Jewish Life & Culture, based in the San Francisco Bay Area. Shana knew about my great-grandfather's art and project, but I wasn't sure she knew there were paintings here at the Jewish Historical Institute.

"My great-grandfather's painting is on display on the top floor of the museum," I said.

Shana looked frazzled; too many people needed her attention. She nodded and said something about taking a look at it. The woman next to Shana looked at me curiously.

"What do you mean?" she asked.

"My great-grandfather, Moshe Rynecki," I said. "This museum has fifty-two of his paintings. One of them is on display upstairs."

"You have to come tell our whole group," she said.

I needed to leave soon. If I wasn't in the POLIN press room within the hour, I would not be admitted for the inaugural celebration, but the opportunity to spread the word about Moshe was too good to pass up.

"Of course, I'd be delighted," I said, signaling Sławek, who was standing nearby, to follow with his camera.

At the upstairs gallery Jakub was telling an engaging story to his tour group about the work of Gela Seksztajn. The woman who insisted I speak to the whole group interrupted Jakub and told him I had a story to tell. I apologized for disrupting his presentation, but Jakub, ever the gentleman, kindly allowed me to lead the group over to where Moshe's painting was on display. I explained why I was in Poland, talked about

Moshe's art career and life, and recounted my quest to find the lost pieces of the original collection. I noticed a rabbi from the temple I used to attend with my parents; he looked pleased to see me. I handed out postcards with information about the *Chasing Portraits* project. A few people asked for more information.

"Good on you," a woman at the back said. "More young people should care about their heritage."

I took one last look at Moshe's painting and took a selfie standing in front of it. Then we had to go, in order to get to POLIN on time.

It was bitingly cold on this late October afternoon, but you could hardly tell from the excited demeanor of the people gathered outside the museum. By the time we made it through security at the exterior of the building, the media room inside the museum was abuzz with conversations in a variety of languages. I heard Polish, of course, but also French, Spanish, German, and several languages I didn't recognize. The room was packed to capacity with reporters eager to tell the story of the museum and what it meant for Polish-Jewish relations. Eventually an announcement was made that if we wanted to attend the ceremony we needed to head outside.

POLIN Museum of the History of Polish Jews is on the site of the Warsaw Ghetto. Its entrance faces the Ghetto Heroes Monument. The monument, sculpted by Nathan Rapoport, was unveiled in 1948. Eleven feet tall, it was a bronze sculpture commemorating those who fought in the uprising as well as a wall meant to evoke not only the walls of the Warsaw Ghetto, but also the Western Wall in Jerusalem. The combination is fascinating—the stones juxtaposed against the memory of the Warsaw Ghetto Uprising and the religious importance of the Western Wall in Judaism.

Amid recent headlines of rising anti-Semitism across Europe, it seemed incredible to those of us in attendance that we were here—a large group of Jews gathered in Poland, a country where 3.3 million

Jews were all but annihilated in the Holocaust, to celebrate a museum of Polish-Jewish history.

There were several formal presentations. The presidents of Poland and Israel spoke, and Marian Turski, a Polish Jew and Holocaust survivor, beseeched us to remember the refrain from a World War Two Polish-Jewish partisan song. "*Mir zaynen do!*" he said. "We are still here!"

It was a strange feeling—to my right was the brand-new museum, to the left was the Ghetto Heroes Monument, and below the trees in front of me was a bench with a statue of Jan Karski, a Catholic Polish resistance fighter who tried to warn the world of the Holocaust. I felt that in the confluence of history, remembrance, and hope for the future, we were here not only for the opening of the museum; we were also here to celebrate that we, Jews from Poland, Europe, America, and Israel, some of us descendants of survivors, had returned to Poland. The museum represented an enormous symbolic step forward in healing Polish-Jewish relations, and as a group we were giddy—thrilled about both the goodwill of the moment and the potential for the future symbolized by the museum.

When the ceremony was over, we returned to the inside of the museum for a continued celebration. There was an extensive buffet. I stood with a small plate of food at a tall table with Cathy, Sławek, and a few new friends. We made small talk and marveled at the history being made.

"What a way to wrap up our trip to Poland," I told Cathy.

"Now are you glad you came?"

"I never imagined I'd say yes, but it's true. I am glad," I said. "If you can believe it, I'm sad to be going home tomorrow."

"We'll be back," Cathy said.

"When the documentary is shown here!"

"Exactly," Cathy said, raising her wine in a toast. Sławek, Cathy, and I clinked glasses, and the sound reminded me of a story, a story central to the museum and the evening's celebration: The first Jews arrived in this land running from persecution in the western part of medieval Europe. Legend has it that when they arrived they heard the birds chirp two Hebrew letters, *Po-lin*, which in Hebrew means "You will rest here." And they did rest, and thrive, in the place they eventually came to call "Polin," Poland. I didn't hear the birds chirp when I arrived, but I was nonetheless drawn to this place, the land of my ancestors, because of the siren's call of my great-grandfather's paintings.

TWENTY-ONE

Roadblocks

The journey back to California was long, and made even longer by the fact that I missed my connecting flight out of Frankfurt. The airline gave me a choice—fly from Frankfurt to Colorado and clear customs there, and then on to San Francisco, or fly to Munich, with a connecting flight to San Francisco. I took the connection through Munich. I sent Dad an email update and told him I was so tired I could cry.

"Don't worry, you'll get here eventually," he wrote back. "In the old days you would have had to walk or take a wagon to the train station, then the train to the ship, and finally a ship to the United States. It took weeks." As exhausted as I was, it could have been worse, and after twenty-six hours of travel time with a nine-hour time difference, I was home.

I was greeted at the airport by Steve and the boys. Everyone was excited to be back together again. We had a big family hug right in the middle of the airport, just outside customs.

"We missed you," Tyler said.

"A lot," Owen told me.

"We're really glad you're home," Steve said.

"I'm glad to be home," I announced.

"Can I tell her now?" Tyler asked.

"Tell me what?"

"Meisha is missing!" Owen blurted out.

Our senile, hard-of-hearing, nineteen-year-old cat, it seemed, had somehow gotten outside, and been missing for two days. Tyler started to cry. As we walked toward the parking lot, the boys told me the last time they'd seen her and how they'd put up missing posters hoping someone might call with information about her whereabouts.

After two plus weeks on the road of intense focus on Moshe's art and my Polish-Jewish roots, it was an unwelcome jolt, but it drew me right back into the pattern of home life. Setting aside my documentary film focus, I put on my Mom hat and rolled up my sleeves. If I could find lost art in Poland, I could find our lost cat. And in the era of social media, it was a lot easier. I found Meisha in a couple of days, thanks to neighborhood friends and Facebook. She had wandered several blocks away and had been temporarily adopted by a kind and loving family with a big heart for cats.

With Meisha back home and Tyler and Owen ecstatic to have her back, I began to long for the next filming adventure. I mused about trips to Israel and New York, but first I needed funding.

The funding came sooner than I'd expected. Just three months after my return from Poland, the Conference on Jewish Material Claims Against Germany, Inc.—the Claims Conference—approved my documentary film grant application. I began to plan another trip—reaching out to those with my great-grandfather's art.

First I emailed Maciej—the man in New York with six of my great-grandfather's paintings—apologized we hadn't spoken in many years, and asked if he would sit for an interview. The email bounced back. I picked up the phone and called—I got a message that the phone number was no longer in service. I dug out a mailing address and sent a letter asking as nicely as possible if I could come for an interview. I heard nothing. I panicked. I posted in a New York Jewish genealogical Facebook group and asked if anyone knew Maciej. I got a reply from, of all people, Sławek. Sławek had a friend of a friend on Facebook who knew Maciej. Maciej, it seemed, was no longer in New York. He had, ironically, returned to Poland. He lived in the same apartment his family had before the war, in Praga-Południe, a neighborhood with modernistic villas and tree-lined streets. Maciej said he would be delighted to meet with me and film an interview, but to do that I would have to return to Poland.

My film budget was as tight as possible, and there wasn't really room for a second trip to Poland. This was a potentially insurmountable problem, but I knew somehow I had to make it work. Eventually I hit upon a solution—I did have a trip to Israel in the planning stages, so I looked into using Poland as an extended layover on the way to Israel. It turned out that if I flew to Poland for a long weekend and then caught a flight to Israel, I could make it all work without too much additional expense. I tracked down my contacts in Israel.

First on my list for Israel was Alex and Moshe Wertheim's cousin. I wrote to the brothers and explained my plan to be in Israel in May. I asked them to connect me with their cousin, but I didn't hear back. I picked up the phone and called Alex Wertheim in Poland, who said he was traveling and would call me when he was back home. I waited several weeks and tried again, but this time my call went straight to voice mail. I left a message pleading for his assistance. I got no reply, so I called Moshe Wertheim in Canada. He told me he would see what he could do. And then word came back—the Wertheim cousin didn't want to see me. I was crushed. I opened up the low-resolution photographs of the works the cousin supposedly had, which Moshe Wertheim had sent me several years back (the ones I first saw on my iPhone in New

York City) and felt myself digging in. The thought that I couldn't see the paintings made my desire to see them even greater. I wrote a thoughtful and composed email explaining to the Wertheim brothers why I really needed to talk to their cousin—that she was part of the story—that she had my great-grandfather's paintings—that I wanted to see the art. I explained that even if I didn't meet with her, she would still be in the story.

I planned my trip to Israel anyway, despite not having an appointment with the Wertheim Israeli cousin. I tried to remain optimistic. Things might yet work out, and I had a number of other reasons to visit. I would meet with Yehudit Shendar to talk about her visit so many years ago to my parents' home. I also planned a trip to Yad Vashem, securing permission to film on-site. And I would meet with family—both my mother's cousin (who made Aliyah, the immigration of Jews to Israel, in the 1950s and raised a large family there) and David Gefen, a relative to whom Perla had gifted a Moshe Rynecki painting after the war. While David and I had exchanged letters, we had never met.

I asked my mother's Israeli cousins to help me find David. They discovered that David had died, but with the name of the kibbutz where he once lived, they located a phone number for relatives. I called, and a woman answered the phone. She spoke English, but it was heavily accented, and we had difficulty understanding each other. She kept telling me I needed to call Shula, David's daughter who lived in America.

"Shula can tell you more," she explained.

I called Shula at a New York phone number. After several rounds of telephone tag we connected.

"Of course you can come and see the painting," Shula told me. "The sculpture too."

"The sculpture?" I asked.

"Perla sent my father the painting you know, but also a sculpture."

It was amazing. In my life I had seen nearly two hundred of Moshe's paintings—more than two hundred if you counted photos of his works—and never a single representation of anything he had sculpted. I was desperate to know, but in a strange way I wanted to see it—to experience it myself—rather than hear it described. "Don't tell me anything else about it!" I pleaded. "I want it to be a surprise when I visit."

Shula and I tentatively planned for me to visit New York in July, and I turned back to planning my trip to Poland and Israel.

A few weeks before departing for Poland, I contacted Anne-Marie O'Connor, the author of *The Lady in Gold*, about Gustav Klimt's masterpiece. We were Facebook and Twitter friends, and I knew she lived in Jerusalem. I asked if I could interview her for the film. Then I also told her about the Wertheim cousin who wouldn't see me. I wondered if she had some ideas about who might help convince the woman to change her mind. Anne-Marie put me in touch with a reporter with many connections. The reporter told me to email Elinor Kroitoru at Hashava, the Israeli organization that dealt with the location and restitution of Holocaust assets. Elinor and I agreed to meet in Tel Aviv. But first on the itinerary was my return to Poland.

Warsaw was warm, sunny, and inviting in May. Cathy and I met in the hotel lobby on Krucza Street, just a few addresses down from what was once my great-grandparents' apartment building. We went for a walk and dinner al fresco, where I ate my favorite Polish meal—mushroom soup. We compared travel notes and went over our itinerary. I had, once again, crammed far too much into a brief visit—a quick trip to POLIN to see the Roman Vishniac photography exhibit; an interview with Agnieszka Yass-Alston, a provenance researcher interested in Jewish collectors from Kraków and who had helped me on more than one occasion; the Jewish Motifs International Film Festival, to see Sławek's new film about Jan Karski; dinner with Barbara Kirshenblatt-Gimblett; a follow-up visit to the Jewish Historical Institute; and the interview with Maciej.

I was slightly worried about visiting Maciej. Our previous letter exchanges and failed price negotiation were now long behind us, but I wasn't sure how it would go. However it turned out, I was determined to see Maciej's Rynecki paintings and hear his stories.

Fortunately, my worries were unfounded. On Saturday, when Sławek, Cathy, and I arrived on his doorstep, Maciej welcomed us into his apartment and proudly showed me the Rynecki paintings on his wall.

"I knew it!" I exclaimed.

"What's that?" Maciej asked.

"I've seen these," I said, pointing to two pieces I recognized. "They were once listed at the Polish auction houses Desa and Rempex."

Maciej nodded.

"But you didn't sell them."

"No."

"I'm so glad you still have them," I said. "It's amazing to finally see them in person." I stood with Maciej, who was about a head taller than me and maybe twenty-five years older, in front of his wall, admiring his art collection. The six Rynecki paintings were scattered among other works of art, and if there was a particular pattern or sequence to the display, I was unable to figure it out. Some might have said the wall was cluttered, but the art was beautiful, and the paintings, more than a dozen in all, were clearly well loved.

"Which is your favorite?" I asked.

"Like you, I grew up with them in my family's home," Maciej said. "I love them all."

I pointed to one I had never seen before. It showed four men kneeling in a street laying bricks. Next to them was a wheelbarrow.

"This one is wonderful," I said.

"I like that one too," Maciej said.

"So tell me," I said, "there's a story, right?"

"My grandfather worked in the Polish government before the war," Maciej said. "He collected art. He traveled. I think maybe he knew your great-grandfather."

"You said when we spoke on the phone that you have a photo album from before the war. That maybe there's a photo of my great-grandfather in it?" I asked.

"Yes, maybe," Maciej said. "I'll have to see if I can find the album."

"And the six pieces," I said, "your family has had them as long as you can remember?"

"Seven."

"Seven?"

Maciej pointed to a piece on the wall I hadn't really noticed. It was an oil, almost an abstract impressionistic painting. It was not entirely abstract; there were just enough details to make me think it was a cityscape, or maybe an open-air market. It was an artist's loose interpretation of a real-life scene, as if observed through a distorted lens. Maciej pulled it off the wall, turned it over, and pointed to two pieces of paper affixed to the back. One slightly peeling tag, a sort of a proclamation, said: "for the Brussels International Exposition." The other piece of paper was a skinny form with blanks to be filled in by the artist. The number "21657" was preprinted on the form. In the space for the artist's name someone had written in elegant cursive, "Rynecki, Maurycy" (my great-grandfather's Polish name). The price for the painting was 150 zlotys, an amount I later learned was about one and a half times what a skilled worker earned in Warsaw in a month at that time. The date on the paper was 1932, which was odd because the Brussels International Exposition was in 1935. So maybe my great-grandfather tried to sell it in 1932 but was unsuccessful, and eventually sent it to be shown at the Brussels fair three years later? I was unsure. Even stranger was the fact that the form said the painting was a watercolor titled *Talmudyści* [*Talmudists*]. This title was one I'd expect from my great-grandfather, but it was certainly not the image painted on the reverse of the canvas.

"The title and the medium don't match the painting on the other side," Maciej said.

"That's strange, right?" I asked.

"Maybe your great-grandfather painted over it."

"Like maybe if the piece was X-rayed we'd see a Talmudic scene underneath?"

Maciej nodded.

A woman walked into the living room. She had her light golden brown hair up in a bun. She was wearing a blue jumpsuit covered in white polka dots. Standing in flip-flops she was about as tall as I was in my chunky-heeled sandals. It was Katherina. She greeted me with a hug.

"He's got too many pieces on the wall," Katherina said.

"I think it's nice," I told her.

"He should have more of a collecting theme."

Maciej shrugged.

"I tried to help him when we were still married," Katherina said. "We were going to give the collection more focus. That's why we sold two pieces."

"The two at Sotheby's?" I asked. "That was you?"

"Her," Maciej said. "I didn't want to sell."

"*The Café Scene* and *The Accordionist*?" I asked.

"I don't remember," Maciej said.

I turned on my laptop and pulled open the black-and-white scanned pages from my Sotheby's auction catalog.

"These?" I asked, pointing at my laptop screen.

"Yes, I think so," Maciej said. "But I don't really recognize them in black-and-white."

"It looks like whoever bought the two you sold in New York tried to sell *The Café Scene* through Sotheby's in Tel Aviv. I know from

Sotheby's that it never sold," I said. "But I'm curious if you know anything about the provenance write-up in the Tel Aviv catalog. It says: 'After the German retreat 150 works by Rynecki were discovered in the basement of a Warsaw apartment block, including the present work.' You had 150 paintings?"

"Oh, no," Maciej said.

"So this provenance isn't accurate?" I asked.

"Like you said, we sold two in New York, nothing in Tel Aviv. I don't know where they got that information," Maciej said.

"The New York catalog says, 'Provenance: Acquired from the widow of the artist, 1945.'"

Maciej and Katherina looked at me.

"Did your family acquire it from Perla?"

"Maciej's mother knew the story," Katherina said. "I don't really remember it. There was something about having some pieces before the war and then some fluttering in the street—that she rescued them."

"The Soviets occupied apartments in this neighborhood," Maciej said. "They trashed the apartment. When my family returned it was a disaster."

"They threw things out, tossed things into the streets," Katherina said. "They didn't care."

"The Russians sat out here during the Warsaw Uprising. The soldiers didn't do a thing for Poland, but they happily drank and destroyed our belongings," Maciej said.

"War is ugly," I said.

I asked about the photo album Maciej promised I could look through.

The album was filled with old black-and-white photographs from before the war. Maciej watched as I flipped through the pages, scanning the faces of people I didn't know. I was searching for a photograph of my great-grandfather, but I had no idea how I would recognize him unless one happened to look very much like one of the few self-portraits

I had seen. Even then, I don't think I would have been sure. Maciej pointed out the people he knew in the photos, but he wasn't sure of everyone's name. Very few photos were labeled. Finding a picture of Moshe would have been a tremendous discovery; it would have made him that much more real to me. But none of the faces registered with me, and when I reached the last page I looked up. If my great-grandfather was in this album, I hadn't spotted him.

Cathy and Sławek gave me a look letting me know it was time to wrap up the interview. Sławek invited Katherina and Maciej to attend tomorrow night's showing of *Karski and the Lords of Humanity*—his new documentary film showing at the Jewish Motifs International Film Festival. We packed up and said our goodbyes.

On Sunday we went to the Karski movie screening. It was a sold-out show, and when it was over Sławek received a standing ovation. There was a question-and-answer period after the film, in Polish. I didn't understand any of it, but I could tell some of the questions were difficult to answer. Sławek did his best to explain why he had made certain editorial choices. Katherina and Maciej came out to the aisle where Cathy and I were standing. They had thoroughly enjoyed the film. I hugged them goodbye and excused myself to get a drink of water in the lobby. When I returned, Sławek was still chatting and answering questions. Unable to converse in Polish and not wanting to impose, Cathy and I decided to grab a cab back to the hotel. We would connect with Sławek again tomorrow at the Jewish Historical Institute.

The return trip to the institute on Monday was for the most embarrassing of reasons; in October I had miscounted. The institute had fifty-two of my great-grandfather's paintings, but when I arrived back home in California at the end of October and reviewed my photographs, it became apparent that I had only photographed fifty-one of my great-grandfather's works.

We arrived a bit early, and neither Teresa nor Jakub was in yet, so we sat down in the bookstore.

"I have something I'm supposed to give you," Cathy said.

"Give me what?" I asked.

"Katherina gave me a package yesterday," Cathy said rather sheepishly. "She gave me strict orders to only have you open it when Sławek was filming."

"Then let's film it," Sławek said, pulling his camera out and setting me up at a table in the bookstore. Cathy handed me a tube. A tube for drawings.

"Do you think they gave me a painting?" I asked.

"Open it."

Inside I found two large photographs and a note in plastic. It said: "We went through our closets, drawers, and shelves, and we found copies of the two sold paintings. The images are slightly cut, but we hope you will be glad to have a chance to see them in color. It was a pleasure to finally meet you."

"Not quite like Edward gifting me a painting," I said, "but it's so sweet."

As Sławek finished up filming, Teresa arrived and invited us into the library room we had used during our last visit. Jakub met us too and asked me which painting I hadn't seen. I pulled out my spreadsheet and pointed to the inventory number and description. He promised to find it.

Jakub returned quite a bit later. He had had a great deal of difficulty finding the work, which helped explain why I missed seeing it in October. He set down the painting in front of me—it was a large group of men inside a synagouge, praying.

"That's not my great-grandfather's work. Are you sure this is the right piece?" I asked.

"It's the right inventory number," Jakub said.

"It's not his style," I said. "It's too photo-realistic. I mean, he painted scenes like this, but the style doesn't look right."

"Maybe it's an earlier piece," Teresa said.

"Is there a date on it? A signature?" I asked.

There was neither.

"But you believe it's my great-grandfather's work."

"Yes. It was identified by a well-respected curator who spent many years here. I don't have any reason to doubt the attribution to Rynecki."

I took photographs of the painting. Teresa was convinced it was one of my great-grandfather's paintings. I was not so certain. Of course, if it wasn't his work, whose was it? Another day, another mystery, another puzzle piece to ponder.

Jakub put the painting away, and Teresa took us upstairs to a room we'd been unable to access during the remodel in October. We were here to see the index inventory cards with information about my great-grandfather's paintings. I didn't have much time. I quickly snapped three photos of every card—one of the black-and-white photo attached to each card, one of the front of the card, and one of the back. These were the same cards that Richard, the Fulbright scholar, had used to create his spreadsheet, the same cards my cousin Aliza was shown during her visit, when she was told she couldn't see the paintings themselves. We left the Jewish Historical Institute, returned to the hotel, grabbed dinner, and then headed for the airport. We had a flight to catch to Tel Aviv.

Flights from Warsaw to Tel Aviv are generally red-eye flights: they leave late at night and arrive very early in the morning. Ours arrived at 3:50 a.m. We started our day in Tel Aviv with a long nap to help us to shift time zones. By the time we got up it was just past 10 a.m. We found a place for breakfast and ordered *shakshuka* (eggs poached in a tomato, chili pepper, and onion sauce) and hummus. Then it was a late morning walk through Carmel Market—a market jam-packed with vendors selling everything from fresh fruit and fish to T-shirts and Judaica souveniers—before we grabbed a taxi to meet Elinor at Hashava.

Hashava was set up by the Israeli government to help Holocaust survivors and their heirs recover assets in Israel. Those assets, mostly in the form of bank accounts or property, were generally investments made before the Second World War. Often those who made the investments perished in the Holocaust, and their surviving heirs didn't always know these assets existed. Hashava was created by the Knesset (the Israeli parliament) to find the heirs and resolve unclaimed property issues, so looted art was not a primary focus. Despite the unusual nature of Moshe's artwork as an asset, Elinor was happy to talk to me about how she might help. I explained my story and that I wanted to see the Rynecki art held by the Wertheim cousin. We went back and forth for over an hour.

"I can't help you unless you file a claim," Elinor said. "Without a notarized claim on my desk, my hands are tied and there is absolutely nothing I can do for you."

"But I don't want to file a claim. I'm acting as a historian."

"I understand," Elinor said, "but unless you file a claim, I can't help you."

Elinor handed me the four-page "Request for Resitutution of an Asset Located in Israel Belonging to a Holocaust Victim" form. It started with basic questions like my name and whether or not the asset was located in Israel. The questions quickly ramped up to more complicated issues, like providing my great-grandfather's last permanent residential address (I had no idea), what sort of evidence I had that supported my right to receive the asset, and a space for me to provide additional and significant information that might help the handling of the application.

Sławek, Cathy, and I returned to our Airbnb apartment rental on Ben Yehuda Street in Tel Aviv, just a few blocks from the beach.

"You sure you really want to file a claim?" Cathy asked.

"No, I don't. I really don't. But if I want to see the paintings, what choice do I have?" I countered. "I'm willing to live with the conflicting stories of the Wertheim brothers, and let go of any provenance issues, but I really want to see the paintings. I don't think access to the paintings is unfair or unreasonable, and this seems like the only leverage I have to see them."

"But if you file a claim, you look like the bad guy," Cathy said.

"It's probably why she doesn't want to show you the paintings," Sławek said. "She was afraid you would file a claim and now her worst fears about you are confirmed."

"But Elinor made it really clear that there is nothing she can do for me unless I file a claim. So I could walk away. Give up seeing some of the few paintings that I know survived, that I know where they are, and who has them. Or I fill out the paperwork in order to receive Hashava's help, try to get some leverage to see them."

"You might lose sympathy if you file," Sławek said.

"Maybe, but won't people understand it's not about making a claim for possession of the paintings, it's a claim requesting access to the paintings?"

"Perhaps she's a really private person," Cathy said.

"She doesn't need to be in the film. I don't even need to see the paintings at her apartment. Let her bring them to a hotel conference room, or anywhere that she feels comfortable. I don't really care where I see the paintings, I just want to see them."

Cathy and Sławek looked unsure. I couldn't just let go, when I felt so close.

"Her position seems so coldhearted. We're both the children of Holocaust survivors. I don't understand why that doesn't hold any sway with her. And besides, she knows I saw her cousin's paintings in Toronto and that I've never made a claim for them."

"Apparently it's not enough," Cathy said.

I needed a break from the conversation. I was exceptionally stressed and distraught. As a way of escaping the conversation, I started filling in the blanks on Hashava's form.

"I should call my dad. He's the actual heir. I need his permission before I submit the paperwork."

It was early morning in California, but Dad was up. Sławek filmed me talking on speakerphone with Dad.

"I need your permission to go ahead with something," I said.

"Shoot. Tell me."

And so I explained. I was angry, but I also felt like I might cry. Emotionally I was all over the map. I was frustrated and dumbfounded by the Wertheim cousin's refusal to allow me access to my great-grandfather's art. Then I told Dad about Elinor and how Hashava had the power and authority to create some leverage.

"Whatever you need to do," Dad said, "I support your decision."

Thursday morning we returned to Elinor's office. I handed her my paperwork, and with a loud thud she imprinted the documents with Hashava's official acceptance of the claim.

"Now what?" I asked.

"Now I track her down and let her know you've filed a claim," Elinor said. "And then you wait. Once I send the letter, she has thirty days to respond."

There was nothing to do now, and there wasn't a lot of time to contemplate my decision. We were late for an appointment at Yad Vashem.

Yad Vashem, the Holocaust Martyrs' and Heroes' Remembrance Authority, sits on forty-five acres on the Mount of Remembrance in Jerusalem. As the cab ascended the winding road to the visitor's center, I could not see all the physical commemorative sites or memorials on the campus, but nonetheless I felt a profound sense of melancholy.

The visitor's center was incredibly busy when we arrived a bit after lunch. I called my contact, who issued me press credentials and then took me to the art museum to meet with Eliad Moreh-Rosenberg. Eliad was the curator and Art Department director of Yad Vashem's art museum, one of more than a dozen places on the campus accessible to visitors. Most people visit the Holocaust History Museum, the Hall of Remembrance, and the Valley of the Communities (a 2.5-acre monument dug out of the bedrock, containing the names of more than five thousand Jewish communities destroyed in the Holocaust) when they come to Yad Vashem. But there are also archives, the Avenue of the Righteous Among Nations, the Cattle Car Memorial, the Warsaw Ghetto Square, the Exhibitions Pavilion, and the Synagogue.

The Museum of Holocaust Art, where we met Eliad, has more than ten thousand works of art, almost all of them from the Holocaust period, so only a tiny fraction of the full collection can be shown at any given time.

"Artists took incredible risks to create art during the Holocaust," Eliad said. "Those who managed to find the materials to create made and produced whatever they could to express themselves. The works in our collection not only provide eyewitness accounts, but they are an incredible testimony to the importance of creativity, even in the face of atrocity and certain death."

I nodded and followed Eliad farther into the museum.

"There it is!" I said, pointing at *Refugees* (1939), my great-grandfather's painting that was prominently displayed right near the entrance to the gallery room.

Eliad and I walked closer.

"Your great-grandfather's piece is important," Eliad said. "It's unique in that it shows the early status of Jewish refugees in Warsaw."

"I love that it shows such a cross-section of life," I said.

"It's true," Eliad said. "There is a young man carrying a bag over his shoulder. Next to him is a woman, perhaps his mother, with a straw bag in her hand. Then there are three other figures—a father carrying a young child too tired to walk. On the far right a woman pushes someone in a wheelchair. The figure in the wheelchair is either very elderly or perhaps disabled."

"How often does the painting get displayed in the art museum?" I asked.

"We rotate through our collection," Eliad said. "You know a copy of the *Refugees* painting is on permanent display in the History Museum, right?"

"I do, and I'd like to see it."

We left the art museum and connected with Niv Goldberg, the collection manager for the Art Department who first shared his Rynecki discoveries with me. He had found a testimony in Yiddish Perla had given after the war, as well as several Pages of Testimony with the names on them of the extended Rynecki family that perished in the Holocaust.

"I should add photographs to some of these testimonies," I said.

"Please," Niv pleaded, "promise me you will. It's really very important. Names with faces help, and you're probably the last generation of your family that can do it."

I promised. It seemed the least I could do, to help document the past. Afterward, we headed out to the History Museum for the fastest guided walking tour of the museum ever. Niv zipped us through gallery after gallery. It was a good thing this was not my first Holocaust museum; we skipped past much of the history and context. After going through several galleries and watching how the displays changed, I got a sense of what year each gallery showed, and what part of the Holocaust was being described. I saw photographs, videos, artifacts, and art scattered throughout all of the exhibits. We weaved through an American tour group, and then Niv directed us to a gallery off the main path. I didn't see a sign, but I knew it was the *Between Walls and Fences* gallery. I had just seen the original in the art museum, but here I paused, and looked carefully at the replica in the context of the display. The museum was busy, but I had this alcove to myself. And here in the exhibit, where it was juxtaposed with black-and-white photographs, artifacts, videos, I understood the painting in a slightly different way. I could really see why Yehudit Shendar had wanted the painting for the museum—not just to show Polish-Jewish refugees as victims, but to give voice to the refugee experience. My great-grandfather's art bore witness to what he saw and experienced before he was murdered in the Holocaust. His painting gave visitors more depth, more empathy, a deeper connection to the past. I was grateful to have a private moment in a very public space, and unexpectedly awed by the testimonial and touchstone, the link Moshe provided to the past. I don't think I've ever been more grateful about growing up surrounded by my great-grandfather's art than I was at that moment. In this space, which shared a profoundly awful and distressing history, I could see how much richness and depth his art added to the story provided by the other artifacts.

We left the History Museum just as all visitors do, on a rising exit that allowed us to look out across the valley. We filmed the grounds of the museum and then packed up for the day.

The following day we filmed some background shots for the documentary in the Old City, at the Western Wall, and in Jerusalem. Everyplace we went there were locals, tourists, and merchants selling their wares. We took respite from the crowds by escaping to the rooftop balcony of a hotel at Jaffa Gate in the old city, where we were greeted by panoramic views of the city below. We had the vista to ourselves. After a short break, we headed deeper into the Old City, wandering its narrow streets, admiring hamsa bracelets, Armenian ceramic candlesticks, and T-shirts. After a short stop in the Christian Quarter to take a look at the nearby Church of the Holy Sepulchre, we went to the Western Wall, where we were required to go through a security checkpoint.

The Western Wall was divided into a men's section (quite spacious) and the women's portion (much smaller, crowded, and less accommodating). I watched transfixed as people prayed and placed offerings into the wall. Eventually, I made my own journey to the wall. I tried my best to respect the women there, to not invade their space. I noticed many of them walked backward away from the wall as they left. I did as they did. I didn't want to offend anyone.

As we left the area, past the rows of Israeli police cars and IDF (Israeli Defense Force) soldiers, we found ourselves on a bustling thoroughfare crowded with taxi drivers. Sławek negotiated with one to give us a ride. It had been a long day and we returned to our apartment. It was extraordinarily quiet on our street, just one block from the Ben Yehuda pedestrian mall. It was Friday night, and all of Jerusalem had come to a standstill for Shabbat.

TWENTY-TWO

A Shared Heritage

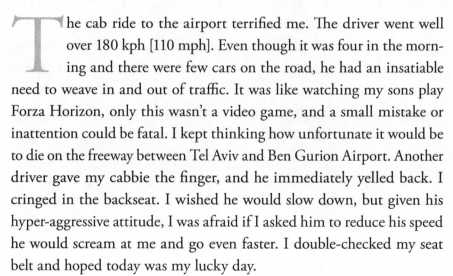

The cab ride to the airport terrified me. The driver went well over 180 kph [110 mph]. Even though it was four in the morning and there were few cars on the road, he had an insatiable need to weave in and out of traffic. It was like watching my sons play Forza Horizon, only this wasn't a video game, and a small mistake or inattention could be fatal. I kept thinking how unfortunate it would be to die on the freeway between Tel Aviv and Ben Gurion Airport. Another driver gave my cabbie the finger, and he immediately yelled back. I cringed in the backseat. I wished he would slow down, but given his hyper-aggressive attitude, I was afraid if I asked him to reduce his speed he would scream at me and go even faster. I double-checked my seat belt and hoped today was my lucky day.

The lines at the airport, even at this hour, were long. Security was tight. As I checked in, I was asked numerous times why I had visited Israel and if my bags had been with me since I packed them. Then I passed through a security checkpoint before entering a second, more thorough screening area. There were supposed to be several different lines, but nobody actually formed lines. It was like we were all in one large group which eventually funneled down into lines, but everyone in the funnel seemed to resist forming lines for as long as possible. People in the crowd were tired and frustrated. One guy and his girlfriend tried to enter what looked like an underutilized line, but others thought they were cutting them off. There were some rude looks and tense words spoken. As the bolus of people sorted into lines, I noticed nearby an older gentleman who looked like he was straight out of one of my great-grandfather's paintings. He was dressed head to toe in black, a traditional Hassidic black hat on the top of his head. His *payos* ["side curls"] were longer than his beard. I wanted to show him the postcard with my great-grandfather's paintings. I was sure Moshe's more religious work would seem very familiar to him, but I said nothing.

My flight to London, just over five hours, was the short leg of my journey. After a layover at Heathrow it was then eleven hours to San Francisco. The travel, the interviewing, the filming were all exciting, but I felt wiped out. And it was not just this trip that had left me feeling drained; it was my personal and emotional investment in the subject and my relentless push to uncover more paintings, more stories, more fragments of information, which left me with little downtime. I still had very mixed feelings about filing the claim with Hashava—my relentlessness might have gone a step too far, though what I wanted seemed so easy to give. I am not sure how I could feel both self-righteous and full of guilt, but I managed it. Aside from that, I felt like my project had a certain momentum, and each discovery added to the momentum. At the same time, each discovery made the prospect of taking even a small break from the project ever more remote. At Passover we say, "Next year in Jerusalem." I kept saying to myself, "Next year I can take a break." I felt that there was no time to rest. It had been so hard to get started, and the war passed out of living memory with each passing day. Each day came with the risk that some clues, and more of the story, would be lost forever.

So as soon as I stepped off the plane in San Francisco, I was already planning my next trip, to New York. And because I always want to get the most out of each trip, I wouldn't just interview Shula, and see her Rynecki painting and sculpture. So I planned more—research at the Frick and at the Watson Library in the Metropolitan, coffee with friends I knew on social media who supported the documentary film project, appointments with those in the Jewish art world who might help me find venues for the film, and meetings with attorneys to film interviews about Holocaust-era art looting and restitution issues.

While I planned my New York itinerary, I received an email from Elinor at Hashava. She had located the Wertheim cousin and written a letter citing clause number 18 of the Hashava law. Clause 18 spoke of providing information regarding an asset suspected to be in the ownership of a Holocaust victim. The other option would have been to invoke clause number 10, a law which would have demanded the cousin hand over the paintings. Elinor explained that given my own reticence to be a claimant and because the provenance of the art was unclear, she wanted to deliver a less demanding letter. The letter, sent by registered mail, gave the cousin thirty days, until late July, to reply.

In early July the Wertheim cousin replied. Her note to Elinor was short and firm, and she made her position clear—she said she had only two watercolors, not the eight the Wertheim brothers had told me she possessed—and that they'd been in her family for three generations and thus were not an asset of a Holocaust victim. Elinor told me she was "disappointed, but not giving up . . ."

In mid-July I went to New York City to meet with Shula.

Sławek drove us out to Shula's home. The "us" this time was Cathy, photojournalist Chuck Fishman, and I. We were early. Sławek was hungry. We stopped at a classic American diner for breakfast. Sławek opened the menu and eyed eggs, flapjacks, and coffee. A group of men in the corner of the diner, maybe ten of them, were speaking a language we didn't recognize. Sławek went closer—he wanted to figure out what they were speaking. My cellphone rang; it was Shula.

"You're coming for breakfast, right?" Shula asked.

"We're at a diner just down the road," I said.

"But I picked up bagels, lox, white fish, fresh fruit, and coffee," Shula said.

I looked at Sławek, Chuck, and Cathy, who were about to order.

"We'll be there in a few minutes," I said, before hanging up.

"But I wanted a diner breakfast!" Sławek moaned.

"Another time."

When we parked outside, it was pouring rain, but it was a warm East Coast summer rain. Sławek and I huddled at the back of his Toyota Land Cruiser, hoping the glass rear hatch would keep us dry while he readied his equipment.

I fiddled with the intercom system outside Shula and her husband's apartment complex until I dialed the right number. Shula answered, buzzed me in, and told me how to find her apartment. When the elevator doors opened on Shula's floor I headed down the long hallway, looking for her door number. Reaching a dead end, I realized that I had somehow missed Shula's apartment despite her detailed directions, so I retraced my steps. Halfway back I saw a woman step out of her apartment.

"Elizabeth?" she said.

"Oh my gosh, I walked right by it!"

"It happens all the time. Not to worry! Come in, come in!"

We stepped inside a small entryway, where we met Shula's husband, Eliran. On the wall that faced the entry was my great-grandfather's painting of two tailors. I had seen both a black-and-white photograph of the piece (my family had made a glass plate negative of the painting in Italy after the war) and a poor-quality Polaroid tossed into Grandpa George's papers.

"The sculpture is right over here," Shula said, gesturing toward the kitchen.

I walked into the kitchen, a somewhat wider-than-typical galley with a large countertop and an opening that looked out into the living room. Shula pointed behind me. I swiveled to see where she gestured, but was unclear where to direct my attention. All she had said on the phone was that it was a sculpture. I was looking for a large carving on a stand-alone base. But then I saw a small wood carving mounted in a wood frame hanging on the wall. I moved closer. It was nothing like I'd imagined, which made the thrill of seeing it that much more intense.

"Can I take it off the wall?" I asked.

"Of course."

I tried to lift it up off a picture hook, but realized it was affixed to the wall with Velcro. I gently tugged until it came loose and then I cradled it in my hands. It was smaller than I'd expected, maybe five by seven inches. The sculpture, more of an assembled group of carvings, was mounted onto a piece of wood set into a frame. The carving was of a man. I could see his eyes, nose, beard, and yarmulke quite distinctly, but I was not sure what he was doing. He was sitting, and his right arm was stretched out to the side.

"Is he saying a prayer?" I asked.

"Oh, I don't think so," Shula said. "I think he's a tailor, just like in the painting. See the fabric draped over his leg? And he must have a needle and thread in the hand of his outstretched arm. He's pulling the thread taut."

I looked at each segment of the carving. It looked as if each piece, carved individually, had been glued into place. The pieces that comprised the man were all slightly different in their tone and color.

I had never seen a Rynecki sculpture or carving. I saw a signature, but it was in pencil, and it was incredibly difficult to read. I thought I saw an R and some of the other letters in Rynecki, but I was not certain.

I tilted the carving forward, left, right, trying to make out the letters more easily. Nothing made it more readable. "You're sure it's my great-grandfather's?" I asked.

"My dad said it was. I have no reason to doubt him," Shula said. "He loved this piece and the painting. They were always together."

Carrying the wood piece, I walked to the painting so I could compare a painted tailor to a carved tailor. I was not really sure what I hoped to see. I knew my great-grandfather's painting style so well, but a wood carving? This was completely new territory, but if Shula's father said it was the work of my great-grandfather, I believed it—he had known Moshe personally. My grandfather had noted in his memoir that Moshe had produced sculptures as well as paintings; I just had no idea what to expect. The subject matter seemed completely appropriate as well. It wasn't a fully three-dimensional carving since it lay flat on the wood backing, but if I could have transformed the tailor in Shula's painting into a multidimensional, textured piece of wood, this is exactly what it would have looked like.

While Shula and I looked at the painting and the wood carving and chatted, her eldest son, Izhar (Izzy) and his wife, Heather, arrived. They were recently back in New York after a bike-riding honeymoon in Italy. They came to listen to our conversation and learn some family history.

Shula and I perched ourselves on a red leather couch in the living room. I had Shula read the letter her father wrote me in 2001. We both focused in on the same sentences: "This original picture hangs in my apartment and was sent to me by my father's aunt, Perla, who was my grandmother's sister. I remember as a child Moshe Rynecki visiting us often and playing chess with my father. I'm very proud of this picture and show it to everybody visiting us."

Neither of us was an expert on family genealogy. We weren't even sure how we were related, except that if we went back far enough we had common ancestors. Shula dug out a family tree someone had written in Hebrew. She pointed to the names and tried to draw the lines for me.

I stared helplessly, since I couldn't even sound out the names. Shula kept reading the names aloud, until two caught my attention. Mittelsbach and Rotzstein.

"Perla is a Mittelsbach!" I said, relieved to recognize her maiden name. "And Rotzstein . . . those are the cousins she went to live with in Le Mans in the 1950s."

"I've met the Rotzsteins!" Shula said.

"Do you still have their contact information?" I asked. "I'm hoping Perla gave them a painting and that I can arrange to see it."

"It's so long ago," Shula said, but she promised that she would see if she could find a name, an address, or maybe even a phone number after my visit.

I asked Shula what her father remembered about Moshe's visits. She didn't have details, just that he played chess and visited often. Shula's father, David, left Poland for Palestine well before the Second World War. He went home only once, in the late 1930s. He brought back a wife, a woman he married to get her out of Poland. Their marriage was one of convenience; each went on to marry someone else. David lost everyone in his immediate family in the Holocaust. After the war, when Perla offered him a Rynecki painting, it was a touchstone to a home that no longer existed. The painting and the carving reminded him of better days. Shula inherited a love of the Rynecki art; to her it was a link to her father as well as a link to her Polish ancestors.

Izzy and Heather sat quietly at the dining room table adjacent to where we were filming. We took a brief hiatus. I stood up and took a sip of water at the table.

"I never knew all this," Izzy said.

"And?" I asked.

"It's amazing," Heather said.

TWENTY-THREE

Looking Forward

I am a writer, a reader, a lover of words on the printed page. The bookshelf in my office is filled to bursting with Holocaust-era memoirs, words put to paper to document the horrors and atrocities of the past. Each shelf has a row of books lined up neatly, but above each row are horizontal stacks of books crammed into every available inch. The shelves are bowed from the strain of holding up the books. Above the bookcase, next to a pair of windows, hangs a painting, *Luna Park* (undated). It's probably my favorite Rynecki painting. It's not large, nineteen by thirteen inches, but the fairground it portrays is somehow larger than the canvas itself—a sprawling carnival with brightly colored tents and the Polish flag, a horizontal bicolor of white and red. At the center is a swing ride, a carousel where eight figures in chairs, suspended from the rotating top, fly across the blue sky. Below, wandering between the green, pink, and blue tents, a large crowd lingers. My great-grandfather's paintbrush rendered them as a multitude so deep and full of life, it's impossible to distinguish individuals. At the right is a merry-go-round with wooden horses.

So often when we think of Jews in Poland, we think of all that was lost and destroyed in the Holocaust. We focus on the devastation and destruction, and we wonder how it is possible the world went so dark, and how there could be such a deep, vicious, and murderous hatred. My great-grandfather's paintings have taught me that while we endeavor to understand this history, we must also remember beyond that, to a time in Poland when Jewish life flourished. I think this is why I love *Luna Park* so much, because I can almost hear exuberant, cheerful music floating across the fairgrounds. It is a painting of hope and joy.

The juxtaposition of a painting of hope and joy above a bookshelf filled with despair became especially poignant upon my return to California, when my overburdened bookshelf finally collapsed under the weight of history. The jumble of hardcover books and paperbacks, a veritable chronicle of the Jewish people, lay piled at the foot of my desk. It was, I surmised, a sign of some sort. Perhaps a simple one to buy a new bookcase, but it also seemed so much more—a reminder of the physical burden of memories the next generation must bear.

I simultaneously felt both guilty and angry about how a past, not exactly my own, weighed so heavily upon me. I craved guidance and approval from my great-grandfather as well as Grandpa George, though of course this would be impossible. I wondered if my ancestors would be pleased by my dedication to the art and the history or if they would tell me it was time to move on with my own life. But I can't, and perhaps I never will, because there are seemingly endless unanswered questions and unresolved issues. With most of the filming for the *Chasing Portraits* documentary completed, the most unsettled question in front of me was whether or not the Wertheim cousin might have a change of heart and allow me to see the Rynecki paintings in her home.

There had been nothing new to report. Elinor at Hashava wasn't sure what next steps to take, and Rosh Hashanah, the Jewish New Year, soon approached. She proposed we touch base after the holidays. It was in the absence of any news, while stacking my books so I could get to my desk, that my mind got stuck in an endless cycle of regret and recrimination regarding the Wertheim cousin in Israel.

"Why did you file a claim if you're a historian?" friends asked, confused by my seeming contradictions. Quite honestly, because I had a fierce and abiding desire to see my great-grandfather's paintings. To be in Israel, to be so very close to the paintings, and not to try one more way to gain access would have meant giving up and accepting the roadblock. I am not so easily dissuaded, and when Hashava offered to intercede on my behalf, it was an opportunity I could not pass up. If I had, I would have forever berated myself for not at least allowing Elinor to broker a chance for me to see the paintings.

Unfortunately, this collector of my great-grandfather's work in Israel, a woman who is not part of my family, but to whom I am inextricably linked by Moshe's art, again said no. She did not want to grant me access to the paintings in her home. I might never know why, and perhaps her reason, whatever it is, didn't matter.

Consumed by thoughts of failure, I alternately felt wronged and guilty. Wronged because the paintings were the works of my great-grandfather and rejecting my request to see them seemed unfair. Guilty because as confident as I was about my moral right to view the paintings, I didn't have definitive proof those paintings were taken from my family.

Personally, I think it is very likely that the Wertheim paintings came from one of the bundles Moshe hid. One could question the conflicting stories of the Wertheim brothers, but given that it was a long time ago and there was a war going on, I don't find their contradictions surprising. No one will ever know the actual story of what happened. I think it's better to try to keep an open mind about where the paintings came from and what possible explanations exist. I know my great-grandfather bundled his paintings unframed and hid them with friends. One explanation would be that the Wertheim paintings were traveling to or from an exhibit. But Perla said the last time the paintings were exhibited abroad was in Brussels in 1935, so these artworks didn't come from an exhibition. Even if they had, if Moshe had sent them, they would still belong to him.

The only other logical alternative is that these paintings were owned by someone else. It's remotely possible Moshe sold this group of paintings, but it is exceedingly rare to purchase bulk unframed paintings by a single artist. Who would have purchased them, and why so many? So for this alternative to be correct, we have to postulate an unknown benefactor of some sort, a collector of Moshe's work, whom Moshe's wife and adult son didn't know about, who then bundled a group of unframed Rynecki paintings for safekeeping during the war and lost them when the Lodz farmer acquired them. Although it is possible, it would be a pretty remarkable set of circumstances.

When all is said and done, regardless of how likely it is that the paintings came from one of my great-grandfather's bundles, and regardless of how unlikely the alternatives are, claims are not judged based on likelihood. While my instincts told me the Rynecki paintings held by the Wertheim family were from a bundle hidden by my great-grandfather, I had no definitive proof.

I could only hope that a letter from Hashava would raise a question in the Wertheim cousin's mind. Perhaps she would begin to see that her provenance was on shaky ground. If so, perhaps the doubt would convince her that the right thing to do would be to allow me to see the paintings. In retrospect, perhaps the opposite happened; perhaps she thought that if I saw the paintings I would want to keep them. I just don't know, but I do know that the initial letter made no difference. My options were to keep going down an uncertain, bitter, and most likely unproductive path, or let it go. Neither option seemed appealing, but I felt I had to choose the lesser of two evils.

Not wanting my request to devolve into a lengthy and acrimonious legal dispute, I opened a blank Word document on my computer and composed a letter: a personal, emotional plea to this woman who loved my great-grandfather's paintings. I wrote of my sorrow and disappointment. "I imagine my great-grandfather would be dismayed to know his art has created a rift between us. I wish that instead of creating tension between us, his art had united us. That together we might have stood in front of his work and admired his beautiful paintings and our shared Polish-Jewish heritage."

I emailed my letter to Elinor at Hashava and asked her to deliver it to the Wertheim cousin. I told her that while it was emotionally wrenching, I'd come to the conclusion that nothing would change and I wanted to drop the claim.

My letter, Elinor replied, was "brave and moving," but she was not ready to give up. After consulting with Hashava's legal adviser, she proposed bringing the Wertheim cousin to the appeals committee for questioning under oath. I thanked Elinor profusely for her help, but said I could not in good conscience press the case any further. I wanted access to the paintings, yes. But I was beginning to feel this approach was overly aggressive. I'm not a bully. I just wanted to see the paintings.

Often people say there is no instruction manual for how to be a parent. Similarly, there is none for how to be a descendant of Holocaust survivors looking for lost art. Like everyone, I have good days and bad days, and often feel pulled in many different directions. Ultimately, I feel a deep and profound connection to my great-grandfather's work that is hard to describe. I have a passion to see all his paintings, to get every view I can of his works.

The paintings are a direct link to my great-grandfather, his ideas made real through the expression of his paintbrush. His works are, in some sense, an extension of his very being. In their own way, they are Holocaust survivors, and as links to him, they feel like members of my family. I don't need to possess all of the paintings, and I wouldn't have a place to display them if I did. But I need to know what survived, and what didn't. Even photographs of the paintings and sculptures that didn't survive are treasures to me. I often wonder what types of art, what styles, what insights I don't know about simply because I have seen only a small portion of Moshe's work.

Beyond the need to see the works themselves, I also feel a great yearning to know their stories of survival. I want to know these works are cared for and that they are in good homes. I feel a kinship and a sense of stewardship for these paintings, because each is a memory of a moment, a story of a vanished culture, and a clue to understanding my family's art legacy. When barriers are raised, when I am blocked from seeing or learning about the surviving works, it makes me deeply angry.

The injustice I feel is magnified by the inexorable march of time. My family and my personal history have shown me just how precious and ephemeral life is. It can vanish in an instant. Mom died unexpectedly. Dad was three at the start of the war and now is almost eighty. Every year there are fewer people alive who know exactly what happened to the paintings, so the works' stories are at risk of being lost in the mists of time. It's already clear that the paintings have scattered more with each passing generation, and that the stories of the works have increasingly faded, conflicted, or been forgotten. Every time a piece changes hands, another potential connection to my great-grandfather is lost.

I know my great-grandfather's collection will never be whole again. There's a part of me that has always been dismayed by this fact. But each discovery of a piece that survived gives me great joy. Grandpa George died believing that nearly 90 percent of his father's paintings had been destroyed and were gone forever, so each new find is a ray of hope for me that he never got to see.

The woman in Israel is not the only one with Rynecki paintings I have never seen. The Wertheim family originally bought a bundle containing close to fifty works, and the whereabouts of most of these, pieces the family gave away, are entirely unknown. There is also a collector who bought two Rynecki paintings at Sotheby's, and I've never been granted access to those works either. Given that the works held by the

Jewish Historical Institute were acquired piecemeal, from various people in the 1940s and on, into the 1980s, it is almost certain that they came from multiple bundles. So I know there are other Rynecki works out there, waiting to be found. To me, that is another motivation to share Moshe's work and the story of my search. The more word spreads, the more likely others with my great-grandfather's works will step forward and share their stories and paintings. The possibility of learning what is still out there, what survived and how it survived, is what has motivated me for the last decade, and will continue to drive me in the future.

I've been told by many well-meaning friends and acquaintances, on more than one occasion, "The paintings are stolen property," "It is an outrage they are not with your family," and "It's despicable others have what properly should be yours." I appreciate this keen sense of fixing historical injustice, and I am aware of how the return of a painting can provide a deep-seated sense of righting the wrongs of history. But justice can come in many forms, and restorative justice—to reclaim the art—is only one measure of success. Even if I successfully recovered some of the artworks, the greater impact would likely be that people would no longer share, and doors that are now open, even a crack, would slam shut. The opportunities to find lost works and learn their stories would dry up, which would be a much greater blow to my search, and ultimately to my great-grandfather's legacy. So despite my tremendous disappointment, I walked away from pursuing the pieces in Israel. Despite the frustration and sadness, I am optimistic, and confident, there will be other opportunities to see more of my great-grandfather's work.

I have a recurring dream. In the dream, I am on my book tour, or it's after the showing of the documentary, during a Q&A session, and a woman (or a man) in the back tentatively raises her hand. She tells a story—a painting has been prominently displayed in her family's living room for as long as she can remember. Her parents acquired it, she doesn't remember how, and now they are gone and so it is too late to ask, but it was always so important to them, and now it means so much to her. It gives her solace at the end of a busy day. It's a reminder of her childhood home, a link to a Polish-Jewish heritage she only vaguely knows. She thinks maybe the signature is my great-grandfather's mark. She wonders if I might take a look at the painting.

My great-grandfather's paintings are an everyday part of my life. Growing up, it was easy to walk by them and take them for granted. Sometimes that is even true today. They have always been in my life and I expect they will always remain with me. But their story is anything but mundane. Moshe Rynecki was an artist of merit. His paintings stand on their own and attest to a unique Jewish perspective on life in Poland. While his individual works can be admired in isolation, it is difficult even now for me to piece together a true understanding of Moshe as an artist from less than a quarter of his art. What I have so far is an incomplete assessment, an unfinished portrait of a man who dedicated his life to painting. To understand my great-grandfather, to get to know him, I must see more. Each new discovery helps bring his life just a bit more into focus. And, as his great-granddaughter, it is this portrait I have been chasing all along, the portrait of the man behind the paintings.

ACKNOWLEDGMENTS

While it is true that getting one's *tuches* (Yiddish for buttocks or bottom) into the chair, fingers on the keyboard, and ideas transforming to bits on the computer is the generally solitary act of the writer, writing a book is far from an individual endeavor. Bringing this true life story to the page has taken a vast team and more than a decade of my time. I am grateful to all who have given so generously of their own time. A particularly heartfelt thank-you to all who appear in the book. The story just wouldn't be the same without each and every one of you. To those individuals who did behind-the-scenes yeoman's work to get me here, thank you.

Thanks also to Natalee Rosenstein and Brent Howard, my Penguin Random House editors, who not only believed in the viability of the book, but helped guide it toward publication. Sharlene Martin, my literary agent, who saw the promise of the book within the pages of my proposal. Jill Swenson, my book development editor, and Jenna Goodman, her editorial assistant.

I owe enormous thanks to my family for their wisdom and guidance in all its various forms, especially Grandpa George, Grandma Stella, and my parents, Alex and Fern Rynecki. I am profoundly grateful to my husband, Steve Knowlton, who edited many drafts (more than should ever have been asked of him). Much love to my sons, Tyler and Owen, for their moral support, and a sincere wish that someday each will navigate the Rynecki legacy on his own terms.

I am especially indebted to Helen Miller, Henry Miller, Adam and Chaia Schneid, Ed Mitukiewicz, Nana Meyer, Linda Mazur, Arlene

Weicsensang Zapata, Mitchell Schwarzbach, Connie Clayton, Martha Jain, Betty Jain, Nancy Goldberg, Sheryl Knowlton, Paige Dansinger, Amira Kendar, and the extended Knox and Niv families for their assistance.

Thank you, Jeanne Diller (Oakland Public Library), Anne Evenhaugen (Smithsonian Library), Logan Kleinwaks (genealogyindexer.org), Sławomir Kitowski (Gdynia historian), and Michael Halber (for sharing Marian Trzebiński's story with me).

An enormous thank-you to extended family and friends. You were among the first to believe in the project and to marvel at each and every discovery. I am particularly grateful to Twitter and Facebook friends who offered guidance and assistance in many different ways, and who generously shared the story within their own networks.

A thank-you to the grantors and individual backers who made donations to the documentary film.

I've worked hard to record the facts and details in the book as accurately as possible. Many have helped me in this endeavor, but ultimately any errors found in the book are, of course, mine.

A NOTE ABOUT SOURCES

The materials I relied on include my great-grandfather's artwork rescued after the war, a substantial number of original documents Grandpa George saved (letters, wartime papers, U.S. military certificates, photographs), and Grandpa George's memoir. All the scenes and conversations in the book are based on historical facts, oral history, and family testimony.

Perhaps the most important primary source I relied on was Grandpa George's memoir. Published posthumously in 2005, *Surviving Hitler in Poland: One Jew's Story* is a collection of vignettes written in the last years of his life about his memories of life in Poland before the Second World War and during the war itself. My family's discovery of the memoir after Grandpa George's death in 1992 is described in Chapter One. At first I approached the memoir with a healthy dose of skepticism. I wondered how Grandpa remembered so many details of his wartime experiences so many years later. But as I researched my family's history, I found, time and again, that his recollections could be corroborated by other sources. The memoir turned out to be a foundational resource. I could not have written the first several chapters of the book without it.

There is a lot of dialogue in my book. I wanted to find a way to actively tell the story, to bring it alive. For me, sharing people's words and conversations helps convey the story with greater intimacy, as it presents the voices of those who feature prominently in the story. There are two types of dialogue in my book. The first is those conversations I personally experienced. When I wrote these, I stayed as true as possible to my memory, notes, and email exchanges. In the second type I took literary liberties to re-create conversations where I was not present. There is tremendous challenge as well as substantial room for error in re-creating conversations where I was not present, but in most cases I had substantial corroboration from secondary sources that gave me guidance as to context, content, and results of the conversations.

I've become familiar with vast numbers of libraries, auction houses, online markets, museums, memorials, private collections, databases, *Yizkor* books (Eastern European memorial books created after the Holocaust), genealogical indices, documentaries, 2G and 3G (children and grandchildren of survivors) organizations, and newspaper archives over the course of my quest for my great-grandfather's lost paintings. I have personally visited many of these storehouses of information in the United States, Poland, Canada, and Israel. I've also been fortunate enough to have assistance from people along the way who have helped me navigate Polish, German, Hebrew, and Yiddish search engines in my pursuit of further information. I've also developed relationships with many museum professionals over the course of more than a decade of research—directors, curators, registrars, art conservationists, and museum educators—all of whom shared book titles, exhibition catalogs, and insights about Polish-Jewish art history with me. Similarly, I've received substantial assistance from provenance researchers, art crime investigators, and art lawyers about where to go in search of answers to my myriad of art ownership questions. And last, but definitely not least, professors and other academics have opened innumerable doors for me—giving me new insight into Judaism, Jewish culture, Jewish history, and Jewish identity.

The impact of serendipity on my project cannot be overstated: you never know where information will come from, how it may land in your lap, or how it may connect to yet another find. When you start collecting bits and pieces of data, it isn't always clear how it will all coalesce to create a coherent whole. Over the years I've learned to be open to different ideas and suggestions. I've repeatedly learned firsthand how disparate pieces of seemingly insignificant research can suddenly become monumentally important when combined. I have worked hard to incorporate many of my finds and discoveries into the book. I hope it makes for a rich and rewarding read.

Chapter One: A Jewish Girl Should Know

["Elżbieta," she said and gave me a large hug.] Elizabeth, in Polish, is Elżbieta. It is pronounced Elzhbyeta.

[He had commingled stories, so that a tale about Poland in 1480 was intersected with a memory of the Second World War.] It has been pointed out to me that 1480 was not a particularly significant year in Polish history. One early draft reader asked if it was a typo; perhaps I meant to write 1410, the year of the Polish-Lithuanian-Teutonic War, or 1980, when Poland's Solidarity movement was founded. But Grandpa George did, indeed, write 1480. In fact, what he wrote was this: "Jews were unknown in Poland in the year 980. They came by invitation of King Kasimir the Great to come and live in Poland in the year 1480. Remember the Spaniards? The Jews were persecuted in Western Europe and took the invitation seriously. They came by the thousands and settled all over the Polish land. They brought with them crafts and arts. They were masters in commerce and banking. They were excellent artisans. They came and worked. Their efforts were tremendous. They brought Poland to be known all over Europe, and they created an atmosphere of confidence, prosperity, and the land started to bloom." As it turns out, Grandpa George's dates are not correct, but the idea that Jewish refugees were allowed to settle in Poland is true and King Kasimir was welcoming and friendly to the growing Jewish population.

[Some say it will never happen again.] *Surviving Hitler in Poland: One Jew's Story*, page 33.

Chapter Two: The Trouble with Moshe

The description of Moshe's interaction with his father was inspired by both Grandpa George's memoir and years of familiarity with my great-grandfather's paintings.

The book *My Name Is Asher Lev* by Chaim Potok, and the play Aaron Posner wrote based on the book, which I saw at the Marin Theater Company in the 2009–2010 season, were exceedingly helpful in thinking about my great-grandfather's struggle with his father about his passion to make art.

[He spent his early childhood in Międzyrzecze, a place whose name meant "Between Rivers."] Międzyrzecze is pronounced: Mee-end-zee-ger-tscher. Grandpa George's memoir states that his father was born in Międzyrzecze. The town is presently known as Międzyrzec Podlaski or just Międzyrzec (no "e" on the end). MapyWIG.org maintains a digital collection of maps and geographical materials published in the interwar period (1919–1939) by the Polish Wojskowy Instytut Geograficzny (WIG, the Military Geographical Institute), which existed in Poland between 1919 and 1949. WIG has maps from the time period that show the town name without an "e" on the end. I have left it with an "e" because this is how Grandpa George wrote it.

Descriptions of Międzyrzecze and Siedlce come from Grandpa George's memoir, a translation of *Żydzi w Siedlcach 1850–1945* by Edward Kopówka (translated from the Polish by Dobrochna Fire and edited by Leonard Levin and Michael Halber), and other various online sources.

[The Rynecki family moved to the larger but still primarily agricultural town of Siedlce when Moshe was about ten years old.] In Polish the Rynecki name is pronounced Rin-EHtski. Dad and his parents Americanized the pronunciation to RYNehkee when they arrived in the United States in 1949.

The scene with Moshe, his father, and Polish artist Marian Trzebiński (1871–1942) is based on Trzebiński's own recollection of their visit, described in his memoir *Pamiętnik Malarza,* published posthumously in 1958. [Wrocław: *Zakład Narodowy im. Ossolińskich*, edited by Maciej Masłowski]. I worked from the section about my great-grandfather translated for me by Marlena Rosłan.

["I'll tell you what. I'll buy you a paper store just like Celnik in Siedlce has."] Trzebiński's memoir mentions Moshe's father referring to a paper store Celnik owned in Siedlce. I was able to verify the name and existence of the store on Virtual Shtetl (http://www.sztetl.org.pl/), which has both history about the Celnik family and their art supply store, as well as a poster advertising the arts supply and paper/stationery store owned by F. Celnik.

["I'm not promising anything, but I thought you might say that. I'll make an appointment with Professor Kotarbiński at the Municipal Drawing School."] Miłosz Kotarbiński (1854–1944) was a painter, art critic, and composer. After studying at the St. Petersburg Academy of Fine Arts in Russia, he returned to Warsaw to teach first at the Municipal Drawing School (*Miejska Szkoła Rysunkowa*) and then at the Warsaw School of Fine Arts (*Warszawska Szkoła Sztuk Pięknych*).

["The store is at 24 Krucza Street."] Moshe and Perla's store was at Krucza 24 in Warsaw. In Polish the number always comes after the street name, but I've written the book with American readers in mind and so have placed the building's number before the street name.

Chapter Three: Paintings

Chapter Three leans heavily on details found in Grandpa George's memoir. If he remembered someone had wavy hair, I included it. His recollection of scenes from the early days of the war, searching for food, and hiding out in the bombed-out skeleton of the apartment building are included, as are his spellings of names. Of course, it was not possible to incorporate everything from his memoir into this book, but I did my best to integrate as many of the relevant stories and situations as possible.

[In 1906, he enrolled at the School of Fine Arts in Warsaw.] Moshe attended the School of Fine Arts in Warsaw in the 1906–1907 school year. From 1904 to 1932 the school was known as the School of Fine Arts in Warsaw. In 1932 it changed its name to the Academy of Fine Arts in Warsaw. In 1907 the school published a report, *Sprawozdanie Z Dotychczasowej Działalności Warszawskiej Szkoły Sztuk Pięknych*, containing a list of pupils, which includes my great-grandfather.

[The school, founded by Professor Kazimierz Stabrowski (1869–1929) among others, did more than train students in classical art techniques; it engaged and developed the broader Warsaw art community and culture.] Kazimierz Stabrowski gave students a foundation in art techniques gained from his own education abroad (he studied at the St. Petersburg Academy of Fine Arts and the Académie Julian in Paris). As an artist Moshe was interested in learning about different styles and techniques, but Grandpa George said Moshe was interested in new techniques never just to be fashionable, but rather as a means to better represent his subjects. My statement that Moshe "wasn't so sure about some of Stabrowski's views on art and technique" is a bit of an educated guess based on two pieces of information: (1) the fact that in 1930 Moshe wrote a brief biography about influential art teachers, which included Stabrowski's name, and (2) Grandpa George recalls in his memoir that his father favored subject matter over technique. Other teachers named in Moshe's brief biography include Ignacy Gajewski from Siedlce, Marian Trzebiński, and Professor Adolf Eduard Herstein.

About *The Dybbuk*, Grandpa George wrote, "One time, the Hebrew theater troupe, Habima, showed up in Warsaw. He came home and painted a scene from *The Dybbuk*. I still have it. I consider it a masterpiece of art. Still, somebody during the war tore away the figure of the rabbi and the *shammash* blowing the *shofar*." (*Surviving Hitler in Poland: One Jew's Story*, page 62.) The painting is dated 1920. In *Jewish Drama & Theatre: From Rabbinical Intolerance to Secular Liberalism*, author Eli Rozik says *The Dybbuk* was premiered in Yiddish by the Vilna Troupe in Warsaw in 1920. Although Habima did perform *The Dybbuk*, it seems they did not do the show my great-grandfather saw in Warsaw.

[Jerzy ran the office in Gdynia.] Grandpa George's memoir talks about living in Gdynia and the fish import business he established with Herman Mathiesen. Details about where he lived in Gdynia, the date the business was established, its registration number, and its payroll come from *Lost in the Whirlwind of War: The Jewish Community in Gdynia, Poland* by Jarosław Drozd. Originally published in Polish in 2007, it was translated to English in 2008. The extended Rynecki family appears in several places in this book. Moshe and Perla appear in a footnote which cites a Szymon Rynecki, which really is Jerzy (Grandpa George) Rynecki. The exact reason for Jerzy's name appearing as Szymon on official documents is unclear to me.

[Jerzy opted to fire the pregnant employee "not because of prudishness, just as an example to others."] Grandpa George wrote in his memoir, "I had to let her go not because of my prudishness, just as an example to others. The last thing I needed was a scandal. Gdynia was a small provincial town. Everybody knew everybody." (*Surviving Hitler in Poland: One Jew's Story*, page 53.)

[Jerzy took him in his small car, a Ford Eifel.] Grandpa George's memoir states the car was an English Ford Eifel. While Ford did produce an English version of the Eifel, calling it an English Ford Eifel isn't quite right. "It is," Sam Roberts, Archivist at Ford Y&C Model Register, explained to me, "stretching the description a tad too far." Sam suggested a more accurate description might be "a Ford Eifel, based on the contemporary English Ford 10hp." This seemed a bit too wordy for the story. While the surest way to resolve this question would be to examine a photograph of the car in question, unfortunately no such photograph exists in Grandpa George's documents.

["I carried him on my shoulders, and we would have gotten here sooner, but the railroad ties and sand under the tracks made for slow walking, and it was hotter than hell."] Grandpa George wrote quite a bit about this memory. I tried to use his exact words when I could. He wrote, "After a day or two, I decided to move to Warsaw. I was stranded and desperate. I could depend on my parents. They still had the large apartment on Krucza. The railroad was out, the car was gone, and the only way to get there was to walk. Along the rails in sandy ground. We started one morning to walk. It was tedious. Sand and more sand. Alex got very quickly tired and I had to take him on my shoulders with a couple packs in my hands. Hotter than hell in this early September 1939. The battlefield losses of the Poles, the rapid progress of German armies, all this was no incentive to live, or act intelligently. A few miles, but how difficult. When we reached the Vistula and the Kierbedzia bridge, I was exhausted. And there, right on the bridge, the Polish soldiers were building a barricade of sorts to protect the approach from the east. As I was thinking, an officer stopped me, requesting my help in building the barricades. I dropped Alex, the bundles, and started to work. Stella and Alex were resting on the side of the bridge. After a while I was released and could proceed, till finally, after a couple of hours, we reached my parents' home. We were refugees, and there was no way out of it. The future looked dim and unpromising. Artillery fire had already started, and the next day we all knew Warsaw to be completely surrounded. German cannon boomed day and night. German Stukas were dive bombing constantly just the city itself without seeking anything of military value." (*Surviving Hitler in Poland: One Jew's Story,* pages 86–87.)

[On the table he kept a pad of paper. As he reviewed, sorted, and divided the collection, he made a list of which pieces went into which pile. It wasn't a terribly descriptive list, but he didn't know how much time they had left, and it just had to suffice. "It's just to help me remember what's where," he said to himself.] Grandpa George distinctly recalled that when the Second World War broke out his father had a collection of approximately eight hundred works (paintings and sculptures). While he was confident about the number of works in the collection, his memory of the precise number of bundles created to hide the work was less certain. I've underlined the number of bundles in each of the following three quotes to draw attention to the varying number of bundles he remembered. In one place in his memoir he wrote, "He packed the canvases and paper paintings into bundles. Some which were framed he took out. Some canvases he had to roll into scrolls. Some flat into packages around one hundred each. He then divided the parcels and entrusted them to ten Polish, so called, friends." (*Surviving Hitler in Poland: One Jew's Story*, page 60.) Then later in his memoir he wrote, "In the first days of the war he decided to hide his paintings and sculpture from the Germans. He divided his works according to materials and sizes, and made eight large parcels. No frames. Rolled canvasses. Flat paper, or parchments were put in one hundred packages each, approximately." (*Surviving Hitler in Poland: One Jew's Story*, page 94.) A 1981 newspaper story by Donna Horowitz of the *Marin Independent Journal* states, "According to Rynecki, a retired steel company owner, his father's 800 paintings were divided into six parcels during the war and entrusted to Gentile friends around Warsaw." On where the bundles were hidden, Grandpa George wrote in his memoir, "He [Moshe] gave me a list, my sister one, and of course, my mother knew where the paintings did go." (*Surviving Hitler in Poland: One Jew's Story*, pages 60–61.) Sadly, I have never seen these lists and do not know precisely what information they did or did not include.

[Unfortunately, what little money Jerzy made selling the fish became worthless, as the zloty was being replaced—no one was willing to take the zloty, no one was sure what would ultimately replace the zloty, and no one had German marks.] Grandpa George's memoir states, "Occupational money—marks—were the legal tender. Nothing else. No one had marks." Initially, bank accounts and deposits were blocked. Then on December 15, 1939, the new Nazi General Government created a new bank and currency. Individuals, depending on whether they were Polish or Jewish, were limited on what they could withdraw. Jews could withdraw only 250 zlotys a week, and were forbidden from having more than two thousand zlotys in cash. A fixed exchange rate of 1 reichsmark = 2 zlotys was established.

[In 1920 the Vilna troupe premiered *The Dybbuk* in Warsaw.] In Jewish mythology, a dybbuk is a wicked possessing spirit believed to be the lost soul of a dead person. Shloyme Zanvl Rappoport, known as S. Anski [sometimes An-Ski], a Russian Jewish author and playwright, popularized interest in the Jewish folklore idea in his play. *The Dybbuk*, set in the Jewish town of Brinitz, took place sometime in the early 1880s. A poor Yeshiva student named Khanan approached the father of Leah, his love, to get approval for marriage, only to find out her father had promised her to another. Khanan's father and Leah's father had long ago agreed to the marriage, and the children had always expected to be wed, but when Khanan's father died, Leah's father reneged on their agreement. In despair, Khanan dropped dead on the spot. Ultimately, in a dream Leah perceived Khanan's spirit, and confided her love to him. She mourned the life they lost together, and the children they would never have. She rose from the bed, walked to his spirit, and the two were united in death. A tragic love story with a spiritually uplifting ending, *The Dybbuk* was a huge artistic and commercial success in Warsaw.

[He couldn't use the type of crates he used for local exhibitions, much less the safer kind he used when he sent his works to the Brussels International Exposition of 1935.] The Brussels International Exposition of 1935 (French: *Exposition Universelle et Internationale Bruxelles de 1935*) was held in Heysel, near Brussels, Belgium, from April 27, 1935, to November 6, 1935. Evidence Moshe exhibited at the Brussels International Exposition comes both from stickers affixed to the backsides of several paintings and information in a newspaper article published after the war that quoted Perla about her husband's work. On July 20, 1946, *Opinia* published "*M. Rynecki I jego twórczość*," [M. Rynecki and his work]. The article also confirms information Grandpa George wrote in his memoir many years after the war. I received translation assistance for the article from Agnieszka Yass-Alston and Ed Mitukiewicz. The opening paragraphs talk about the Shoah in, I am told, poetic terms. The remaining paragraphs of the article introduce my great-grandfather and say: "On September 19, 1942, M. Rynecki, 57 years old, was facing death. His wife, who miraculously crossed to the 'Aryan' side, survived and saved 70 of her husband's works. There were moments when Rynecki could have saved his life—however, he chose not to do so. 'I will not leave my brothers,' he cried. 'What will happen to them, will happen to me!' and he kept his word. M. Rynecki, known and acclaimed in painting circles in the capital city, exhibited his work in Warsaw for over 20 years at Zachęta, IPS [*Instytut Propagandy Sztuki/Institute for Propaganda of Art*], and Baryczków [note: in 1937–1938 Baryczków House was one of three purchased for the purpose of establishing a museum, which today is known as the Historical Museum of Warsaw, a branch of the National Museum. It is located in the Old Town Square in Warsaw]. Most recently over 60 of his works were shown at the Brussels World Exhibition. Rynecki's scenes depicted Polish Jews and those from the Orthodox community. His pictures were sincere representations, filled with expressive dynamism and extraordinarily sober yet rich colors."

[In 1942 Jerzy arranged her escape, and she spent the remainder of the war with a Polish Christian woman, Emilia Komarnicka, in Służewiec, a neighborhood in Warsaw's Mokotów district.] Grandpa George wrote in his memoir, "My mother listened to me, got out of the ghetto in 1942 and spent the war years in peace hidden with a Polish lady, a certain Komarnicka, in a suburb of Warsaw, who did it for money." Perla recorded testimony in Yiddish after the war, a copy of which is in Yad Vashem's archives (record group M.49.E.; Perla's testimony was dictated to a K. Meiska, who transcribed her testimony; Perla signed the document). In the testimony Perla recalled that the woman she stayed with had two brothers, one of whom was the painter Marian Trzebiński. After cross-checking the genealogy on Geni.com (the online ancestry family tree website), I learned that Komarnicka was, in fact, Emilia Komarnicka (née Trzebińska). Additionally, it is interesting to note that Perla's testimony states she did not pay Ms. Komarnicka at all for hiding her, but Grandpa George distinctly remembers he did pay Ms. Komarnicka. I left the detail of money out of the book because of the conflicting information. Translation of Perla's Yiddish testimony was provided to me by Nick Block, PhD Translations.

Chapter Four: Defying Hitler

["You better do what I tell you," Jerzy growled . . .] It is not clear to me what Grandpa George meant by "Army of the People," but I've included it here because it is what he wrote in his memoir. His recollection of the event in the memoir reads, in part, "It took more than money and time to persuade the Polish bullies. In sheer desperation I told them in a very quiet voice, 'You better do what I tell you, because in five minutes from now, if I don't show up downstairs with her and the kid, this whole complex will blow sky high. You are here surrounded by my colleagues from the Army of the People. I am not making jokes. This time you are trapped, not me.' My desperate position made an impression and in a minute or so the 'transaction' was made. I had to show up the next day at noon in a local restaurant with five thousand złoty and buy them a lunch with drinks. This is how it happened. I grabbed Alex in my arms and we ran out. The curfew was already on, and there was a chance we'd be shot on sight. We came to the apartment in one piece, and all of us in shock." (*Surviving Hitler in Poland: One Jew's Story*, page 103.)

Chapter Five: Displaced

[These lists, produced by the United Nations Relief and Rehabilitation Administration (UNRRA) and the International Refugee Organization (IRO), shared names and locations of DPs spread across Europe—it was a way for people to search for and reconnect with family and loved ones.] In the course of my research I came across an interesting document held by the American Jewish Joint Distribution Committee in regards to these lists and my family. On February 21, 1946, David Guzik of the Joint Distribution Committee in Warsaw sent a cable to the Joint Distribution Committee in Paris. The cable said Perla was living in Lodz and, having learned her son was alive, wished to send him this message: "I am the wife of an artist-painter, aged of 65 years. I am quite alone and I am very happy to learn that my son is alive. Having no possibility to write to him directly, I ask you very kindly to forward this message to my dear son under the quoted address. I should like to join him, as I have to live quite alone in hard conditions. I am very anxious for news from him.—P. Rynecka, unhappy mother."

[ex-political prisoner of the Concentration Camp SD Prag is travelling to Linden for the purpose of looking for his deported family.] Prag is a German name for Prague. SD is an abbreviation of German *Sicherheitdienst*, the SS Security Service, declared a criminal organization at the Nuremberg trials. In addition to the Polish Committee Expeditionary Forces Military Government certificate, Jerzy had two other documents for his trip to Linden. One, a four-by-six-inch preprinted form with the header "Military Government Det. Displaced Persons Transit" stated, "Dr. Trzaska-Rynecki Jerzy with car Vehicle No. 3 M 1155 is authorized to go from Bad Aibling to Hamburg and come back with approval of authorities of zones to be crossed [for purposes of] contact of Linden concentration camp." It is signed by First Lieutenant R. Genot, Medical Corps, U.S. Third Army. A second document stated that "The gasoline used by Mr. Trzaska-Rynecki Jerzy, chief of Polish Committee, is supplied by UNRRA Team 710 in Bad-Aibling." It is stamped and signed by: Lt. C. Duplan.

[A woman screamed. Not a scream of fear or pain, but a screeching, astonished sort of scream. After a moment, Jerzy realized it might be someone calling his name, but he wasn't certain. He turned to look, and saw a boy running toward him.] Grandpa George did not write about this moment in his memoir, but he did tell a Denison, Texas, reporter about it in 1949. In a newspaper clipping titled "Polish Family First Displaced Persons to Settle in Denison," the reporter wrote, "The day the family was reunited after six years was a memorable one, the doctor recalls. He drove in an army staff car to the camp where Mrs. Rynecki and Alexander were staying. She became hysterical when she saw her husband as she had given him up for dead." Whoever clipped out the article neglected to save the header, so I'm not sure of the name of the newspaper or the exact date on which it was published.

["The Germans took us all on the street and put us in a coal wagon."] Grandma Stella's recollection of leaving Warsaw in a coal wagon after the uprising comes from an interview I recorded with her in 1994.

["The last home we stayed at in Warsaw, before the uprising, was with the Stefański family in the Żoliborz district."] I know from the interview I made with Grandma Stella that she lived with a family named Stefański. The fact that they were in the Żoliborz district comes from Grandpa George, who wrote in his memoir, "My wife and Alex lived at that time in a district of Warsaw called Żoliborz." Historians believe Żoliborz was largely saved from complete devastation because in the first days of the 1944 Warsaw Uprising the Polish Home Army forces failed to secure their key military targets in the district. Consequently, some members of the Polish resistance retreated into the forests just outside of the city, thus sparing the neighborhood of heavy fighting. Dad once wrote, "I remember turmoil on the streets, dead horses, and trenches cut into the streets to allow passing from one side to the other. I was nearly eight years old and the circumstances made an impression of great impact on me."

[In the rural area surrounding the town, he found a farmer who had stored an old BMW in his barn, under bales of hay, for the duration of the war.] The military government motor vehicle registration application and permit for the BMW Grandpa George bought, dated July 26, 1945, notes it was a six-cylinder passenger vehicle with room for four passengers. It was engine number 95 923. Under "Purpose for which registration is desired" it states: "Jewish Information Office C.C. Dachau Misbach."

[Perhaps sensing a fresh start would be good for his eventual plans of a Communist government, Josef Stalin supported the rebuilding project.] In early 1945, with Soviet forces in place in Poland, the new Communist authorities considered moving Poland's capital to Lodz, a major city still largely intact. Many officials thought it would be easiest to turn the entirety of Warsaw into a kind of memorial. Ultimately Warsaw was rebuilt for two essential reasons. First was the steady influx of people into the city after the war, many of whom began reconstruction on their own. The second was political. The particulars of the Warsaw Uprising were politically inconvenient for Stalin; they suggested that the uprising had failed because of the Soviet Union's lack of military involvement. Stalin, preparing for the Yalta Conference (the 1945 meeting between President Franklin D. Roosevelt, British Prime Minister Winston Churchill, and Soviet Premier Joseph Stalin to discuss and make decisions regarding the future progress of the war and the postwar world), needed international support for his presence in Poland. Announcing his intention to rebuild Warsaw was intended to show Stalin's goodwill toward the Polish people.

[Perla knew from the list Moshe had given her where the bundles had been hidden, but many of the locations had been completely destroyed.] There are two places in Grandpa George's memoir, twenty pages apart, where he reminisces on his mother's discovery and recovery of the paintings. He wrote: "My mother was the one who with the help of a cousin of mine, Sophie Binstock, found two broken packages in Praga in a cellar across the river Vistula from Warsaw, which my mother eventually brought to me in Italy." And then, "They were looking for all the hidden parcels. The only one found was in a cellar in Praga. The people were away, and the paintings, all on paper or parchment, fairly small, were strewn on the basement floor in the cellar. Some damaged, some cut in half with scenes missing. They seemed to have gone through the same fate as the Jewish people—massacred and destroyed." This chapter gave me the greatest heartache to write. A point so central to the story and so poignant, and there was little direct information, with the number of packages conflicting in the two places they were mentioned. I hope the reader will forgive me for adding some detail here regarding the recovery of the art, but several secondary sources were used to add descriptive depth as well, regarding the condition of the neighborhood, where the Vistula could be crossed, etc. Given the conflicting nature of the two references, I chose not to specify the number of bundles Perla found, but instead to focus on the paintings themselves. What I do know is that Grandpa George believed the rest were destroyed in Warsaw's ruins. Grandpa George wrote, "Six hundred eighty were lost, probably destroyed." (*Surviving Hitler in Poland: One Jew's Story*, page 60.)

Chapter Six: Italy

["So when exactly did Perla come to Rome?" I asked.] Information from the American Joint Distribution Committee on a document titled "Emigration Service: Warsawa—Index Cards for April 1947," shows Perla's name (number 96 on the list), her Warsaw-Emigration file (number 1672-E), and her country of destination (Italy).

[And that was how I ended up on the floor of my office reading a stack of letters from a Chicago relative, Charles Weicensang.] Stella wrote to her uncle Louis from Bad Aibling. Unbeknownst to her, Louis had died in 1940. Her letter was forwarded to Louis's nephew, Charles Weicensang, her first cousin. Letters sent between Charles Weicensang in Chicago and the Rynecki family in Italy (February 1946 to December 1949) are part of the Rynecki family's private collection. In addition to saving Charles's letters, Grandpa George also kept copies of some letters he sent Charles. Early letters were in Polish, but he subsequently wrote in English.

[because Grandpa George noted a financial requirement to possess one thousand Australian pounds to even be considered for immigration, it was out of the question.] One thousand Australian pounds would have been worth about $3,200 at the time and, correcting for inflation, would be worth over $40,000 today. Australia once required landing money for incoming immigrants, but in the postwar period it had a policy promoting mass immigration, with the slogan "populate or perish," that did not include such a condition. So while Grandpa George's belief that he needed a thousand pounds for landing money appears to be incorrect, what I do know is that immigrating to Australia held little appeal for him.

[Would it have been better if we were between the other ~~6,000,000~~ victims of our family?] Grandpa George originally wrote out the number six million (indicating the number of

Jews murdered in the Holocaust), and then crossed it out. Perhaps what I have is a draft of the letter rather than a final version he sent Charles. I left it in precisely as I found it because it suggests an internal struggle to understand his survival in relationship to the millions who died as well as the known Holocaust victims within his own family.

[for the first time since total war] *ArtNews*, Art News Annual 1948, "Art News of the Year," 45a.

[let's hope for a short stay in this ~~hell~~ prisonlike place.] Again, perhaps a draft, but leaving it in reveals more of what Grandpa George thought about the Bagnoli camp than editing it out and leaving only the words "stay in this prisonlike place."

I found *The Long Road Home: The Aftermath of the Second World War* by Ben Shephard particularly helpful for understanding and contextualizing my family's postwar struggle.

["Refugee ship leaves Italy for U.S. Carrying 673 Jewish Displaced Persons."] *Jewish Telegraphic Agency*, November 16, 1949.

[As the ship got farther from Europe's shores and closer to America, he convinced many of the other Jewish passengers to pool their resources and send President Truman a thank-you-note telegram. "844 Displaced Persons from Italy on USAT 'Marine Jumper' thank you Mr. President and the people of the United States for giving them the possibility to emigrate to your free country."] Grandpa George saved the draft of the message along with calculations that I believe show the cost of sending the telegram to the White House: $7.56.

[After arriving in the U.S., they settled in Denison, Texas, where Sidney Karchmer, their sponsor, lived.] Sidney Karchmer was married to Irma Karchmer [née Weicensang], who, like Charles, was a first cousin to Grandma Stella.

Chapter Seven: Legacy

["He painted scenes of the Polish-Jewish community from the interwar period," I said, and pulled out the abbreviated catalog that had been put together for the 1981 exhibition and passed it to him across the desk.] The catalog I showed Jacek Nowakowski was the exhibition catalog produced in 1981 for the Moshe Rynecki exhibition at the Judah L. Magnes Museum in Berkeley, California. Catalog credits include Ruth Eis, Florence B. Helzel, Alex Lauterbach, and Irena Narell.

["I'm sorry," Mr. Nowakwoski said. "I'm really afraid it just won't be possible."] I later learned that the U.S. Holocaust Memorial Museum wasn't the only Holocaust museum that felt my great-grandfather's paintings didn't fit with their mission. The director of collections and exhibitions at another Holocaust memorial museum explained to me, "We are a historical museum, and as such we do not collect art, except as documentation of the Holocaust (i.e., art done during or immediately following the Holocaust)." I was told by another Holocaust museum, "It's a beautiful story and a very touching piece of Holocaust history, but it does not fit into our strategic plan at the moment." In other words, since my great-grandfather's work was done before the war, his work does not fall under the category of Holocaust art. Conversely, to Jewish museums specializing in fine art, Moshe's work is considered related to the Holocaust. Several Jewish art museums explained a lack of interest in displaying an exhibit of my great-grandfather's works because it would necessitate a Holocaust narrative.

[I had already applied to graduate school at that point, and began studying at UC Davis in the field of Rhetoric and Speech Communication in the fall.] Rhetoric and Speech Communication is often offered as the study of rhetorical traditions from classical (Greek philosopher Aristotle's description of the means of persuasion and appeals into the three categories of Ethos, Pathos, and Logos) to more contemporary studies of human communication. In addition to classes on theory and criticism, public speaking, and group communication, my course work included studies of documentary film, television, and politics. I was particularly interested in representations of Jews in popular culture.

[After a long silence, I gave in to the tension. I blurted out, "I have a friend who taught herself HTML. She said it's easy to learn."] I hand-coded the original rynecki.org website with HTML in 1999. The website was significantly updated and redesigned in 2012 by Sara Glaser, a graphic designer. The ChasingPortraits.org website was established in 2014 to offer more information and resources about the documentary film and the book.

[The subject line, "To Ms. Elizabeth Rynecki," was from a Katherina and Maciej Rauch-Grodecki, in Queens, New York.] Perhaps a more correct Polish spelling of Katherina's name would be "Katarzyna," but she signed her emails with "Katherina," so that is what I used.

[But I also had to admit, despite my outrage, that I didn't know the provenance of the pieces he had, since the mysterious letter from the mother-in-law explaining their relationship to the Rynecki family had never materialized.] Provenance is a record of ownership, whether for a work of art, an antique, or other object of historical significance. It is, essentially, a chain of title. Traditionally used by art scholars and researchers to primarily address issues of attribution and authenticity, it is also used in legal claims by heirs of Holocaust victims whose artworks were looted or forcibly taken during the Second World War.

[Sincerely, Maciek] Maciek is a common Polish diminutive for Maciej. It is also exactly how he signed his letter.

Chapter Eight: Cultural Assets—Lost Art

[Renata, it seemed, was currently employed at POLIN Museum of the History of Polish Jews, but she had formerly worked at the Jewish Historical Institute.] The Jewish Historical Institute (Polish: *Żydowski Instytut Historyczny*, or *ŻIH*) is also sometimes called the Emanuel Ringelblum Jewish Historical Institute. The Association of the Jewish Historical Institute of Poland (Polish: *Stowarzyszenie Żydowski Instytut Historyczny w Polsceis*) is a nongovernment organization established in 1951 to preserve and commemorate the history and culture of Polish Jews. The association initiated and helped cofound POLIN Museum of the History of Polish Jews (Polish: *Muzeum Historii Żydów Polskich*) and provides support to both POLIN and the Jewish Historical Institute, which are separate institutions.

[This, Renata said, was why my great-grandfather's pieces had appeared in several exhibitions, most notably the Kraków exhibition, *Polish Jews*, put together by Polish art historian Marek Rostworowski, which included twenty-two Rynecki paintings.] In 1989 the National Museum in Kraków, Poland, under the Ministry of Culture and Art had an exhibition included twenty-two Rynecki paintings. The exhibition, "Żydzi-Polscy," organized by Marek Rostworowski, showed at both Muzeum Narodowe in Kraków and at Zachęta in Warsaw.

[In so doing, she happened upon eight Rynecki paintings included on the pages of a Polish stock photography website called Lookgalleria.] Lookgalleria, the Polish stock photography website, is online at www.photospoland.com/.

[She had no interest in contacting the Shoah Foundation's survivor testimony program.] Steven Spielberg founded the Shoah Foundation Institute in 1994 to videotape and preserve interviews with survivors and other Holocaust witnesses. The foundation moved to the University of Southern California in January 2006.

[With grand visions of documentary filmmaking dancing in my head, in the summer of 2008 I hired Johnny Symons and S. Leo Chiang, both accomplished documentary filmmakers, to film an interview between me and my father.] I should note that I met Johnny Symons at my sons' preschool. Johnny's younger son and my older son had the same teacher. Johnny later became a consulting producer for the *Chasing Portraits* documentary film project. Johnny is an Emmy-nominated independent filmmaker based in the San Francisco Bay Area. He introduced me to S. Leo Chiang. Leo is a documentary filmmaker born in Taiwan and based in San Francisco. He received his MFA in film production from the University of Southern California. Cathy Greenblatt, who appears later in the story, was also at the initial filming session with Dad, but because of an effort to simplify the scene, she is not introduced here.

[Around the time of the interview, I exchanged emails with Chris Marinello, then the executive director and general counsel for an organization called the Art Loss Register (ALR).] Chris

Marinello was the Executive Director and General Counsel for the Art Loss Register (ALR). He later left the company and went on to form a rival business called Art Recovery International. The *New York Times* published an article (September 20, 2013) about some of the controversy surrounding ALR, "Tracking Stolen Art, for Profit, and Blurring a Few Lines."

[One document we found from the Conference on Jewish Material Claims Against Germany, Inc. (the Claims Conference) painted a grim picture of Poland.] "Restitution in Poland, Hungary, Romania and Other Countries in Eastern Europe," Claims Conference website.

[After further searching, I eventually found an article on Bloomberg.com about the Max Stern estate.] "Max Stern Estate Pursues Nazi-Seized Art in German Collections," *Bloomberg*, December 10, 2008. Clarence Epstein, Ph.D., is the senior director, urban and cultural affairs, at Concordia University and oversees the Max Stern Art Restitution Project.

Chapter Nine: A Loan Request

[The new museum, a 45,000-square-foot institution dedicated to the more than thousand-year history of Polish Jews, was set to open in two years, in 2012.] Although POLIN Museum of the History of Polish Jews was originally scheduled to open in 2012, it did not have its soft opening until April 19, 2013. Its official grand opening was October 28, 2014.

[This might sound absurd, but it didn't seem entirely far-fetched in light of the case of Dina Babbitt.] Bruce Webber, "Dina Babbitt, Artist at Auschwitz, Is Dead at 86," *New York Times*, August 1, 2006.

[I waited until almost the end of the Q&A to ask my question—essentially, how I could get more information from Sotheby's about the 1993 auction of two of my great-grandfather's paintings.] I eventually did see photographs of the two paintings sold at Sotheby's, but it was several years later. Please see the note in Chapter Twenty-one for more details.

["The Ministry of Foreign Affairs regrets that it will be unable to assist you in Poland."] Email from Marek Lesniewski-Laas, the honorary consul of the Republic of Poland, received in November 2010.

["the Union of Parisian movers was forced"] Lynn H. Nicholas, *Rape of Europa: The Fate of Europe's Treasures in the Third Reich and the Second World War* (New York: Knopf, 1994), page 139.

[In 2006 Altmann sold *Portrait of Adele Bloch-Bauer I* to cosmetics heir Ronald Lauder for a supposed $135 million.] Carol Vogel, "Lauder Pays $135 Million, a Record, for a Klimt Portrait," *New York Times*, June 19, 2006.

[The first problem related to the stance of the Polish government.] On April 18, 2011, in "Holocaust Survivor: Shame on Poland," the Associated Press (AP) reported, "The government of Prime Minister Donald Tusk argues that the financial crisis has left it too broke to pay even partial compensation for seized property. Government spokesman Paweł Graś said on Wednesday that if the law took effect, the state would have to immediately pay out 20 billion złotys (7 billion US dollars) to former property owners, most of them non-Jews. He said that was 'impossible' for the debt-burdened state to come up with for the next two years. That marks a change of tone from 2008, when Tusk vowed during a visit to Jerusalem to get a law passed." In October 2013 the World Jewish Restitution Organization (WJRO) called for stolen property to be returned and noted that their efforts would focus on Poland, "the only major country in Central or Eastern Europe that has not passed legislation for the restitution of private property stolen during the Holocaust." In August 2015 WJRO welcomed the decision "by President Bronisław Komorowski of Poland not to sign legislation that would limit the ability of Holocaust survivors, their families, and other rightful owners to recover property in Warsaw they claimed after the Second World War." While this was promising, Poland has still not dealt with Holocaust-era looted art restitution issues regarding items on Polish soil. Then, in November 2015, the *Jerusalem Post* ran an article, "Holocaust Historians Run into Political Opposition in Brussels Over Data Protect Law," which noted, "Twenty-four out of 28 EU member states that are members of IHRA [International Holocaust Remembrance Alliance] voted for the international body to push for the inclusion of a reference to the Holocaust in the legislation. However, many of the countries involved have stood on the sidelines during IHRA's lobbying campaign. Members Estonia and Poland have actively opposed the inclusion of IHRA's addition." The IHRA, in a November 2015 press release titled "Holocaust Research and the Draft General Data Protection Regulation," noted that while the IHRA supported the EU's decision to "ensure the protection of personal data, *it is crucial that the right to be forgotten does not conflict with the responsibility to remember*" [emphasis in the original].

Chapter Ten: Gifting Moshe's Paintings

[Marei Von Saher sued the Norton Simon Museum in 2007 for the return of Cranach the Elder's *Adam* and *Eve* paintings.] Mike Boehm, "Nazi-looted-art Case Against Norton Simon Museum Set for 2016 trial," *Los Angeles Times*, July 15, 2015.

["Because my father was not only heir, we had to sell *Two Riders*."] Peter J. Toren, "How My Family Recovered a Painting Stolen by the Nazis and Sold It for $2.9 Million," Yahoo! Finance, July 7, 2015.

["None of these paintings are for sale, and they won't ever be."] Donna Horowitz, "Art That Survived the Holocaust," *Marin Independent Journal*, November 27, 1981 (A1).

Chapter Eleven: Serendipity

[One, to find and print out pages from *Nasz Przegląd Ilustrowany* (a Polish-language Zionist paper published on a daily basis in Warsaw between 1923 and September 1939) containing images of a few Rynecki paintings I'd seen referenced in print.] [There are microfilm copies of this newspaper in the United States. The library closest to me with a copy was the Stanford University's Green Library. In May 2012, Mom joined me on a trip to Stanford University campus in Palo Alto to see if we could spot the Rynecki paintings believed to be in the paper. We scrolled forward and backward through the microfilm, ultimately finding nothing. While Stanford's library had *Nasz Przegląd*, we could not find the *Ilustrowany* insert, the section with my great-grandfather's paintings. Our trip to the library was not a complete failure, as we did discover Jerzy Malinowski's *Malarstwo i rzeźba Żydów Polskich w XIX i XX wieku* [*Painting and Sculpture of Polish Jews in the Nineteenth and Twentieth Centuries*], published in 2000, while in the stacks. On page 270 we found a lengthy paragraph on the work of my great-grandfather and his extensive studies of poor Jewish neighborhoods in Warsaw, and on page 271, six color photographs of Rynecki paintings neither of us had ever seen before. I eventually found out that five of these paintings were held by the Jewish Historical Institute in Warsaw, Poland. The whereabouts of the sixth piece (and even whether it survived the Second World War) is unknown. Ironically, at the back of the book was information about the missing painting indicating Malinowski's source of the sixth photograph was *Nasz Przegląd Ilustrowany*, the same paper I had trouble accessing.

I should note the Jewish Historical Institute's more recent efforts to digitize their archives and to make them accessible via the online searchable Central Judaic Library (Polish: *Centralna Biblioteka Judaistyczna*). My most recent search of the archive yielded photographs of twenty-four of my great-grandfather's paintings held by the Institute.

Chapter Twelve: Toronto, Canada

["During the Second World War they went into Russia and became partisan fighters—part of the resistance."] Moshe Wertheim detailed to me his parents' time as partisan fighters, but later I searched for further information. Anatol Wertheim's testimony, "With Zorin in the Family Camp," can be found in the Minsk Yizkor book. It can also be found in Yad Vashem's archives (0-3/3861).

[*Na Wywczasach* . . . in which a man (presumably my great-grandfather) is painting, a small crowd watching him.] The clipping held by the National Museum in Warsaw has no information about the newspaper source. In early 2015 I discovered the newspaper with the image in it for sale on Allegro.pl. I successfully bid on the paper and now own a copy of the October 11, 1931, edition of *Kurjer Warszawski Niedzielny Dodatek Ilustrowany* [Warsaw Courier Illustrated Sunday Supplement] in which the image appeared. The clipping held by the National Museum of Warsaw is in their Iconographic and Photographic collection as inventory item [inv. DI] 59 217.

[In August the documentary film received its first donation.] The *Chasing Portraits* documentary film has 501(c)(3) nonprofit status under the fiscal sponsorship program run by the National Center for Jewish Film (NCJF). NCJF serves as the film's nonprofit tax-exempt umbrella organization, which accepts and administers contributions made to the film. Fiscal sponsorship makes it possible to solicit and receive tax-deductible donations from individuals and gifts from foundations without having to create a 501(c)(3) nonprofit corporation.

Chapter Thirteen: University of Toronto

["I'm Fern Smiley," she said. "I'm an art researcher and consultant for Holocaust-era cultural property. Do you mind if I come with you to the library? I sometimes write for the *Canadian Jewish News*."] Fern Smiley, "Search for Lost Pre-WWII Art Bears Fruit in Toronto," *Canadian Jewish News*, October 31, 2013.

["So, Otto Schneid?" I asked. "Who is he?"] In two separate donations (first in 1998 and then again in 1999), Otto Schneid's widow, Miriam, donated Schneid's work, including the manuscripts of his books, Schneid's own articles on art history, correspondence with artists, photographs of art by some 180 European Jewish artists from the early 1930s, exhibit catalogs, and autobiographies of some of these artists, to the Thomas Fisher Rare Book Library.

Photos of items from the Otto Schneid archive are courtesy of the Thomas Fisher Rare Book Library, University of Toronto. The reference code for the entire Schneid collection is: CA OTUTF MS COLL 00350.

Chapter Fourteen: Schneid Archive

[As soon as I returned home from Toronto, I had the letters translated.] Moshe's letters to Otto Schneid in Polish were translated by Dad's cousin, Helen Miller.

[In addition to the letters, there was a document written in Yiddish.] Moshe's Yiddish biography was translated by Khane-Faygl (Anita) Turtletaub.

["I am enclosing a German newspaper and several reviews of my paintings."] The archive includes a German newspaper clipping with no publisher information. In March 2015 Assistant Professor Kerry Wallach (Department of German Studies at Gettysburg College) identified the article as being from the illustrated supplement to *Israelitisches Familienblatt* [*Israelite Family Paper*] published on May 15, 1930, issue number 20. A translation of a transcribed version of the article, which was printed using Fraktur font, was provided for me by Rita Goldhor. Rita, originally from Vienna, was a child refugee rescued in the early days of the Second World War by the Kindertransport efforts.

Chapter Fifteen: Poland

[We got off near Tamka Street, the street where my great-aunt, Bronisława, had had her dental practice.] Grandpa George's sister, Bronisława, was a dentist in Warsaw. I discovered her Tamka 29 address in a series of interwar telephone directories made available on GenealogyIndexer.org.

["the paintings of your grand-grandfather were coming back to Poland,"] All the Polish-speaking natives I've spoken to in English about my great-grandfather, always say "grand-grandfather." I didn't change Alex Wertheim's words both because I wanted to stay true to how he told the story, but also because I think it helps to better hear Alex's voice.

Chapter Sixteen: The Jewish Historical Institute

The Jewish Historical Institute is located at ul. Tłomackie 3/5 in Warsaw. Before the war it housed the main Judaic library and the Institute for Judaic Studies, which opened in 1928. During the Second World War the building was one of the centers of Jewish social life in the Warsaw Ghetto.

["Many artists went there for plein-air sessions," Teresa said.] "Plein-air" refers to the idea of painting outdoors, which was popular in the late nineteenth century, when the proliferation of paints in tubes made it more feasible for artists to transport their easel and paints (they no longer had to grind and mix dry powders). Proponents of painting outdoors loved working in natural light and painting what they actually saw versus having to later remember the outdoor scenes inside a studio. A great deal about Jewish painters in Kazimierz Dolny was written in the catalog for the 2008 exhibition at the Museum Nadwislanskie in Kazimierz Dolny.

[I was happy to find out that these were in the art conservation studio being prepared for display in the *Ocalałe/Salvaged* exhibition, which was opening in a few days.] *Ocalałe/Salvaged* was an exhibit put together by the Jewish Historical Institute meant to coincide with the opening of the core exhibition at POLIN. The paintings on display, all from the interwar period and part of the institute's collection, had not been shown for many years.

Chapter Seventeen: A Tour of POLIN

[I recognized my great-grandmother's name "P. Rynecka."] Rynecka is pronounced RinEHtskAH

["On the application you can see the price he asked for each of the works: 74 złotys and 150 złotys."] These amounts would have been roughly equivalent to fifteen dollars and thirty dollars in 1934/35. As I note in Chapter Twenty-one, 150 złotys was more than a skilled worker made in Warsaw in a month.

["It's from the magazine *The Synagogue and the Hazzans' World*," Renata said. "It's a publication for cantors. On the cover is this Rynecki painting of a Passover seder."] An image of the Rynecki Passover seder painting can be found in two places: (1) on the cover of *The Synagogue and the Hazzans' World*, Vol. 3, Warsaw, April 1939; (2) in *Nasz Przegląd Ilustrowany*, number 16 (1938), page 5.

Chapter Eighteen: Majdanek

[Grandpa George's memoir said Perla received a postcard from Moshe telling her he was well and hoped to paint at Majdanek.] I do wish there was more definitive data about whether my great-grandfather perished at Majdanek or Treblinka. It would be helpful if I could somehow verify Grandpa George's assertion that the family received a postcard from Moshe written from Majdanek. Sadly, I do not have that postcard. I've written to the International Tracing Service (ITS) at Bad Arolsen twice to request information about where my great-grandfather was deported and murdered. They've come up empty-handed.

Chapter Nineteen: Kazimierz Dolny

[My favorite line about the historical importance of Kazimierz Dolny comes from *The River Remembers* by S. L. Shneiderman. He wrote, "The Vistula is to Poland what the Mississippi is to America and the Volga is to Russia."] S. L. Shneiderman, *The River Remembers* (New York: Horizon Press, 1978).

[In the early twentieth century, the Warsaw School of Fine Arts sent groups of students to the historic town of Kazimierz Dolny for plein-air workshops.] The end of the eighteenth century brought the first Polish artists to Kazimierz Dolny to paint the town. The twentieth century saw the biggest influx of artists into the town when the Warsaw School of Fine Arts was established and art professors brought students to Kazimierz Dolny to paint. 1909 is considered an important year in the town's artistic history because it was the year Władysław Ślewiński, a Polish artist who painted at Pont-Aven (in northwestern France) and was a friend of Paul Gauguin's, brought his students to paint along the Vistula River. In 1923 the president of the Academy of Fine Arts in Warsaw, Professor Tadeusz Pruszkowski, brought a group of students to paint for the summer, marking the beginning of a long-held tradition. See: http://www.kazimierz-dolny.pl/en.

Chapter Twenty: Playing Ball

["My great-grandfather's painting is on display on the top floor of the museum," I said.] The opening of the *Ocalałe/Salvaged* exhibit in October 2014 contained a single Rynecki painting. On a return trip in May 2015 I saw that the first one had been taken down, but three different Rynecki pieces were on display.

Chapter Twenty-one: Roadblocks

["I've seen these," I said, pointing to two pieces I recognized. "They were once listed at the Polish auction houses Desa and Rempex."] There's another thing about the two paintings that made them seem more familiar. Oddly enough, I'd seen copies of these two works for sale on a website run by a company in China called Nice Art Gallery (www.niceartgallery.com). The company employs artists to make "100 percent handmade oil paintings, hand painted by experienced artists. These are oil on canvas genuine masterpieces and each stroke, texture and nuance is created by hand—in the same way the original paintings were created. We use no printing, pressing or technological tricks to create our paintings." While admiring the originals on Maciej's wall, I explained I had ordered copies of the two works from the Chinese company. Maciej was outraged. "They can't do this!" he said. I agreed, but wasn't sure what to say as it was my understanding that a work is no longer copyright protected seventy years after the death of the artist, and my great-grandfather had perished seventy-one years before. When I had first seen them, I too was shocked to discover it was possible to order copies of Rynecki paintings in China. There was something about it that felt like a violation of the spirit of my great-grandfather's work. And while it is true the artists in China did copy the painting, and matched his composition, the copies paled in comparison to the originals in Maciej's apartment. The brushstrokes were wrong—they didn't match my great-grandfather's style—and the colors in the copy didn't properly match the originals either.

[The price for the painting was 150 zlotys, an amount I later learned was about one and a half times what a skilled worker earned in Warsaw in a month.] "*Panie Marszałku, jak żyć? Ceny i zarobki w II RP* [Mr. Speaker, how to live? Prices and earnings in the Second Republic]," *Polska Newsweek*, May 29, 2013.

["The two at Sotheby's?" I asked. "That was you?"] Maciej and Katherina sold two Rynecki paintings through Sotheby's Arcade auction in 1993. I believe the buyer was in California. I have so far been unsuccessful in arranging an opportunity to see the originals. Although I learned about the Sotheby's auction from the art appraiser Dad spoke to many years earlier, I didn't actually see a photograph of the paintings until January 2015, when Polish provenance researcher and friend Agnieszka Yass-Alston was doing research in Israel. In fact, prior to that I didn't even know photos existed; when I had called Sotheby's and asked for photos from their files, I was told they didn't have any. Agnieszka's email arrived innocently enough, accompanied by a snapshot from a Sotheby's Israeli auction catalog and the question, "Do you know the piece?" I got chills seeing the photo of *Café Scene* for the first time—although the subject was so different from the rest of Moshe's work I had seen, the style and signature were instantly familiar. And although I knew about the New York auction, I was stunned to learn about the Israeli auction. As I tried to connect the dots between the fragments of information I knew and did not know, it seemed that after the New York auction the buyer had turned around and tried to sell *Café Scene* through the Israeli branch of Sotheby's. When I contacted Sotheby's Israeli office for information about the sale of the painting, I learned that the painting had failed to sell at auction. There wasn't room in the chapter to quote in its entirety the provenance of the Rynecki paintings cited in the Sotheby's catalog, but it is worth sharing here, especially given that Maciej had nothing to do with the sale at the Sotheby's Israeli auction and the provenance details leave me with additional questions. The New York Sotheby's catalog separates information about the artist and provenance. The first paragraph states, "Moses Rynecki (1885–1943) graduated from the Warsaw Academy of Art in 1910. Working mainly in watercolors, he depicted scenes of Jewish life. He died in the Warsaw Ghetto rebellion in 1943." While I know my great-grandfather attended the Warsaw Academy of Arts, I am not certain if he graduated from the school. As for the death information, it contradicts my family's own understanding that he was deported to Majdanek. Then the catalog has one sentence under the heading for provenance, "Acquired from the widow of the artist, 1945." Maciej recalls growing up with the Rynecki paintings in his family's home, but he's always been a bit unclear with me on exactly how his family acquired the works. The Israeli Sotheby's catalog contains a paragraph combining history and provenance and states, "Rynecki (1881–1943) was born in Warsaw and graduated from the Warsaw Academy of Art in 1910. In 1929–30 he exhibited at the Warsaw Association of Jewish Art and the Warsaw Society of Fine Art and in 1935 he exhibited at the Brussels International Art Exhibition. On the 17th September 1942 he was imprisoned in the

Warsaw Ghetto and he died in the Ghetto uprising in 1943. After the German retreat 150 works by Rynecki were discovered in the basement of a Warsaw apartment block, including the present work." This last statement, if true, is absolutely jaw-dropping; it would be a find larger than what Perla found after the war. Interestingly, Maciej is not the source of this information—when I asked, he said his family did not recover 150 works. It is possible that Sotheby's confused what Perla recovered with the paintings found by Maciej's family, but the painting at issue, *Café Scene*, was not one of the works my family recovered.

["That's not my great-grandfather's work. Are you sure this is the right piece?" I asked.] Painting number 52 at the Jewish Historical Institute—I have asked a few well-respected art historians familiar with Polish-Jewish art history, and my great-grandfather's work in particular, if they think this painting is the work of my great-grandfather. So far no one can definitely say who painted the piece, but there are many question marks about it being a Rynecki work.

[He had found a testimony in Yiddish Perla had given after the war, as well as several Pages of Testimony with the names on them of the extended Rynecki family that perished in the Holocaust.] "Pages of Testimony are special forms created by Yad Vashem to record the personal identities and life stories of the six million Jews murdered by the Nazis and their accomplices. Submitted by survivors, remaining family members or friends in commemoration of Jews murdered in the Holocaust, these one-page forms contain the names, biographical details and, when available, photographs, of each individual victim. They are essentially symbolic 'tombstones.'" (http://www.yadvashem.org/yv/en/about/hall_of_names/what_are_pot.asp)

Chapter Twenty-two: A Shared Heritage

["Perla is a Mittelsbach!" I said, relieved to recognize her maiden name. . . . "Do you still have their contact information?"] Shula did not have the French family's contact information, but four months later, during a second trip to New York (I'd come back to the city to speak on a panel for the New York County Lawyers' Association 8th Annual Art Litigation and Dispute Resolution Practice Institute about Holocaust-era looted art), I received another clue, during an afternoon get-together with Roz Jacobs and Laurie Weisman. Roz and Laurie are friends (whom I met through Barbara Kirshenblatt-Gimblett) who run the Memory Project, a multimedia exhibit, workshop, and film that engages students in the history of the Holocaust while enabling them as "artists, storytellers and creators—to connect to their own family histories of memory, of loss and of the power of the creative process." Roz and Laurie spend every summer in France, and at one point I mentioned that there might be a Rynecki painting in Le Mans, France.

Roz looked bewildered and said she had a good friend, Margi Bressack Kupferstein, from high school, who lived in Le Mans and might be able to help. I laughed. What were the odds she knew my family in Le Mans? As unlikely as it seems, it turned out Margi did know several members of Perla's extended family. She put us in touch, and on Christmas Day in 2015, I received an email from the family with two photographs: one of the Rynecki painting in their home, a woman doing embroidery work, sitting by a window, and another of a large portion of the family, twelve people in all, gathered around the Rynecki painting. It was, Roz and Laurie proclaimed, our own Jewish Christmas miracle! But even better, if there can be such a thing in a story already so wonderful, was the kind accompanying email which said, "I am very pleased that a beautiful painting painted in the 1930s, is the link that connects our history around the world. I hope that it will enable us to meet." Indeed, I expect that someday soon it will.

[Shula's father, David, left Poland for Palestine well before the Second World War. He went home only once, in the late 1930s.] David was born David Rotsztein, but when he left Poland for Palestine before the Second World War, he changed his last name to Gefen. In a letter he wrote to me, David said his grandmother and Perla were sisters.

ANNOTATED BIBLIOGRAPHY IN REGARDS TO THE RYNECKI FAMILY STORY

Bartoszewski, W., & Lewinówna, Z. (1969). *Ten jest z ojczyzny mojej: Polacy z pomocą Żydom, 1939–1945*. Kraków: Znak. Rough translation: He is of/from my Fatherland. The book is all in Polish. On page 1029, the book states that on the eve of the liquidation of the "small ghetto" of the Warsaw Ghetto a man named Jozef Kulig moved out three women and two children (including Perla, Grandpa George, his wife Stella, their son Alex, Stella's sister-in-law and her daughter, Halina) and placed them in Podkowa Lesna ("Warsaw life" 1968, 31 III–1 IV). It should be noted that this information conflicts with Grandpa George's assertion that he never lived inside the Warsaw Ghetto.

Biernacka, M., Bernatowicz, A., Makowska, U., Polanowska, J., Różalska, J., & Polska Akademia Nauk. (2013). *Słownik artystów polskich i obcych w Polsce działających (zmarłych przed 1966 r.): Malarze, rzeźbiarze, graficy*. Warszawa: Instytut Sztuki Polskiej Akademii Nauk. Work on this Dictionary of Polish Artists by the National Institute of Arts began in the 1950s. It includes a four-page entry about Moshe Rynecki (pages 388–391).

Drozd, J. (2008). *Lost in the whirlwind of war: The Jewish community in Gdynia, Poland.* The extended Rynecki family appears in several places in this book. Moshe and Perla appear in a footnote, which cites Szymon Rynecki, who really is Jerzy/George Rynecki, and the fish import business he ran with Herman Mathiesen.

Dulęba, Agnieszka. *Ikonografia Żydów w Polsce 1874–1945.* This appears to be an academic paper that Ms. Dulęba wrote for the Institute of Art History, College of Interdisciplinary Studies in the Humanities, UW. Pages 16–17 contain some commentary about my great-grandfather's work.

Eis, Ruth. "Moshe Rynecki: 1881–1943." Museum Exhibition Catalog (Judah L. Magnes Museum, Berkeley, California, November 8, 1981–January 17, 1982). Features commentary by curator Ruth Eis as well as reprints of many of the works included in the exhibition.

Instytut Historii Kultury Materialnej (*Polska Akademia Nauk*) & *Instytut Archeologii i Etnologii (Polska Akademia Nauk)* (1953). *Kwartalnik historii kultury materialnej.* Warszawa: Państwowe Wydawnictwo Naukowe, Volume 16, 1968. Pages 426–427 contain a few paragraphs about the history of the Jewish Historical Institute in Warsaw and the creation of its collection. At the time of the publication of this piece, the museum said its collection of Jewish art (painting, sculpture, graphics) included more than eleven hundred items, including the works of Moshe Rynecki.

Kopówka, E. (2001). *Żydzi Siedleccy.* Siedlce: E. Kopówka. Written in Polish, this book contains an excerpt of the Marian Trzebiński book about an encounter with Moshe Rynecki, pages 90–92.

Kruszewski, Z. P., & Kansy, A. (2004). *Kultura żydowska na Mazowszu.* Płock: Towarzystwo Naukowe Płockie. This journal contains essays from a 2004 conference. An approximate translation of the title is "Mazovia, the Jews, history, architecture, customs." The article written by Renata Piątkowska (pages 34–44) translates to roughly "Weekday and feast of the Jews in the work of Moshe Rynecki." The piece also includes some black-and-white images of several Moshe Rynecki paintings.

Malinowski, J., & Brus-Malinowska, B. (2000). *Malarstwo i rzeźba żydów polskich w XIX i XX wieku.* Warszawa: Wydawn. Naukowe PWN. Page 270 contains a lengthy paragraph on the work of Mojzesz Rynecki and his extensive studies of poor Jewish neighborhoods in Warsaw. Malinowski also cites the titles, subjects, and dates of several paintings to illustrate the types of subjects Rynecki focused on in his work. Page 271 contains six color photographs of Rynecki paintings. These works portray market scenes, men in Temple, and people at work. The book is in Polish.

Musierowicz, Małgorzata. *Kiedyś, w Polsce* [Once, in Poland]. This review of the 2004 exhibition *Nasi Bracia Starsi* [Our Older Brothers] appears on the website Dialog: Platform for Jewish-Polish Dialogue (http://www.dialog.org/dialog_pl/kiedys-w-Polsce.html). The piece, written by Małgorzata Musierowicz, a popular Polish author of books for children and teenagers, is a review of the exhibition. In the piece she writes, "We all know who was and how painted Jan Gotard, Maurycy Gottlieb and Roman Kramsztyk—but how many of us are familiar with the names of great painters such as Mojżesz [Moshe] Rynecki, Maurycy Trębacz, Artur Markowicz, Wilhelm Wachtel or Samuel Hirschenberg?"

Odorowski, W., & Muzeum Nadwiślańskie w Kazimierzu Dolnym. (2008). *In Kazimierz the Vistula River spoke to them in Yiddish: Jewish painters in the art colony of Kazimierz.*

Kazimierz Dolny: Muzeum Nadwiślanskie in Kazimierz Dolny. Chapter One, written by Renata Piątkowska, is titled "I Come from Kazimierz . . ." Printed in both Polish and English, it is a piece about the artistic wonders and literary legends who came to Kazimierz Dolny to draw, paint, and write. It speaks of the art colony's charm and the atmosphere it offered successive generations of artists. Pages 31 and 37 contain mention of pieces Moshe Rynecki made in the town. The back portion of the book contains a brief biography of Mojżesz [Moshe] Rynecki (page 201) with a self-portrait, and on pages 202 and 203 there are photographs of five of Rynecki's paintings, four in color and one in black-and-white: *Magid* (1937), *Market in Kazimierz on the Vistula* (1937), *Kazimierz on the Vistula, Market* (undated), *At a Market* (1937), and *Two Jews on a Street of a Little Town* (1932).

Piwocki, K., & Akademia Sztuk Pięknych w Warszawie. (1965). *Historia Akademii Sztuk Pięknych w Warszawie, 1904–1964.* Wrocław: Zakład Narodowy im. Ossolińskich. History of the Academy of Fine Arts in Warsaw. Page 211 of the book lists Rynecki as having attended the Warsaw Academy of Fine Arts during the 1906/1907 school year. Moshe would have been in his mid-twenties during this time period. Also of note, in 1907, "a Report of the hitherto activity of the School of Fine Arts in Warsaw for the period: March 1904–June 1907" was published, and this document contains information about Moshe's attendance at the school.

Pogonowski, I. (1998). *Jews in Poland: A documentary history: the rise of Jews as a nation from Congressus Judaicus in Poland to the Knesset in Israel.* New York: Hippocrene Books. Page 218 contains a painting by Moshe Rynecki of men playing chess.

Rynecki, George. (2005) *Surviving Hitler in Poland: One Jew's Story.* Victoria, Canada: Trafford Publishing. A collection of vignettes written by Moshe Rynecki's son, George. The stories recall prewar Europe, his father's life, and the Holocaust.

Sandel, J. (1957). *Umgeḳumene Yidishe ḳinsṭler in Poyln.* Ṿarshe: Farlag Yidish Bukh. Information about Jewish artists from Poland who perished in the Holocaust. The book contains a passage about Moshe Rynecki and includes two of his paintings.

Schneid, Otto. Schneid's papers at the University of Toronto's Thomas Fisher Rare Book Library in Canada include research materials for his unpublished book on twentieth-century Jewish artists in Europe. The materials related to Moshe Rynecki include handwritten correspondence from Moshe Rynecki in Polish and Yiddish as well as a typed letter in German, black-and-white photographs of Moshe Rynecki paintings, and newspaper clippings.

Sotheby's (Tel Aviv). (1993). *Important judaica: books, manuscripts, works of art and paintings.* Tel Aviv: Sotheby's. Page 52, item #216, *Café Scene* by Moshe Rynecki, dated 1934.

Sotheby's Arcade Auctions (New York). (1993). *Modern and Contemporary Paintings, Drawings and Sculpture. Sale 1433.* Item #76, *Café Scene* and *The Accordianist*: Two Watercolors, each dated 1934.

Tanikowski, A. (2007). *Malarze żydowscy w Polsce: Cz. 2.* Warszawa: Edipresse Polska. The second volume of a book about Jewish painters in Poland. The book is written entirely in Polish. Page 18 contains a brief paragraph about Moshe. Page 19 shows a self-portrait. Pages 20 and 21 contain images of three Rynecki paintings.

Tanikowski, A., & Galeria U Jezuitów (Poznań, Poland). (2004). *Nasi bracia starsi: Malarstwo, rysunek i grafika ze zbiorów Żydowskiego Instytutu Historycznego w Warszawie: katalog wystawy.* Poznań: Księg. Św. Wojciecha. (Our older brothers: painting, drawing and graphics from the collection of Jewish History Institute in Warsaw). Pages 49–50 contain seven black-and-white 1.5- by 2-inch prints of Moshe Rynecki paintings. The catalog contains two essays. Both are in Polish.

Trzebiński, M., & Masłowski, M. (1958). *Pamiętnik malarza.* Wrocław: Zakład Narodowy im. Ossolińskich. *Diary of a Painter.* Pages 170–173 discuss Trzebiński's recollection of an encounter with Moshe Rynecki and his father, Abraham. These pages are also available in Polish in excerpt format in *Żydzi Siedleccy* by Edward Kopówka, pages 90–92.

Żak, J. (2010). *Z dziejów miasteczka w kolorze niebieskim: O społeczności żydowskiej Żyrardowa i okolic.* Żyrardów: Muzeum Mazowsza Zachodniego w Żyrardowie. (From the history of a little town in the shade of blue: on the Jewish community in Żyrardów and neighboring areas.) A sixty-seven-page catalog from an exhibition. The catalog contains the photograph of a 1929 painting by Moshe Rynecki.

Związek Gmin Wyznaniowych Żydowskich w Rzeczypospolitej Polskiej. (1996). *Almanach żydowski.* Warszawa: Związek Gmin Wyznaniowych Żydowskich w Rzeczypospolitej Polskiej. This book is sometimes referred to by its Hebrew title, *Luah li-shenat.* This journal contains fifteen five-inch-by-seven-inch color prints of Moshe Rynecki paintings, plus an almost three-inch-by-four-inch image on the cover of the journal. The journal is 117 pages, plus an appendix. It is in Polish and Hebrew. In addition to the Moshe Rynecki paintings, the journal includes a two-page commentary (pages 94–95) written by Renata Piątkowska, titled "*Mojzesz Rynecki—Piewca zydowskiej Warszawy*" [Moshe Rynecki: Bard of Jewish Warsaw].

Żydowski Instytut Historyczny w Polsce. (1995). *The Museum of the Jewish Historical Institute: Arts and crafts.* Warszawa: Auriga, Wydawnictwa Artystyczne i Filmowe. The introduction contains mention of Mojzesz Rynecki.

Żydowski Instytut Historyczny w Polsce. (1981). *Trzydzieści pięc lat działalności Żydowskiego Instytutu Historycznego w Polsce Ludowej: Dzieje Instytutu i jego zbiory.* Warszawa: Państwowe Wydawn. Nauk. [Thirty-Five Years of the Jewish Historical Institute in

Poland: The History of the Institute and its Collection. Pages 111–12 contain commentary about Mojzesz Rynecki (1885–1942). Museum and exhibition catalog.

Zydzi-Polscy. Muzeum Nardowe w Krakowie. Czerwiec-Sierpien. (1989). *Wystawa Pod Protektoratem Ministra Kultury i Sztuki. Aleksandra Krawczuka.* [Loose translation: Polish Jews. National Museum in Krakow. (1989). Exhibit under the protection of the Ministry of Culture and Art.] Page 81 of this museum catalog lists twenty-two Rynecki paintings included in the exhibition.

SELECTED BIBLIOGRAPHY

Ackerman, D. (2007). *The Zookeeper's Wife*. New York: W. W. Norton.

ARTnews. (1923). New York, etc.: ARTnews Associates, etc.

Baksik, Ł. (2012). *Macewy codziennego użytku = Matzevot for Everyday Use*. Wołowiec: Wydawnictwo "Czarne."

Berge, R., Newnham, N., Cohen, B., Edsel, R. M., Shenk, J., Allen, J., Nicholas, L. H., . . . Oregon Public Broadcasting. (2008). *The Rape of Europa*. Venice, CA: Menemsha Films.

Brendon, P. (2000). *The Dark Valley: A Panorama of the 1930s*. New York: Knopf, distributed by Random House.

Cahn-Tober, T. (2003). *Hide and Seek: A Wartime Childhood*. Albuquerque: University of New Mexico Press.

Chapman, F. S. (2000). *Motherland: Beyond the Holocaust: A Daughter's Journey to Reclaim the Past*. New York: Viking.

Cowan, P., & Mazal Holocaust Collection. (1982). *An Orphan in History: Retrieving a Jewish Legacy*. Garden City, NY: Doubleday.

Cutler, I. (1996). *The Jews of Chicago: From Shtetl to Suburb*. Urbana: University of Illinois Press.

Davies, N., & Mazal Holocaust Collection. (2004). *Rising '44: The Battle for Warsaw*. New York: Viking.

De, W. E. (2011). *The Hare with Amber Eyes: A Hidden Inheritance*. New York: Picador.

Edsel, R. M., & Mazal Holocaust Collection. (2006). *Rescuing da Vinci: Hitler and the Nazis Stole Europe's Great Art; America and Her Allies Recovered It*. Dallas: Laurel Pub.

Edsel, R. M., & Witter, B. (2009). *The Monuments Men: Allied Heroes, Nazi Thieves, and the Greatest Treasure Hunt in History*. New York: Center Street.

Eisenstein, B. (2006). *I Was a Child of Holocaust Survivors.* New York: Riverhead Books.

Epstein, H., & Mazal Holocaust Collection. (1979). *Children of the Holocaust: Conversations with Sons and Daughters of Survivors.* New York: Putnam.

Epstein, H., & Mazal Holocaust Collection. (1997). *Where She Came From: A Daughter's Search for Her Mother's History.* Boston: Little, Brown.

Fass, P. S. (2009). *Inheriting the Holocaust: A Second-Generation Memoir.* New Brunswick, NJ: Rutgers University Press.

Feliciano, H., & Mazal Holocaust Collection. (1997). *The Lost Museum: The Nazi Conspiracy to Steal the World's Greatest Works of Art.* New York: BasicBooks.

Fremont, H., & Mazal Holocaust Collection. (1999). *After Long Silence: A Memoir.* New York: Delacorte Press.

Gensburger, S., & Bundesarchiv (Germany). (2015). *Witnessing the Robbing of the Jews: A Photographic Album, Paris, 1940–1944.* Bloomington: Indiana University Press.

Gola, J., Sitkowska, M., Akademia Sztuk Pięknych (Warschau), & Galeria Zachęta. (2012). *Art Everywhere: Academy of Fine Arts in Warsaw, 1904–1944 [exhibition 4 June–26 August 2012, Zachęta National Gallery of Art, Warsaw].* Warszawa: Akademia of Fine Arts.

Goodman, S. T., Cohen, R. I., Jewish Museum (New York), & Jewish Theological Seminary of America. (2001). *The Emergence of Jewish Artists in Nineteenth-century Europe.* London: Merrell.

Haffner, S. (2002). *Defying Hitler: A Memoir.* New York: Farrar, Straus and Giroux.

Hanson, J. K. M. (1982). *The Civilian Population and the Warsaw Uprising of 1944.* Cambridge: Cambridge University Press.

Harr, J. (2005). *The Lost Painting.* New York: Random House.

Hoffman, E. (1993). *Exit into history: A Journey Through the New Eastern Europe.* New York: Viking.

Hoffman, E. (1989). *Lost in Translation: A Life in a New Language.* New York: E. P. Dutton.

Hoffman, E. (1999). *Shtetl: The History of a Small Town and an Extinguished World.* London: Vintage.

Houghteling, S. (2009). *Pictures at an Exhibition.* New York: Alfred A. Knopf.

Howard, D. (2010). *Lost Rights: The Misadventures of a Stolen American Relic.* Boston: Houghton Mifflin Harcourt.

Hundert, G. D., & Yivo Institute for Jewish Research. (2008). *The YIVO Encyclopedia of Jews in Eastern Europe.* New Haven, CT: Yale University Press, online edition.

Karski, J., & Mazal Holocaust Collection. (1944). *Story of a Secret State.* Boston: Houghton Mifflin Co.

Keidar, Amira. *Lalechka* (2011). Printed in Israel.

Kruk, H., & Harshav, B. (2002). *The Last Days of the Jerusalem of Lithuania: Chronicles from the Vilna Ghetto and the Camps, 1939–1944.* New Haven, CT: YIVO Institute for Jewish Research.

Kurtz, G. (2014). *Three Minutes in Poland: Discovering a Lost World in a 1938 Family Film.* New York: Farrar, Straus and Giroux.

Lansky, A. (2004). *Outwitting History: The Amazing Adventures of a Man Who Rescued a Million Yiddish Books.* Chapel Hill, NC: Algonquin Books of Chapel Hill.

Lauder, R. S., Price, R., in Peters, O., Fulda, B., Heftrig, R., Lüttichau, M. & A., Müller, K., et al. (2014). *Degenerate Art: The Attack on Modern Art in Nazi Germany, 1937.* Neue Galerie New York.

Linenthal, E. T., & Mazal Holocaust Collection. (1995). *Preserving Memory: The Struggle to Create America's Holocaust Museum.* New York: Viking.

Miller, N. K. (2011). *What They Saved: Pieces of a Jewish Past.* Lincoln: University of Nebraska Press.

Modan, R., & Cohen, J. (2013). *The Property.* Richmond, B.C.: Drawn & Quarterly.

Müller, M., & Tatzkow, M. (2010). *Lost Lives, Lost Art: Jewish Collectors, Nazi Art Theft, and the Quest for Justice.* New York: Vendome Press.

Mundy, J. (2013). *Lost Art: Missing Artworks of the Twentieth Century.* London: Tate Publishing.

Nicholas, L. H. (1994). *The Rape of Europa: The Fate of Europe's Treasures in the Third Reich and the Second World War.* New York: Alfred A. Knopf.

O'Connor, A. M. (2012). *The Lady in Gold: The Extraordinary Tale of Gustav Klimt's Masterpiece, Portrait of Adele Bloch-Bauer.* New York: Knopf.

Paulsson, G. S. (2002). *Secret City: The Hidden Jews of Warsaw, 1940–1945.* New Haven, CT: Yale University Press.

Pell, J., Rosenbaum, F., & Western Jewish History Center. (2004). *Taking Risks: A Jewish Youth in the Soviet Partisans and His Unlikely Life in California.* Berkeley, CA: Western Jewish History Center of the Judah L. Magnes Museum.

Posner, A., Potok, C., & Dramatists Play Service (New York, NY). (2010). *My Name Is Asher Lev.* New York: Dramatists Play Service.

Potok, C. (1972). *My Name Is Asher Lev.* New York: Knopf, distributed by Random House.

Prawica, A., & Amerykafilm. (2013). *The Fourth Partition: Czwarta Dzielnica.*

Reszke, K. (2013). *Return of the Jew.* Brighton: Academic Studies Press.

Ross, H., in Sutnik, M. M., & Art Gallery of Ontario. (2015). *Memory Unearthed: The Lodz Ghetto Photographs of Henryk Ross.* Toronto, Ontario, Canada: Art Gallery of Ontario.

Schönhaus, C. (2008). *The Forger: An Extraordinary Story of Survival in Wartime Berlin.* New York: Da Capo Press.

Shea, A. B., D'Arcy, D., Morgan, B., & Seventh Art Releasing (Firm). (2012). *Portrait of Wally: P.O.W.*

Shephard, B. (2011). *The Long Road Home: The Aftermath of the Second World War.* New York: Alfred A. Knopf.

Shneiderman, S. L. (1978). *The River Remembers.* New York: Horizon Press.

Śliwowska, W., & Mazal Holocaust Collection. (1998). *The Last Eyewitnesses: Children of the Holocaust Speak.* Evanston, IL: Northwestern University Press.

Spiegelman, A. (1986). *Maus: A Survivor's Tale.* New York: Pantheon Books.

Spiegelman, A. (1991). *Maus II: A Survivor's Tale: And Here My Troubles Began.* New York: Pantheon Books.

Spiegelman, A., & Small Press Expo Collection (Library of Congress). (2011). *MetaMaus.* New York: Pantheon Books.

Steinfeld, J. J. (1993). *Dancing at the Club Holocaust: Stories New & Selected.* Charlottetown, PEI: Ragweed.

Steinman, L. (2013). *The Crooked Mirror: A Memoir of Polish-Jewish Reconciliation.* Boston: Beacon Press.

Steinman, L. (2001). *The Souvenir: A Daughter Discovers Her Father's War.* Chapel Hill, NC: Algonquin Books of Chapel Hill.

Sucher, C. P. (1997). *The Rescue of Memory: A Novel.* New York: Scribner.

Szpilman, W., & Hosenfeld, W. (1999). *The Pianist: The Extraordinary Story of One Man's Survival in Warsaw, 1939–45.* New York: Picador USA.

Tec, N., & Mazal Holocaust Collection. (1993). *Defiance: The Bielski Partisans*. New York: Oxford University Press.

Thornton, S. (2008). *Seven Days in the Art World*. New York: W. W. Norton.

Trienens, H. J. (2000). *Landscape with Smokestacks: The Case of the Allegedly Plundered Degas*. Evanston, IL: Northwestern University Press.

United States Holocaust Memorial Museum online resources.

USC Shoah Foundation: The Institute for Visual History and Education. Miriam Schneid-Ofseyer. Interview Code: 3858. August 1995.

Vale, L. J., & Campanella, T. J. (2005). *The Resilient City: How Modern Cities Recover from Disaster*. New York: Oxford University Press.

Vishniac, R., & Mazal Holocaust Collection. (1983). *A Vanished World*. New York: Farrar, Straus, and Giroux.

Wildman, S. (2014). *Paper Love: Searching for the Girl My Grandfather Left Behind*. New York: Riverhead Books.

Witek, J. (2007). *Art Spiegelman: Conversations*. Jackson: University Press of Mississippi.

Witek, J. (1989). *Comic Books as History: The Narrative Art of Jack Jackson, Art Spiegelman, and Harvey Pekar*. Jackson: University Press of Mississippi.

Wittman, R. K. (2010). *Priceless: How I Went Undercover to Rescue the World's Stolen Treasures*. New York: Crown Publishers.

Yezierska, A. (1975). *Bread Givers: A Novel: A Struggle Between a Father of the Old World and a Daughter of the New*. New York: Persea Books.

Young, J. E. (2000). *At Memory's Edge: After-images of the Holocaust in Contemporary Art and Architecture*. New Haven, CT: Yale University Press.

Young, J. E. (1990). *Writing and Rewriting the Holocaust: Narrative and the Consequences of Interpretation*. Bloomington: Indiana University Press.

Young, J. E., & Mazal Holocaust Collection. (1993). *The Texture of Memory: Holocaust Memorials and Meaning*. New Haven, CT: Yale University Press.

Young, J. E., Mazal Holocaust Collection & Jewish Museum (New York). (1994). *The Art of Memory: Holocaust Memorials in History*. New York: Prestel.

KNOWN EXHIBITIONS

26 January–3 April 2016: *Art from the Holocaust: 100 Works from the Yad Vashem Collection.* Deutsches Historisches Museum, Berlin Germany.

October 2014–March 2015: *Ocalałe/Salvaged.* Jewish Historical Institute. Warsaw, Poland.

October 2010: Muzeum Mazowsza Zachodniego w Żyrardowie.

2008: Museum Nadwislanskie in Kazimierz Dolny.

April 15–May 7, 2003: Works by Jewish artists in Warsaw at the Gallery of the Jewish Historical Institute.

1989: National Museum in Kraków, Poland.

November 8, 1981–January 17, 1982: Judah L. Magnes Museum, Berkeley, California.

June 1951: Jewish Community Center, Dallas, Texas.

1948: *Wystawa dzieł żydowskich artystów plastyków męczenników niemieckiej okupacji 1939–1945.* [Exhibition of Works of Jewish Artists, Martyrs of the German Occupation 1939–1945].

1939: Fifth Jubilee Salon of Paintings and Sculpture, Organization of Jewish Artists and Sculptors.

1937: Bazaar of Pictures.

1936: Jewish Art Salon, The Jewish Society for the Advancement of Art.

1932 and 1931: Zachęta.

1930: Jewish Society for the Promotion of Fine Arts (*Żydowskie Towarzystwo Krzewienia Sztuk Pięknych- ŻTKSP*). The 44th Annual Show, 26 Dluga Street, Warsaw, Poland.

1929: Society for the Advancement of Fine Arts, Warsaw.

1928: Spring Salon of Jewish Art, Gallery at 6 Rymarska Street, Warsaw.